Web Publishing with XML in 6 Easy Steps

Web Publishing with XML in 6 Easy Steps

Bryan Pfaffenberger
University of Virginia

AP PROFESSIONAL
AP PROFESSIONAL is a division of Academic Press

San Diego London Boston
New York Sydney Tokyo Toronto

This book is printed on acid-free paper.

ACADEMIC PRESS
525 B Street, Suite 1900, San Diego, CA 92101-4495
A Division of Harcourt Brace & Company
http://www.apnet.com

Academic Press
24-28 Oval Road, London NW1 7DX
http://www.hbuk.cc.uk/ap/

Library of Congress Cataloging-in-Publication Data
Pfaffenberger, Bryan, 1949-
Web Publishing with XML in 6 Easy Steps / Bryan Pfaffenberger.
p. cm.
Includes index.
ISBN 0-12-553166-4 (paper : alk. paper)
1. XML (Document markup language) 2. Web publishing. I. Title
QA76.76.H94P52 1998
005.7'2--dc21 98-30427
CIP

Printed in the United States of America
98 99 00 01 02 IP 9 8 7 6 5 4 3 2 1

For Suzanne, always

Contents

Acknowledgments

Many thanks to everyone who helped me bring this book to completion. Special thanks are due to Tom Stone for believing in this book's mission, namely, to make XML intelligible to Web authors who know HTML—but know very little about SGML. As you'll learn in the pages to follow, this is the first "Web-up" rather than "SGML-down" treatment of this exciting new technology. Assistant acquisitions editor Thomas Park was a constant source of support and inspiration, as always.

A superb technical edit was performed by David Seaman, director of the University of Virginia's pioneering Electronic Text Center (etext.lib.virginia.edu), a world leader in SGML and XML application development. Sally Elliot, creator of the Internet Sleuth (www.isleuth.com), provided helpful comments on an early draft of this book.

In the production stage, my daughter, Julia, brought her superb grasp of English to the preparation of the final manuscript, including the onerous task of indexing. Thanks, too, to production editors Linda Hamilton-Korey and Julie Champagne, and everyone else at AP Professional who labored long over a complex manuscript.

Very special thanks are due to my family for putting up with lengthy work hours and periods of crankiness when I couldn't get various computer programs to cooperate.

And as always, thanks to my agent, Carole McClendon, and all the great folks at Waterside Productions.

I would also like to thank Big Mouth, Chipper, and Bob, the three wren hatchlings whose mommy—for some reason—built a nest in my office window air conditioner. You kept me company through many long hours in front of the computer. Long may you fly, my friends.

Introduction

You're among the many millions of people who have learned some HTML and created a Web page. Perhaps you're a professional Web designer, and you've created award-winning sites that get thousands of visitors per day. Perhaps you're a small business owner, and you've developed a modest site that's attracting new business—or maybe you're a hobbyist, student, or senior citizen who works on a Web page in your spare time.

Whether you're a Web professional or not, you share something in common with just about everybody who uses HTML: You've heard about eXtensible Markup Language (XML), and you're wondering what all the fuss is about. Do you need to learn XML? What does XML have to offer you?

Why This Book is Unique

This is the first book to address the needs of Web authors who are wondering what to make of XML—and it's about time. Most of the XML books on the market were written by professionals whose real interests lie in the Standard Generalized Markup Language (SGML), the "metalanguage" used to create HTML. (As you'll learn in this book, XML is a simplified version of SGML.) It's not an evil thing that these authors tend to be SGML professionals; it's just that they tend to assume a lot of knowledge about SGML, and they sometimes write as if they were coming down from the heights to try to explain all these wonderful, mysterious concepts to the unwashed masses.

This book is different. It began as an HTML author's personal inquiry—I asked the same questions you're asking right now. I'm not an SGML missionary and I have no vested interest in SGML; like you, I'm an HTML author, and my sole interest in XML lies in figuring out whether I can use it for Web publishing. And frankly, I'm skeptical. More than a few innovations have come along that were supposed to revolutionize the Web, but then fizzled out—like VRML (the Virtual Reality Modeling Language), and just possibly Java. I don't mean to belittle VRML or Java here; people are doing wonderful things with VRML and Java. I'm just pointing out that neither VRML nor Java have really affected the way the broad mass of Web authors prepare their Web pages.

Will XML be any different? The short answer: I believe that XML *will* affect the way that virtually all of us author and publish on the Internet. XML offers the simplicity that helped to make HTML so wildly popular, but it also offers something that XML can't: The ability to create your own tags to describe your data.

XML could very well prove to be one of the key enabling technologies for the next generation of Web publishing—and you owe it to yourself to learn what it could mean for you.

What Is XML?

In brief, XML is a simplified version of SGML, and both are tools for creating markup languages. Unlike SGML, XML is very easy to learn and use. It frees Web authors to create their own tags to capture the richness of the data they publish. But this doesn't mean that the Web will dissolve in a cacophony of mutually unintelligible markup schemes. Because the markup languages you can create with XML are self-describing, browsers can read and display XML documents even if they've never encountered the document's tag set before. And in contrast to SGML, XML is Web-friendly in its support for hyperlinking and style sheets. The following sections explain these points.

Toolkits for Making Markup Languages

You've been using HTML, so you're familiar with the basic idea of document *markup*. You prepare documents by surrounding document components (such as headings or lists) with tags; browsers know how to "read" these tags and display the components on-screen. Because all the markup uses plain text characters, our HTML documents are easily exchanged via the Internet and can be viewed on just about any type of computer.

What you may not realize is that HTML's authors used SGML to create HTML. SGML, short for the Standard Generalized Markup Language, is a toolkit for making markup languages. If you know SGML, you can make your own markup language, one that's better attuned to your particular needs.

But SGML is difficult to learn—and what's worse, popular browsers don't support SGML. As a result, they wouldn't be able to make any sense out of your markup.

A Simplified Version of SGML

Here's where XML fits in. Like SGML, it's a toolkit for making markup languages. But it's much easier to learn and use. For example, if you try to make a new markup language with SGML, you must create a *document type definition (DTD),* which is an arduous process. Although XML provides simplified tools to construct DTDs, you can create your own markup languages without making a DTD, and an XML program can read your tags. (This type of XML is called *well-formed XML.)* Anyone who knows HTML can learn how to use XML make a custom markup language in short order. And if lots of people start doing this, the big browser publishers (such as Netscape and Microsoft) will start supporting XML in their products.

In sum, XML isn't a markup language, like HTML. Rather, it's a toolkit for *making* markup languages. And that's precisely why it's so exciting. HTML isn't fine-grained enough to express the nuances of the information people want to publish on the Internet. As a result, the Web is really just a mass of undifferentiated text. With XML available, people will be able to express much more finely grained document structures. This could lead to tremendous improvements in the retrievability of information by means of Internet searches, to name just one benefit.

Self-Describing Document Structures

You're probably saying, "Wait a minute. If everyone uses XML to make a personal, idiosyncratic markup language, how can browsers understand and display the pages they create? Won't this lead to a breakdown in communication?" On the Web, HTML got into trouble when people pushed for new tags, and the browser publishers introduced their own versions of these tags in an attempt to corner the market. HTML browsers are hard-coded to respond to a specific set of HTML elements. So you see a lot of pages that say, "This site requires Internet Explorer" or "This site requires Netscape Communicator."

But XML is different. Thanks to XML's careful and logical design, the markup languages you create with XML are *self-describing*. A program called an XML processor can read your document, figure out how you've structured it, and display the information accordingly. Unlike HTML, XML doesn't force everyone to use the same tag set, at the cost of losing some of their audience should they introduce something new.

The implications of this will take a while to sink in, but here's a taste: With XML, there's really nothing to stop you from inventing whatever tags you want. And instead of isolating your information, your creativity makes your information all the more accessible!

A Web-Friendly Version of SGML

Unlike SGML, which is most often used for nonpublic corporate or research applications, XML was designed from the beginning to be useful on the Internet. It incorporates all the fundamentals of HTML hyperlinking—and, as you'll learn in Chapter 7, it adds some very attractive new linking options that every Web author will appreciate. Another way in which XML differs from SGML (and, in so doing, shows XML's Web-friendliness) lies in its support for easy-to-use style sheet languages. Web authors want their documents to look good, but they don't want to learn a programming language to style their documents the way SGML requires. As you'll learn in this book, Cascading Style Sheets (CSS) provides the ideal tool for presenting XML documents with magazine-quality layouts, fonts, and graphics.

The Two Approaches to XML

Although it's still early in the game—the XML 1.0 specification was just published at this book's writing—early activity suggests that people are looking at XML in two very different ways:

- **Approach 1: As a means for storing structured data so that it can be processed by customized applications.** Microsoft's Channel Definition Format (CDF), explored in Chapter 19, exemplifies this approach. Created with XML, CDF is a markup language that enables Web authors to set up site subscriptions. Web users never see the CDF document directly; instead, it's read by an XML-savvy browser, and the CDF information enables the application to make subscription options available.
- **Approach 2: As a means for publishing structured documents that people can browse and read directly.** As you'll see, one of the terrific things about XML is that it's self-describing—which means that applications can automatically detect and represent your markup scheme's underlying structure. This enables applications to display your document in two

ways: as a text document, the way HTML does, and also as a navigable tree structure.

To date, most XML activity is characterized by Approach 1, but that's to be expected—after all, at this writing there aren't any browsers that can read and display XML documents. You'll see a lot more interest in Approach 2 once XML-ready browsers appear. This book examines both approaches.

Where Did XML Come From?

A project coordinated by the World Wide Web Consortium (W3C), headquartered in Cambridge, Mass., the basic XML 1.0 language specification has the status of a W3C Recommendation—which means that it's a firmly established standard.

In mid-1998, however, three key components of the XML recommendation (XLink, XPointer, and namespaces) existed in W3C Working Drafts. In the W3C scheme of things, a Working Draft represents reasonable consensus among the committee members, but the draft is intended to promote discussion—and that discussion may result changes to the specification when the final Recommendations are published.

Other components of the technology that are usually considered part of XML, such as the eXtensible Style Language (XSL), exist only as unofficial proposals submitted to the W3C, or as Notes (W3C publications that are intended to stimulate discussion without representing any W3C commitment to the material contained in them).

Please note that this book's treatment of XLink and XPointer hyperlinking is based on the W3C's Working Drafts, and some of the details covered in this book will change when the final Recommendations are published. For the latest information on XML, be sure to visit the W3C Web site, located at www.w3.org.

The XML language specification is the product of a collaboration between the SGML and Web communities. Their goal was to create a simplified version of SGML that would be optimized for use on the Web. As I think you'll agree after reading this book, they succeeded brilliantly.

How This Book Is Organized

I've titled this book *Web Publishing with XML in 6 Easy Steps*—but that doesn't mean you have to take all six of them. The steps correspond to the various parts of this book, summarized in the following sections.

Part One: Understanding Document Structure

Part One provides a conceptual foundation for everything that follows. Don't let that sound threatening—it's actually interesting stuff. As you'll learn in Chapter 1, computers produce huge benefits only when the underlying structure of information is understood. Then, and only then, it becomes possible to represent and manipulate this structure with all the speed and power that a computer provides. Although most of humanity's knowledge exists in text-based documents, it's only recently that the underlying, flexible tree structure of these documents has been discovered.

As you'll learn in Chapter 2, SGML arose from an attempt to mark this structure and make it available for computer processing. In spite of its enormous promise, though, SGML has failed to have much of an impact. It's too complex, too difficult to learn, and doesn't provide usable tools for presenting information attractively.

Part Two: Appreciating the Need for XML

In Part Two, you'll learn why HTML has been so dramatically successful, even as SGML languished in obscurity. You'll also learn about HTML's shortcomings, and why so many people believe that it's near the end of its useful life. You'll learn why people from the Web and SGML communities joined hands to create a simplified version of SGML called XML. As you'll see, XML solves not only the Web's problems but many of SGML's as well. This could lead to a major shift in the way people and organizations work with document-based information.

Part Three: Writing Well-Formed XML

Part Three shows you how easy it is to create your own markup languages with XML. When you write *well-formed* XML, you must follow certain easily learned rules, but you don't have to write a document type definition (DTD). Anyone can learn how to make a markup language in short order—and, if you follow the simple rules, an XML browser can understand your document's structure and display it accordingly. In Part Three, you'll also learn the fundamentals of XML's hyperlinking languages, XLink and XPointer, and you'll learn how to use an XML editor to compose XML documents.

Part Four: Creating Document Type Definitions (DTDs)

Should you decide that you'd like to try your hand at creating a DTD, you'll find that doing so has many advantages—and, with XML, it's much easier than you'd think. The chapters in Part Four are designed to meet your needs; you're a typical Web author who knows HTML but doesn't really want to do this as the first step in learning how to write full-fledged SGML. Accordingly, these chapters present just the information you need to know, and do it as clearly as possible. You'll be surprised to learn how easy it is to create a DTD with XML.

Part Five: Assigning Styles to XML Elements

XML does something HTML doesn't: It completely separates the *structure* of markup from the *presentation* of the marked-up information. This makes XML documents easy to read and maintain, but raw XML doesn't look like much on-screen. To present your XML markup, you need to use a style sheet language. This book stresses Cascading Style Sheets (CSS), an easy-to-learn style sheet language that will meet the needs of almost all XML authors. Also discussed is the proposal for a more sophisticated style sheet language called XSL.

Part Six: Exploring XML Vocabularies

To help you understand what people are doing right now with XML, Part Six examines two XML-derived markup languages in detail: the Channel Definition Format (CDF) and the Synchronized Multimedia Integration Language (SMIL). One has already had a significant impact on Web publishing, and the latter seems likely to do so. You'll also find less detailed descriptions of many other XML-based projects. From these examples, you can get a better idea of how people are learning to apply XML right now.

Where Should You Start?

This book is designed so that you can approach its subject in a way that suits your interest level and the amount of time you have.

- Would you like to start with a conceptual overview, one that puts XML in perspective? Start with Part One, "Understanding Document Structure."
- Do you need an introduction to the XML before you start coding? Start with Part Two, "Appreciating the Need for XML."
- Do you want to jump right in and start learning XML? Start with Part Three, "Writing Well-Formed XML."
- Would you like to see what other people are already doing with XML, before you dive in? Start with Part Six, "Exploring XML Vocabularies."

The only parts of this book that really ought to be read in order are Parts Three, Four, and Five.

Keeping Informed

Learning XML is like trying to change a tire on a moving truck—there's a new development, it seems, every couple of weeks. This book will give you a solid foundation in the principles of XML, but you'll be wise to keep in contact with what's happening now, months after this book hits the shelves. Naturally, the best place to do this is the World Wide Web.

Here are some sites you'll want to visit:

- **World Wide Web Consortium (W3C)** (www.w3.org) Here, you'll find news concerning the latest status of XML and XML-related standards, including XLink, XPointer, Namespaces, and XSL.
- **Robin Cover's SGML/XML Web Page** (www.sil.org/sgml). This is *the* place on the Web to find information related to any aspect of SGML and XML. Updated several times per week, the XML section provides links to standard documents, press releases, announcements of XML software, Internet-accessible tutorials, technical documents, mailing lists, and much more.
- **Microsoft's XML Workshop** (www.microsoft.com/xml) This site includes useful information on XML support in Microsoft Internet Explorer.
- **XML.com** (www.xml.com) Jointly published by Seybold Publications and O'Reilly & Associates, this professionally-designed and maintained site includes up-to-date links and original articles by key XML players.

From Here

To get started with this book's conceptual overview, go directly to Chapter 1. To learn more about XML before you start learning it, go to Chapter 3. If you've had enough introduction and you're ready to start coding, go to Chapter 6.

Part One

Understanding Document Structure

1

Discovering Document Structure

According to a recent estimate, U.S. corporations create 92 billion documents a year. It's not because anybody really enjoys killing trees, writing reports, filing all the documents, or—perish the thought—actually *reading* them. And it's also not because the information contained in these documents is readily accessible or easy to manipulate—quite the opposite, as you'll see. Organizations create so many documents because there's simply no other way to encode information that's new and complex. As this chapter explains, though, computers haven't yet helped to make this information more readily available and useful.

For several years, though, SGML's advocates have argued that they've found a solution. In this chapter, you'll find out why.

Word Processing Makes Paper, Not Data

In the early, heady days of the PC revolution, computer experts confidently predicted that word processing software would lead to major gains in white collar productivity. After all, they argued, professionals, managers, and executives write a lot of reports, and word processing software enables them to do it more quickly. As any writer, myself included, will tell you, word processing frees writers from the drudgery of revisions (which used to require retyping the whole document). You'd think that word processing would lead to major productivity gains.

The productivity gains didn't happen. Researchers found that people use word processing programs to write longer documents, and they spend more time fussing over their document's appearance. And in the end, they produced the same old product: paper. To be sure, paper documents look better today, with cool fonts and laser-printed quality. But they're still just marked-up paper. And that's exactly the problem.

Word processing embodies a publication model that goes all the way back to Gutenberg, the inventor of printing: You make marks on paper. However, as organizations everywhere are discovering, *paper isn't information.* You can read the documents, of course, but you can't easily reuse or manipulate the information. You'll need to find the file in order to do so. But you'll have to jump through a series of hurdles:

- **Where is it?** "Who's got the original file?"
- **What format is it in?** "Sombody wrote this thing up in MacWrite II. How the heck do I open this file with WordPerfect?"
- **Is the formatting correct?** "Oh no, they typed this up using the wrong style sheet. Darn, I'm going to have to reformat the whole thing."
- **Did the author use standard techniques for entering text?** "Can you believe this? This guy indented every paragraph by pressing the spacebar five times. I'm going to have to delete all those spaces manually."

Lost files, incompatible file formats, formatting inconsistencies, idiosyncratic text entry techniques—all these problems explain why so little document-based information is available when and where it's needed. Often, people conclude that it's cheaper and easier to retype documents rather than deal with these problems. Not surprisingly, several major late-1980s studies of the impact of word processing software on whitecollar productivity were unable to demonstrate any gains—and some suggested productivity decreases.

The Hidden Costs of Word Processing

The time and money wasted on these problems add up in terms of both misdirected effort and lost opportunities:

- A documentation conference held in Toronto in 1996 concluded that 90 percent of all corporate data is contained in documents.
- A Gartner Group study found that 60 percent of the work of a typical corporation involves creating and dealing with documents.

- Much of this effort involves fussing with formatting and file incompatibilities. A major software firm reported that its technical writers spent up to 30% of their time on the rote chores of managing word processing files.
- A university research team found that the effort expended on creating, printing, revising, and distributing documents consumes 12 to 15 percent of a typical corporation's revenue.
- According to a 1994 article in *Credit Union Executive*, the typical banking executive spends 150 hours per year looking for lost information.
- A study reported in *The Wall Street Journal* found that computer users spent nearly a third of their time trying to organize files on their systems and deal with file incompatibilities.
- In a typical manufacturing firm, the costs of updating documents to reflect a single engineering change can exceed $50,000.

The inaccessibility of data contained in word processing files causes horrendous problems. But that's not the worst of it.

Report Card: "Not Performing Up to Potential"

Big as they are, the problems with word processing that I've just enumerated are only the tip of the iceberg. There's something even worse underneath them: *Word processing doesn't improve white collar productivity because it didn't make full use of the computer's potential.*

Computers bring about revolutionary changes only when people (1) learn how to penetrate down to the underlying structure of whatever type of information you happen to be dealing with and (2) represent this structure in a digital form that computers can manipulate.

The major breakthrough in digital audio, for example, occured when audio engineers discovered that a single, 16-bit digital number could almost perfectly represent a tiny fraction of a second's worth of the sound produced by a 120-member symphony orchestra.

From this discovery stems the digital audio industry, which brings us beautiful noise-free recordings and a host of new possibilities for creative expression in digital composing.

Word processing software doesn't do anything like this. It's just a way of cranking out paper, more paper, and still more paper. It doesn't penetrate down to the underlying structure of documents, and doesn't provide a method for representing and manipulating this structure.

What about Database Software?

Database software does get down to the underlying structure of the information recorded in databases, and that's why databases are revolutionizing information storage and retrieval. So! (Bright idea!) Why not put documents into databases? This is the typical computer nerd's first reaction to the problem. As you'll see, though, it's not the right solution—and in fact, it's not a solution at all, at least for the challenges posed by the 90% of information that's contained in documents.

In a database, you create fields that hold certain types of information, as in the following example:

```
MARINA     Happy River Yacht Heaven
SLIPS      128
SHOWERS    10
FUEL       Yes
PUMPOUT    Yes
POWER      120v 30a
TERM       1 year
LEASE      Yes
RENT       $1400
STAFF      Surly
```

Suddenly, the information becomes much more usable. The computer can sort it, summarize it, group it, total it, print it, and more. From my marina database, I can figure out the average cost of an annual boat slip rental—and lots of other facts, such as which marinas have friendly staff and lots of showers.

But databases work only where you can impose a rigid, predefined structure on information, and plug facts into these fields. As many companies have found to their dismay, database programs are close to useless for most document production tasks. Documents contain fluid natural language and often develop new ideas. They contain fuzzy concepts and ideas that aren't easy to fit into predetermined categories. Documents often deal with novel situations in which previous classifications and categories are all but useless—in fact, that's why a lot of documents are written in the first place!

Using database software for writing purposes is like trying to pound a square peg into a round hole—at some point, you'll have to give up. Documents don't have the same structure as information that's susceptible to encoding in a database. But what is the underlying structure of a document?

The Hidden Structure of Everyday Documents

In every career or profession, people learn to write documents according to conventionally defined templates, which specify which part of the document goes where. For example, a business letter includes the correspondent's address, the date, the salutation, the message, and the closing. Take a look:

```
May 21, 1998

Alfred J. Billing
Attorney at Law
129 Milvern Palace Drive
Culver Heights, CA 90299

Dear Mr. Billing:

This is just a note to thank you for your
rather confusing, but ultimately illuminat-
ing, advice concerning my plans to patent my
invention. I've given up the plan because,
obviously, it can't be understood by mere
mortals such as yourself, and I guess I'll
never be able to market the darned thing.

Sincerely,


Janet Genius, Inventor
```

Almost all of the documents we write conform to some sort of overall structural plan like this one, which can be called a *document type*. A document type consists of a number of *structural units* or components (such as "title," "abstract," and "key words"), each of which contains a certain type of information.

It's Flexible — That's Why We Love It

Wait a minute! Is a letter's underlying structure really any different than the type of information that you could plug into a database? If we're just talking about letters, maybe not. Business letters have a fairly rigid structure. But there are all kinds of documents, and most of them have a much less rigidly defined structure. In fact, that's exactly *why* documents are so useful as means of recording and transmitting information: They *don't* lock you into rigid, straitjacket structures. There's room for novelty, creativity, and invention.

Take poems, for instance. A lot of poems consist of nothing but a collection of lines, like the following from the pen of Alexander Pope. The poem's made up of a whole string of two-liners called *couplets:*

> A little learning is a dangerous thing;
> Drink deep, or taste not the Pierian spring:
> There shallow draughts intoxicate the brain,
> And drinking largely sobers us again. . . .

Other poems may contain structural units called *stanzas,* as in Poe's "Annabel Lee"*:*

> It was many and many a year ago
> In this kingdom by the sea
> That a maiden there lived whom you may know
> By the name of Annabel Lee;
> And this maiden she lived with no other thought
> Than to love and be loved by me.
>
> I was a child, and she was a child
> In this kingdom by the sea,
> But we loved with a love that was more than love,
> I and my Annabel Lee,

With a love that the winged seraphs in heaven
Coveted her and me. . . .

Poets vary the basic structure of lines and stanzas in endless interesting ways. Here, Byron combines a type of six-line stanza called a *sestet* with a following stanza containing two lines (a *couplet*):

In the first year of Freedom's second dawn
Died George the Third; although no tyrant, one
Who shielded tyrants, till each sense withdrawn
Left him nor mental nor external sun:
A better farmer ne'er brushed dew from lawn,
A worse king never left a realm undone!

He died—but left his subjects still behind,
One half as mad — and t'other no less blind.

What's going on here? Simply this: A document type contains structural units that authors *manipulate* in order to shape and convey their meaning. They combine them and repeat them in endlessly creative ways. You can see this quite plainly in poetry, but the same goes for dissertations, newspaper articles, engineering reports, novels, or any other kind of writing that isn't subject to a straitjacket structural mold.

Seeing the Trees (Forget the Forest)

So what type of data structure are we talking about here? It's a *tree structure*. A tree structure is a way of organizing information in a hierarchy, in which the top-level units encompass lower-level units. It's called a tree structure because it looks something like an inverted tree—or heck, maybe a windswept bush—as shown in the following diagram:

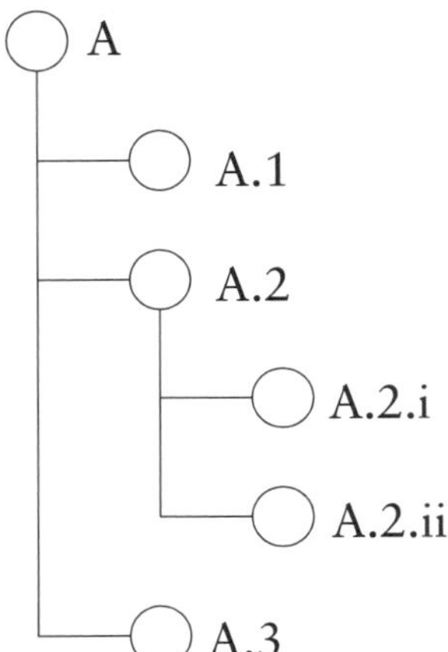

At the top of this diagram you see the top-level unit (A), which is a very general category. It encompasses three second-level units—more specific categories (A.1, A.2, and A.3). One of the second-level elements (A.2) encompasses a couple of third-level units (A.2.i and A.2.ii), which are even more specific.

It's useful to think about tree structures in terms of *nesting*. Nesting refers to units being placed *within* other units in a tree structure. For example, A.1, A.2, and A.3 are nested within A. Another way to put this is to talk in terms of "parents" and "children." A is the parent of A.1 and so on.

The neat thing about tree structures is their *extensibility*—the way you can nest and repeat the units to create infinitely varied and complex structures. Obviously, this is a whole different world than the kind of fixed-field database structures we were talking about earlier in this chapter. Tree structures enable authors to combine units in endlessly creative ways—and that enables them to deal with new, complex information that couldn't be conveyed by means of a rigidly defined structure. Here's an example that suggests how fluid and flexibile tree structures can be:

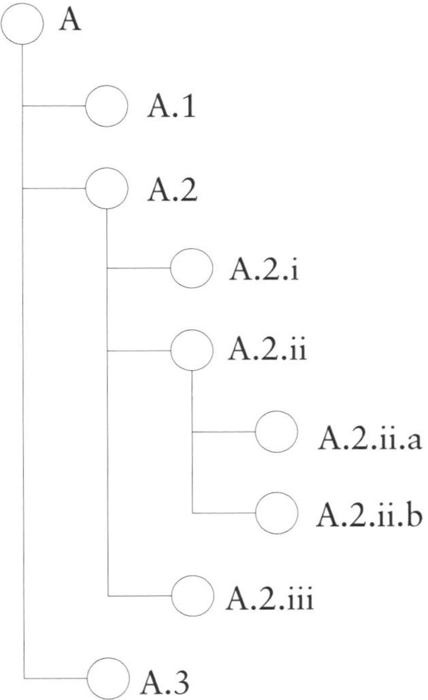

Note that, in this version of the tree shown earlier, another unit has been added at the third level, and this has produced two "children" at the fourth level. With this kind of flexibility, you can organize and express *any* information, no matter how complex or novel it might be.

Poets Do It (You Can Too)

Poets are noted for thinking in structural terms and for finding cool structures—often entirely new ones that they themselves invent—in which to express their ideas. To put this another way, poets think structurally in terms of *lines* and *line groups*, organized as tree structures. Here's how you could see Byron's poem as a tree structure:

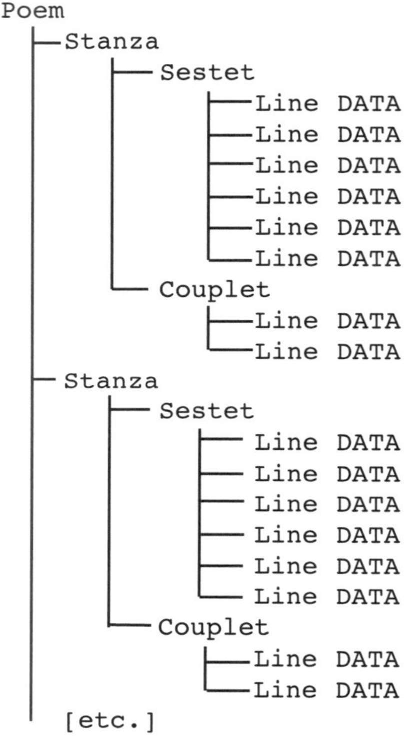

You're probably thinking, "What is this, a literature class?" No, it's not. As I just mentioned, all kinds of writers use extensible, nested structures to embed knowledge in documents. Poets are just more aware of what they're doing, so it's wonderful to look at poetry as a way of understanding what extensible nesting is all about. Consciously or not, you make use of tree structures in almost every document you write. I could make this point by showing you such structures in engineering reports, but they'd be a lot less fun to read than "Annabel Lee."

So What's the Big Deal?

"OK," you're probably saying. "Documents have tree structures, and that's why they're extensible, and that's also why they're such tremendous vehicles for encoding complex and even novel information. But SO WHAT?"

Here's what. *Once you've realized that documents have extensible tree structures, you're on your way to realizing that you can mark these structures—and once you've done that, you're on your way to making the information contained in documents susceptible to computer processing.*

That's what the big deal is. Take a deep breath, and ponder the implications. In every previous area where computers have revolutionized the way we work and play, they've done so because some way has been found to *represent* and *process* the data's underlying structure. The discovery of document structure is the first step toward making document knowledge susceptible to computer processing.

My Structure, Your Structure

I don't mean to imply here that every type of document has only one type of structure, like all cats have the same basic skeleton underneath all that fur. The structures are there, but people perceive them differently depending on their purposes. For example, we've been looking at the underlying structure of poetry in order to learn how writers use nested trees in a creative process. A literary scholar preparing a critical edition of a work might be more interested in describing stanzas and line breaks with precision.

So people see different aspects of the structures in documents, depending on what their purposes are. For some, what's of interest is the way the author has put the document together using structural units that can be described with quantitative precision; for others, what's of interest is the *meaningful content* that's expressed within the structural units. These are very different perspectives, so it's important to remember that the structure you see depends on what you're after.

You can see this distinction by comparing HTML and the markup languages that people have been creating with XML. HTML is a very simple language for markup of a document's structural components, such as titles, headings, lists, and paragraphs. Most of the emerging XML vocabularies show much more interest in the *content* of these structures, largely because HTML makes it so difficult to find this content. For example, in HTML, I can write about environmental organizations in Virginia, but I can't mark this information so that it's clear to a computer that this document actually contains a lot of information about this subject. As you'll see, XML enables me to do so in a way that HTML just can't.

Although scholars have valid reasons for marking up structural components, Web authors will prefer to discover and mark the meaningful content so that this content is more accessible to search programs and human readers. Both approaches are valid—they just have different ends in mind.

Whether you're identifying structural components or meaningful content, the next step involves *marking* these structures so the computer can tell where they begin and where they end. And that's were *descriptive markup* comes in.

Introducing Descriptive (Structural) Markup

In *descriptive markup* (also called *structural markup*), you insert codes (called *tags*) that make the document's structure obvious, even to something as stupid as a computer. Once you've done this, the knowledge contained in a document becomes susceptible to computer retrieval and processing: You can search for it, display it, retrieve it, recombine it, reuse it, embed it in other documents, file it, mail it, share it, and much, much more.

The tags describe the structure and indicate which data are contained in each unit. The tags are made from plain ASCII characters, the ones you see on the usual, garden-variety computer keyboard. (The use of ASCII characters gets us beyond the expensive word processing problem of incompatible file formats, incidentally, because every computer can handle these characters.)

Here's what the Byron poem looks like when marked up using the tags defined by the Text Encoding Initiative (TEI), a consortium of folks who are working to bring literature into the Digital Age:

```
<LG type = "stanza">
    <LG type = "sestet">
      <L>In the first year of Freedom's second dawn
      <L>Died George the Third; although no tyrant, one
      <L>Who shielded tyrants, till each sense withdrawn
      <L>Left him nor mental nor external sun:
      <L>A better farmer ne'er brushed dew from lawn,
      <L>A worse king never left a realm undone!
    </LG>
    <LG type = "couplet">
```

```
            <L>He died—but left his subjects still behind,
            <L>One half as mad—and t'other no less blind.
        </LG>
    </LG>
```

"LG" is short for "Line group," and as you can see, there are three different types of them: stanzas, sestets, and couplets. The "L" stands for "Line."

Note that this isn't the only way you could mark up this document. If you're interested in Byron's political message, for example, you might wish to modify the markup language. In the following, for example, I've modified TEI's <L> tag with an attribute that enables me to indicate which lines contain political commentary:

```
<L class="commentary">A better farmer ne'er brushed dew
from lawn,
<L class="commentary">A worse king never left a realm
undone!
```

As this example suggests, it isn't such a good idea to try to create one standard markup language and expect everyone to use it. People look at document structures in different ways, and they should be able to describe the structures they see. The result multiplies and enriches our perspective on the knowledge contained in textual documents.

What Is Descriptive Markup Good For?

Nothing, initially—but that's the cool thing about it. Descriptive markup is done without making any assumptions about how the information is going to be processed. A program could detect these tags and format the various elements pleasingly for presentation (printing or display) purposes.

Alternatively, programs could be written that analyze the poem in various ways; for instance, you could ask, "How many of Byron's couplets include dashes?" Patterns hidden within an undifferentiated sea of text suddenly become amenable to computer processing, sometimes with startling results: Computer-based analyses of marked-up texts have resolved a number of controversies over just who authored a poem or novel—and in some cases have revealed frauds that went undetected for a century or more. If your interests lean to the meaningful content side, you could write a program that groups all of Byron's political commentary, so that you could compare the lines that contain this content.

There's another payoff to descriptive markup, and it's a biggie. If it's done with ASCII characters—just the ones found on the computer keyboard—the marked-up text can be transferred with ease over computer networks, even those that hook up a variety of mutually incompatible computer systems.

Another huge payoff: With descriptive markup, you can transfer your file over the Internet with absolutely no hassles. Any computer can deal with the files. In a network with a multitude of different computers, this fact alone can pay off very handsomely.

There are more wonderful things about descriptive markup. To understand them, though, let's go back to word processing software.

Procedural Markup Considered Harmful

This chapter began with the evils of word processing files, with their embedded proprietary formats, which are incompatible with software made by other software publishers. Word processing files actually do contain markup of a sort, called *procedural markup*. Procedural markup contains specific instructions for specific types of hardware devices (computers, displays, and printers) that tell them exactly what to do.

Procedural markup is a Bad Thing because the minute you use it, you've limited your file's usefulness to a certain type of computer and certain types of displays and certain types of printers. When new computers and displays and printers come along, your file may not work.

Descriptive markup is wonderful because it doesn't make any assumptions at all about which software, computer, display, or printer you're going to use. Instead, it leaves all these matters to the programs people run when they access your file. These programs are optimized for whatever environment they're running in. That's fine. The important thing is, your file is useful to *anyone* who wants to access it.

Structure at Your Fingertips

There's one other extremely wonderful thing about descriptive markup—maybe the most wonderful thing of all. I'll just hint at it here; the next chapter explores this point in detail. Here's the point: If you've marked up the structure of a document using a recognized set of rules, there's software out there that can read the document's structure and display it in a tree diagram. These programs can display the text in one pane and the tree in the other, giving you a very neat and powerful way to navigate a document.

The following figure (Figure 1.1) illustrates the possibilities. You're looking at a collection of Aesop's Fables. On the left, you see the titles of the fables. On the right, you see the fable you've selected. What's cool about this is that the browser—here, Microsoft Internet Explorer equipped with the Panorama plug-in for reading SGML files—auto-

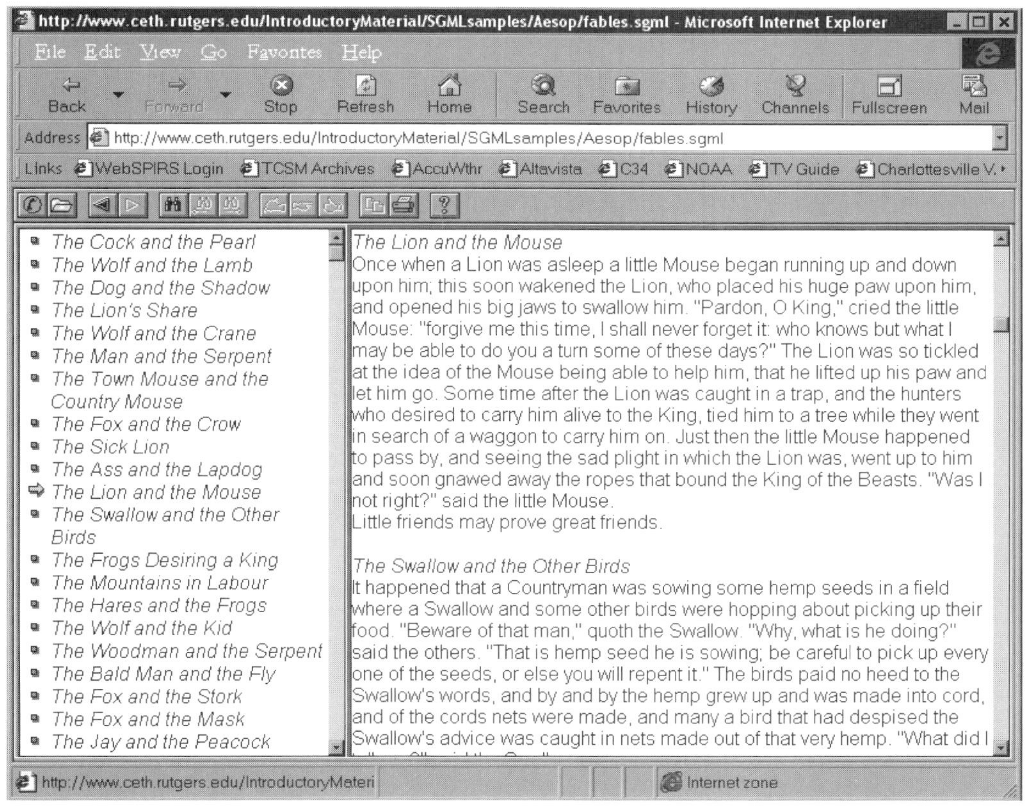

Figure 1.1 SGML browsers can detect and display document structures.

matically detects and displays the document's tree structure, enabling you to navigate the document with ease.

From Here

Word processing software makes writing easier, but it doesn't enable organizations to represent and manipulate the information contained in documents. As this chapter has explained, people write documents because documents offer an elegantly flexible way of encoding information that couldn't be expressed if you had to plug it into rigid, predefined categories.

Descriptive markup makes this information available for computer processing. It also enables document authors to distribute ASCII files, which can be read without difficulty by almost any text-processing program on any computer. Best of all, descriptive markup enables specially prepared programs to detect and display the document's structure, providing an alternative to paging through an ocean of text.

In Chapter 2, you'll learn about SGML, the leading tool for creating descriptive markup languages. Although you don't need to learn SGML to learn XML, it's useful to know just what SGML achieved—and why it failed to achieve the great things some people predicted.

2

Getting a Handle on SGML

As you learned in the last chapter, descriptive markup promises to make document structure available for computer processing—and what's more, it does away with file conversion hassles and opens cool new possibilities for document navigation. But it doesn't make any sense to mark up documents using some sort of proprietary markup scheme. You'd be back in exactly the same box that proprietary word processing software puts you in: stuck with one company's supported software and hardware.

That's why *markup languages* have been created. A markup language defines a set of specific markup symbols, called *tags*, that you can use to identify the structure of your document.

The whole subject of markup languages is dominated by SGML, short for Standard Generalized Markup Language. This chapter focuses on SGML, for a couple of very good reasons. First, understanding SGML's plusses and minuses will enable you to grasp just why XML is such an important innovation. Second, you need to know a bit about SGML's basic concepts to understand XML, which is—after all—a simplified version of SGML.

In the Beginning (GML)

Great ideas have a habit of popping up in more than one place. In the late 1960s, at least two people (William Tunnicliffe, chairman of the Graphic Communications Association, and Stanley Rice, a New York book designer) seem to have independently come up with the idea of structural markup.

What was apparent from the outset, however, was a very serious problem: You'd have to develop a whole series of different markup languages, each suited to the particular requirements of document types.

In 1969, Charles Goldfarb, Edward Mosher, and Raymond Lorie, researchers at IBM, developed a *generalized markup language* that dealt with the problem of multiple, incompatible markup languages. Essentially, a generalized markup language would consist of tools needed to *define* a document type and the requisite tags. Anyone who wanted to mark up a document could look to the *document type definition (DTD)* (a formal document specifying what tags are allowed) to learn how to perform the markup correctly. These researchers went on to create the Generalized Markup Language (GML), which IBM uses to mark up a reported 90 percent of its documents.

What GML Didn't Do

GML first saw the light of day in 1973, but Goldfarb realized that it was far from perfect. One problem was the lack of a *validating parser*, a program that could check a document and make sure its markup actually conformed to the document type definition. Without a validating parser, human editors would have to scan the markup manually—a time-consuming and error-prone procedure, one that could derail some of the productivity benefits of using descriptive markup in the first place.

There's another problem, too. To make marked-up files truly *portable*—easily transferred to any type of computer—isn't as simple as you might think. It's not enough to refrain from procedural markup (although that's a good start). As you quickly realize when you try to read a Windows file on a Macintosh, computers have varying *character sets*. A character set is a list of standard characters (letters, numbers, punctuation marks, and symbols) that the computer is designed to represent and process. Almost all computers recognize the basic, 128-character American Standard Code for Information Interchange (ASCII), but they use proprietary character sets to represent additional characters (including foreign language characters, technical and math symbols, currency symbols, opening and closing quotation marks, and other special-purpose characters).

Some people think that the answer to file incompatibility problems is to create "plain text files" with no markup.

As the character set problem demonstrates, it's actually impossible to create a computer file with no markup. The proprietary character sets are a kind of markup in themselves. Even in plain text files, authors try to insert some presentation markup by creating blank lines, page breaks, page numbers, and spacing.

GML's shortcomings pointed the way. And the result was SGML.

Enter SGML

In 1978, the American National Standards Institute (ANSI) recognized the value of generalized markup languages and created a committee charged with creating a nonproprietary, standardized version of GML. The committee's objective was to develop the basic insights of GML and solve the problems of validation and character set incompatibility.

Goldfarb participated in this effort, which—with several reorganizations along the way—eventually resulted in the publication of draft specification in 1985. After a period of review, the specification, duly revised, was published as an international standard by the International Organization for Standardization (ISO) in 1986 (ISO 8879).

The work that went into SGML took eight years to complete and represented a remarkable collaboration among academic researchers, industry practitioners, and professional organizations worldwide.

What's So Special about SGML?

SGML's great achievement lies in making document type definitions computer-readable (which enables automatic validation) as well as in solving the character set incompatibility problems. The following sections explain how SGML does this.

It's a Metalanguage

SGML is not actually a markup language. Rather, it's a *metalanguage*, a language that can be used to create markup languages. For example, SGML was used to create HTML. With SGML, an organization can create customized markup languages that are designed specifically for its document types.

People use SGML to create *document type definitions (DTDs)*. A DTD specifies the structure of a document type as well as the tags that can be used to mark this structure.

SGML assumes that every type of document has the type of hierarchical structure introduced in Chapter 1, in which structural units (called *elements*) are organized in a nested hierarchy. In HTML, for example, there are two large-scale structural units—the HEAD and the BODY. Within the HEAD, you can insert (nest) a TITLE element.

A DTD also specifies rules that govern just where you can use a given element—and where you can't use it. In HTML, for example, you can place an H1 (Heading 1) tag within the BODY, but you can't place it within the HEAD.

It Enables Automatic Validation

SGML isn't easy to learn because its notation system—the one you have to use to create a DTD—is designed to be readable by computers as well as (trained) humans.

When you've marked up a document in an SGML-created markup language, you can open the document with a program called a *parser*. The parser checks the document to make sure that you've used all the required elements and that they've been nested correctly. If the parser finds errors, you see an error message, and the document may not be displayed. In this way, SGML enforces structural consistency.

Making the DTD computer-readable has another advantage. When an SGML-compatible display program runs across an SGML document, it looks for hidden code that indicates which DTD has been used to prepare the document. This code also tells the program where to find the DTD. In this way, a display program can quickly discover how to parse the document's structure and arrange the various elements properly.

It Assures Portability

To deal with character set incompatibilities and foreign languages, SGML introduces *string substitution* as a way of representing non-ASCII characters. For example, to represent an ampersand, you type the string *&* (a string being a series of characters).

Display devices (such as Web browsers) know how to display these character codes, called *entities*, on the specific type of hardware for which they're designed. For example, the Windows version of Internet Explorer knows how to display open and closed quotation marks on a Windows system, just as the Macintosh knows how to display open and closed quotation marks on a Macintosh.

The Three Components of SGML Markup

Besides content, an SGML document contains three components: elements, attributes, and entities. The following sections introduce these components in a nontechnical way.

Elements

As you learned in Chapter 1, documents turn out to have a hierarchical structure, in which content units are organized into nested trees. To describe a document structure, then, you need to identify the content units—and what's more, the rules that specify just which units can be used where. In a poem, for example, you can't put a stanza inside a line.

When you create an SGML document type definition, you create two things:

- A list of the content units (called elements) that can be used in this type of document.
- The rules that specify where elements can be used (and where they can't be used).

To do this, you first need to conceptualize the document as a tree structure, as explained in Chapter 1. Here's an example. In a memo, there's a head and a body. In the head, elements include the following:

- **To.** The memo's recipient.

- **From.** The memo's author.
- **Date.** The memo's date.
- **Re.** The memo's subject.

In some corporations, memo structure is rigidly defined; the head elements must all be present and must be typed in the same order. In any memo format, the heading elements don't belong in the body. In SGML, you can write rules that enforce this, so that any document that doesn't conform gets rejected by the validating parser.

What's in the body? From a structural perspective, it contains paragraphs. Within paragraphs, the memo might also contain words or phrases that the author chooses to emphasize.

A memo's tree structure, then, looks like this:

```
MEMO
    HEADING (must contain To, From, Date, Re)
        TO (required, must be first)
        FROM (required, must be second)
        DATE (required, must be third)
        RE (required, must be fourth)
    BODY (may contain one or more paragraphs)
        PARAGRAPH
            EMPHASIS (optional)
```

This isn't SGML, but creating a tree structure diagram of this type is the first step toward creating a DTD.

For each element, there's a *content model* that specifies the type of information the element should contain. For example, you could specify that the DATE element should contain a date typed according to a specified format. Like the rules that govern tree structures, content models help to make sure that authors enter information correctly; if an element contains data that violates the element's content model, the validating parser returns an error message.

Note that the term element *isn't synonymous with* tag. *An element is an identified and named structural unit within a document type. A tag is the code that's inserted into the document to mark an element's location. Most elements have start tags and end tags, as in the following HTML example: <H1>Here's a Level 1 Heading</H1>.*

Attributes

An element can have *attributes*, which qualify the element in some ways. Here are some examples:

- Giving the element a unique identifying number.
- Specifying the source of the data to be used as the element's content.
- Stating the status of an element (i.e., a report could be a draft or a finished version).

Every attribute has two parts: a name and a value. When you create a DTD, you can specify the type of data that can be used as a value.

Entities

As you've already learned, entities provide a solution to the problem of character set incompatibilities. They work by means of string substitution. For example, when an HTML browser sees &, it removes the string & from the document and inserts an ampersand (&).

The term *entity* isn't synonymous with *fancy character*, though. An entity, properly defined, is simply a named unit of text that, when processed, is replaced by something else. Here's an example of a use of an entity that doesn't have anything to do with character set incompatibilities: A writer could create an entity &ciatp; to stand for "Center for Integrated Applications in Text Processing." When the document is displayed or printed, the software removes the entity and substitutes the lengthy phrase. This saves a lot of typing.

Entities can also be used to refer to "boilerplate" text that must have a single, fixed wording, often for legal reasons. For example, suppose a writer in an insurance firm must make sure that every document contains exactly the correct language concerning the terms of an insurance policy. The entity &renewal; could refer to a passage of text that explains the company's policy on policy renewals. In this example, you can see that entities can be used to make sure that there's only one authoritative version of important text. This use of entities makes it very easy to update documents; you make just one change, and presto! It's automatically reflected in every document that contains the entity.

SGML Software

Once you've used SGML to create a document type definition, you'll need additional software to create documents, parse them for validity, display them on-screen, and output them to printers.

Editors

To create an SGML document, you can simply type up the text in an ASCII text editor or word processor, and type in the appropriate tags manually. But this solution isn't very satisfactory. The least little mistake in typing the tags (or placing them improperly) results in the document's failure to pass the parser's validity test—and as a result, it can't be displayed or printed.

Some word processing programs enable authors to create named styles, and it's possible to create translation programs that automatically transform these styles into marked-up elements.

It's much better to create documents using a structured editor, a program that's specially designed to enable

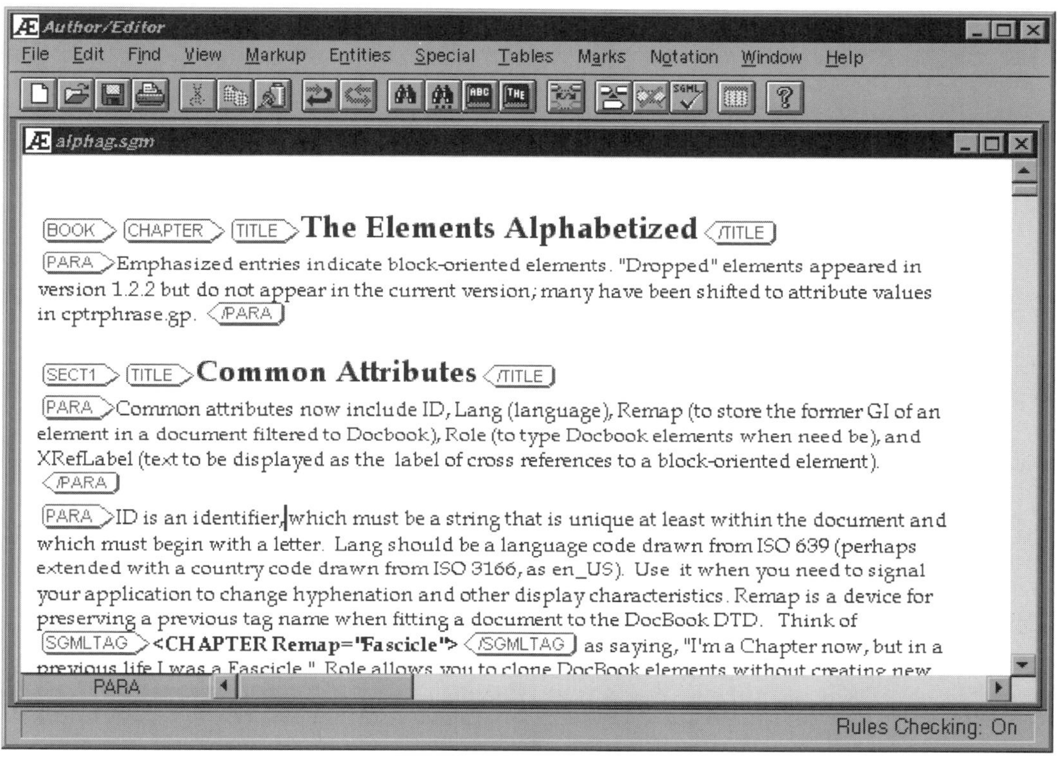

Figure 2..1 With Author/Editor, you can see the tags you've entered.

authors to work conveniently with text even as they're marking the text with tags. SoftQuad's Author/Editor provides an excellent example. The program enables authors to work with the tags on or off. With the tags on (as shown in Figure 2.1, on the previous page), authors can see just where they've inserted tags—and what's more, the program's real-time validity checker immediately alerts them if they've used a tag incorrectly.

If you prefer, you can hide the tags for easy editing (Figure 2.2). You're looking at an entirely new way of writing, and it's a safe bet that it will dominate document

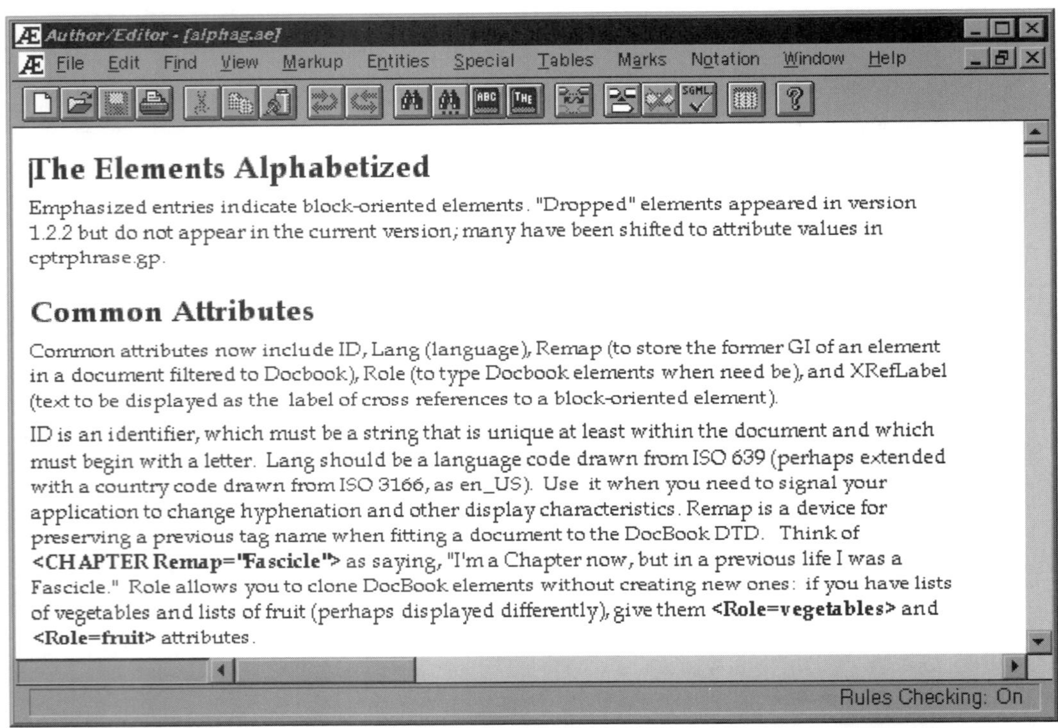

Figure 2.2 Author/Editor enables you to hide the tags for easy editing.

production the next century. It has to—the alternative (proprietary word processing) is just too expensive.

Formatters

So what happens when you want to output your SGML documents to a printer? Although most organizations that use SGML are sold on the idea of separating structure from the presentational aspects of documents, they still need to produce printed output. Unfortunately, the original SGML specification did not provide convenient tools for doing this. Soon, a standard arose (called the Formatting Output Specification or FOS) for specifying presentation styles for specific elements, but this was an interim solution at best. In 1996, the ISO has formalized a standard for SGML style sheets called Document Style Semantics and Specification Language (DSSSL, pronounced "dissel"). Essentially, DSSSL is a complex programming language that enables organizations to create style sheets for document types.

"Sounds Great, Maybe Later"

SGML is rightly regarded as a feat of technical brilliance. But organizations have been slow to adopt it. Part of the reason lies in SGML's complexity; as mentioned previously, the SGML specification runs to some 500 pages. In addition, writers hate it. They don't like giving up word processing programs and typing in horrible-looking tags. DSSSL has only added to SGML's complexity; it's equally complex, if not more so. SGML still doesn't have a workable style language that would enable authors to produce and print pretty-looking documents. Corporate authors are not about to give up their nice-looking printouts in favor of an incomplete SGML.

However, there's a deeper reason for SGML's slow acceptance. It's just too rigid. SGML was designed from the beginning with the assumptions that there's one and only one "correct" way to describe a document's structure and code it, and that SGML's advantages would be lost if parsers did not enforce absolute conformity to this dictated structure. Although this approach has proven valuable and attractive to technical organizations that must produce documentation according to rigid structural specifications, it has not proved workable or attractive elsewhere.

Why has SGML gained acceptance only slowly outside of technical documentation contexts? As Chapter 1 explained, people love writing documents because their tree structures can be extended and modified in all kinds of ways. And that's where SGML falls down. It's a great tool for *constraining* authors to follow the rules in a controlled writing environment; it's a relatively cumbersome tool for trying to *capture* the structure that authors use when they're free to invent whatever structures they like. By saying this, I don't mean to denigrate SGML or the achievements of the people who created this brilliant technology; it's simply that SGML is an incredibly useful tool for constraining authors, but it's not such a great one for describing what they've done when they're given free rein.

Had HTML not suddenly conquered the world, it's likely that very few people would have ever heard of SGML or thought that something like SGML is a wonderful thing. As the next chapter explains, the history of HTML exposes the shortcomings of SGML. For example, in comparison to the rigid and detailed DTDs developed in corporate, military, and industrial uses of SGML, HTML is very simple and flexible. It's simple, easy to learn, and capable of capturing all kinds of Web documents without imposing a rigid structure—which is precisely why it's been so wildly popular.

From Here

SGML is a *metalanguage*, a language that enables you to create and define markup languages for specific document types. HTML is an example of a markup language created with SGML. You use SGML to create a document type definition, which specifies which elements can be used (and where they can be used). Authors insert tags into documents to mark these elements, and parsers validate the structure to make sure that it conforms to the DTD.

Although SGML is a brilliant technical accomplishment, it initially provided no means for producing formatted output—a serious shortcoming. The recent DSSSL specification provides the formal foundation for formatted output by means of style sheets, but it's as complex as the SGML specification itself. And although SGML suits the needs of certain organizations to impose rigid control on the document creation process, it's too rigid, authoritarian, and unwieldy for most purposes.

In the next chapter, you'll take a new look at HTML, the markup language used to define the appearance of documents on the World Wide Web. As you'll learn, SGML was actually used to create HTML, although HTML isn't (strictly speaking) SGML-conformant. And what's more, HTML's popularity (as against the obscurity of other markup languages created with SGML) teaches some important lessons about why SGML has not gained wider acceptance.

Part Two

Appreciating the Need for XML

3

The Lessons of HTML

SGML would probably have remained a curiosity if it weren't for HTML, the SGML-defined markup language that set the World Wide Web in motion. In this chapter, you'll learn why HTML was such a rip-roaring success, compared to SGML's previous (and enduring) obscurity. But you'll also learn why HTML has outlived its usefulness and why the world needs a simpler version of SGML.

HTML: Simplicity Is the Key

In Switzerland, there's a physics research institute called CERN. (The acronym comes from the institute's French name.) CERN was one of the first European research centers to go whole hog for the Internet. By the mid-1980s, CERN was a hotbed of Internet computing. The institute was using the Internet to enable current research fellows to stay in close contact with researchers located elsewhere, including previous fellows of CERN. But the Internet protocols at the time didn't include anything as usable as the Web. And usability mattered.

Physics researchers have always been a chummy, network-oriented community. But computer-literate? Not necessarily. A CERN computer specialist named Tim Berners-Lee was looking for a way to enable physics researchers to share their materials—preprints, commentaries, proposals—that wouldn't force them to spend days or weeks learning complicated codes.

Word Processing Software? Nope

Why not just let these researchers contribute word processing files? No way. Word processing files contain special formatting characters that won't work on computers other than the one designed to run the word processing program. These formatting codes specify exactly how the document is supposed to look when it's printed. You can't use one of these files unless you have the same program (and, generally, the same type of computer as the one on which it was created).

The people at CERN knew all about these file incompatibility problems due to their experiences with the Internet. At CERN, the network included lots of different kinds of computers. These computers could exchange data only if the data contained nothing but the standard *ASCII characters* (the ones found on an ordinary computer keyboard).

Strict SGML? Nope

Berners-Lee knew about SGML and its ability to create markup languages, which enable the exchange of ASCII documents despite computer file system incompatibilities. But SGML, in itself, wasn't enough. At the time, SGML lacked any kind of navigation metaphor—something that could make the files more accessible. And what's more, it was too rigid. Berners-Lee knew that he couldn't ask these physics researchers to learn a bunch of complex elements. He also realized it didn't matter whether their documents passed a validity test. The point was getting them to exchange documents, not to force their documents into a rigid mold.

The HTML Secret: Simplicity, Hypertext, and Freedom!

The brilliant insight soon followed. Why not create a markup language with the following characteristics:

- **Simplicity.** Don't overwhelm these poor physicists with a huge set of elements. Keep it simple—just enough to enable them to create straightforward working documents for intellectual exchange.
- **Hypertext.** It's a simple navigation model suited to nontechnical types.
- **Freedom.** These physicists don't need an error message informing them that their HTML stinks. Better to set the whole system up so that browsers simply ignore inept markup. So HTML browsers aren't validating parsers, like SGML display programs. The HTML is hard-coded into the browser, which doesn't do any validation. It just displays the stuff it knows how to display, and ignores unknown tags.

The rest, as they say, is history. Originally developed for CERN and physics researchers, HTML quickly grew out of its original context and took the world by storm. HTML's been through several versions since then—see Table 3.1—and millions of people use it every day.

Table 3.1 Versions of HTML

Version	Description
1.0 (1989)	This is the original version of HTML created by Tim Berners-Lee for an obscure European research lab. It couldn't do a lot of the things that current versions of HTML can do, such as tables, frames, Java, and all the other snazzy things that we've come to expect of the Web. But it could display inline graphics (pictures mixed with text), and it enabled Web authors to create hyperlinks. And that's what got the ball rolling, big time.
2.0 (1994)	This version, officially ratified as an Internet standard, captured prevailing practice at the time, but was quickly outpaced due to the Netscape extensions (including tables).
3.0 (1996)	Never formally approved by the W3C (World Wide Web Consortium, headquartered in Cambridge, Mass.) or ratified by Internet standards bodies, this standard attempted to capture prevailing practices (such as tables and font tags) but was abandoned due to its internal inconsistencies.
3.2 (1996)	An updated version of the 2.0 standard, HTML is the work of the W3C. HTML formalized many of the popular extensions to HTML 2.0, including tables and text wrapping around images. Formally approved as a standard in January 1997, HTML 3.2 is the current baseline version of HTML; most Web authors continue to write assuming that people are using HTML 3.2–capable browsers.
4.0 (1997)	First published in the summer of 1997, the

proposed HTML 4.0 specification has now been issued as a World Wide Web Consortium Recommendation. HTML 4.0 deprecates (discourages) presentation-related elements and recommends moving presentation to eternal style sheets.

Creeping Presentationalism

HTML is a rip-roaring success thanks to its simplicity, navigability, and freedom. From a straight-laced SGML perspective, though, it isn't *pure*—and it hasn't been since its inception. In SGML terms, purity means upholding the distinction between structure and presentation. (From the SGML angle, that means little presentation, except when it is absolutely necessary for minimum rendition.) Yet from the beginning, HTML has included presentation markup. After all, those physicists wanted their papers to look nice. So even the earliest versions of HTML included some attributes that enabled authors to choose paragraph alignment and other presentation aspects. And soon, more prodigious forces came into play.

The Web Goes Commercial

No sooner had the Web burst onto the public scene than commercial Web authors started expressing disgust with HTML. How the heck could you use this overly simple markup language to create good-looking corporate Web sites?

Commercial Web authors want precise control over the appearance of their company's Web sites. They want tags that will enable them to create complex, magazine-style layouts, with fonts, multiple columns, and other eye-catching formats.

The Browser Opportunity

This creates an irresistible opportunity for browser publishers. If a browser publisher unilaterally introduces a nonstandard HTML tag that gives formatting control or enables authors to push content in your face, and supports it in their browser, the company might be able to get everyone or almost everyone to use its browser. These new tags are called *extensions*.

The Extensions Game—Everyone Does It

The extensions game got going in a big way when young Marc Andreesen left the National Center for Supercomputing Applications (NCSA), the birthplace of Mosaic, and co-founded Netscape Communications. The company added a whole lot of new HTML tags (including tags to create tables) to version 2.0 of Netscape Navigator. They were features that Web authors really wanted. At the time (1995), these features weren't present in the standard version of HTML (1.0). Web authors used these features and put messages on their welcome pages that said, "This site looks best with Netscape Navigator." Lots of free advertising for Netscape, and too bad for you if you're using another browser!

This strategy effectively knocked a lot of the smaller browser players out of the picture, unless they had the money to update their product so that it could display the new Netscape tags (called the Netscape extensions).

Microsoft plays this game, too. For example, Version 2.0 of Microsoft Internet Explorer introduced new tags for creating marquees (scrolling text banners) as well as watermarks (background graphics that don't scroll with text).

Simplicity Lost

What's wrong with the extensions game? By putting presentation aspects into HTML, extensions transform HTML into a coding nightmare, difficult to write and very expensive and time-consuming to maintain. Here's an example of what's needed to center a heading that's formatted with large Helvetica type:

```
<CENTER><FONT face = “Helvetica” size=”7”>A
Heading</FONT></CENTER>
```

All the presentation tags transform what should be a simple expression into an editing and maintenance nightmare. Using tables, for instance, you can create magazine-type layouts—see Figure 3.1 for an example drawn from one of my Web publishing efforts—but only

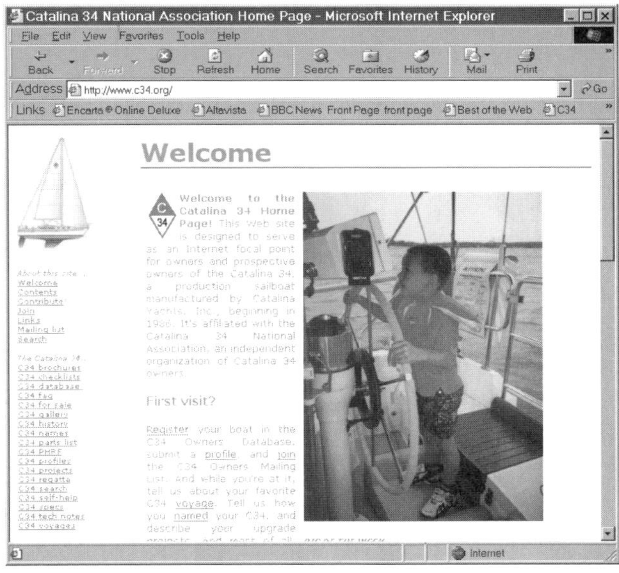

Figure 3.1 HTML authors use tables to emulate magazine layouts.

at the expense of creating code that's a headache to maintain. In the push for presentation, the vital distinction between structure and presentation has been lost.

The Standardization Process (Such as It Is)

It would be nice if the World Wide Web Consortium (W3C) could step in and force companies to stop introducing extensions to HTML. But W3C has absolutely no enforcement power. And besides, this probably wouldn't be desirable. Both Netscape and Microsoft have introduced useful new extensions to HTML—extensions that might not have existed were the task of HTML standardization left up to some academically oriented committee.

To its credit, W3C recognizes this point. Currently, the standardization process consists, essentially, of bringing all the industry participants to the table and getting them to agree on new standards that reflect the best and most widely accepted innovations—and everyone agrees to support the new, standardized version once it's approved and published. The W3C has been very successful in its effort to reduce the amount of proprietary meddling with the HTML standard, but all these efforts—commendable as they are—do not address HTML's underlying deficiencies. As long as people are using a tag set that's hard-coded within browsers, there's going to be a temptation to introduce extensions to the tag set in an attempt to corner the browser market.

Putting Presentation in Its Place (Style Sheets)

The latest version of HTML, 4.0 reduces the temptation to introduce proprietary presentation tags into HTML by taking the presentaion *out* of HTML entirely and transferring it to *style sheets.* A style sheet is a series of style specifications that tell a browser how to display a given element. For example, you can choose 18-point Helvetica for H1 headings, if you wish. Because the style sheet is kept away from most of the HTML code (and even kept in a separate document, if you wish), your HTML code is cleaner and much easier to maintain.

In theory, HTML 4.0 can work with any standardized style sheet format, but browsers support the Consortium's Cascading Style Sheets (CSS) standard. Currently, CSS is in its second version (Level 2).

But wait a minute. Doesn't the use of style sheets constitute an admission of sorts that HTML has lost the battle against presentation? Well, yes. But that's another of the lessons that HTML teaches. Nothing like the "purist" philosophy of SGML is ever going to wash on the Internet. People *want* presentation. The question is, how do you give it to them in a way that doesn't mess up the document's structure, and can be displayed on a variety of mutually incompatible computer systems? CSS is a good step in the right direction. Essentially, it enables people to have their presentation and their structure too. *And that's what they want.*

Getting Long in the Tooth?

Despite HTML's success and the promise of CSS style sheets, it's apparent that HTML is running up against its inherent limitations. Here's a quick survey:

- **It's *too* simple.** The very simplicity that makes HTML so popular also makes it close to useless for expressing the text structures found in specialized areas, such as medical records, electronic commerce, academic bibliographies, and much more. It's simple, yes, but the simplicity comes at a price.

- **There's no way to introduce new elements without setting off a new round of browser wars.** HTML browsers are hard-coded with an HTML element set. You can invent a new element for your needs, but the browser just ignores it.
- **Searching is a nightmare.** With no way to give specific structural labels (such as STANZA or LINE GROUP) to specific units of text within an HTML document, there's no way to search meaningfully for structural elements within documents. As a result Web search engines are very clumsy and retrieve far too many useless documents.

Very possibly the Web can't go much further unless something gives. There needs to be a way for people to express the text structures within their own subject or expertise areas, and still have browsers display the documents correctly. But all this needs to be done without throwing the baby out with the bath water. The solution needs to recognize the lessons of HTML: Simplicity counts! So does freedom of expression; validation may not be needed all the time. And presentation is very important, too.

As you'll see in the next chapter, these are exactly the principles that went into XML.

From Here

HTML was an enormous success precisely because it did what most SGML markup languages don't: It keeps things simple, it provides a user-friendly navigation metaphor, it doesn't force you into the straitjacket of parser validation, and it finds a place for presentation. That's why people love it.

But HTML has a couple of big problems. HTML's design doesn't enable browsers to discover and display the document's structure. What's more, the elements are so general that they can't really capture the nuances of information contained in documents. HTML put descriptive markup on the map, but it fails to make Internet-based knowledge available for computer discovery and processing. (That's one of the reasons, incidentally, that it's so hard to search for information on the Web.)

The cure for HTML's woes isn't another version of HTML (although there's one in the works). Instead, it's something much more radical. Why not bring to the Internet a simplified version of SGML, one that would enable people to create their own markup languages? They could then use these languages to mark up their data in a way that captures the data's richness. That's the basic idea of XML, which is introduced in the following chapter.

4

XML to the Rescue!

The HTML lesson is clear: People *are* willing to use descriptive markup. They want simplicity, they don't care about validation, and they want their documents to look good, whether on the screen or in print. That's why they love HTML. But HTML could be compared to the former U.S. 55-mph federal speed limit. Its "one size fits all" approach isn't fine-grained enough to suit specific needs. HTML code doesn't tell you very much at all about a document's structure—it's just a bunch of headings, paragraphs, images, and tables. And because HTML incorporates a lot of coding shortcuts, browsers can't figure out an HTML document's tree structure in any way that would prove meaningful or useful.

So what's the solution? Keep adding elements to HTML, so that it finally becomes capable of finer-grained markup (such as tags for bibliographies and footnotes)? If this goal were pursued, HTML would quickly become too complex, and it would lose the very simplicity that has made it so popular. It's a much better idea to create a simplified version of SGML—a version that doesn't require a DTD or validation—and let people write their own markup languages, suited to their specific needs. As you'll see in this chapter, that's precisely the idea that underlies XML.

Defining XML

In brief, the Extensible Markup Language (XML) is a simplified version of SGML; it omits many of the hard-to-learn, advanced features of SGML that prevented SGML from gaining widespread acceptance. Like SGML, XML isn't a markup language in the sense that HTML is; rather, it's a *tool* for creating markup languages. Using XML, you can create a markup language that elegantly captures the data that you want to publish. To put the point plainly, with XML, you can create whatever elements you believe are necessary to capture the data you're trying to publish. You're not locked in to anyone's preconceived tags for your data.

But doesn't that imply that your data will be inaccessible to browsers? In HTML, you can create all the new tags you want, but browsers will simply ignore them. But not in XML. In fact, that's precisely the beauty of XML. *An XML-aware browser can "read" an XML document's tree structure, represent this structure graphically, and make this structure available to application programs for further processing.*

Hold on, though. Doesn't this mean that you have to spend weeks or months of work to create your own DTD? No! You can create DTDs with XML or use other peoples' DTDs, but the XML specification is written in an enormously clever way that *guarantees* the discoverability of document structure *even if* the DTD is omitted. SGML can't do this; HTML can't do this. Only XML can do this. And it's terrific. What this means, put simply, is that you can invent your own tags for your data, stick them in your document, and presto! An XML document can read the tree structure, display the tree, and enable all sorts of cool navigation and display possibilities, even if it's never encountered your tags before. Skeptical? I'll prove this to you at the end of this chapter.

XML brings the power of SGML to the Internet—but it leaves out SGML's steep learning curve, the constraint of mandatory DTDs, validation hassles, and complexity. And in so doing, it opens the door toward the explosive growth of discoverable and searchable knowledge structures that will someday span the globe.

XML's Origin

By the mid-1990s, the SGML community learned the lessons that HTML teaches. They realized that SGML wouldn't fulfill its promise unless it was made simpler—and moved to the Internet.

In 1996, the World Wide Web Consortium (W3C) formed a working committee of nearly 100 SGML and Web experts. Chaired by Jon Bosak of Sun Microsystems, the committee—dubbed the XML Working Group—discussed the problems of SGML and opportunities presented by the Internet. Specifically, the committee was charged with the following goals:

- Simplify SGML by removing its least-used and least-understood capabilities.
- Make the simplified version of SGML available for use on the World Wide Web. This means incorporating hyperlinking capabilities.
- Provide a means for authors to specify presentation information by means of style sheets.
- Make the simplified version of XML so easy to use that anyone who knows HTML will be able to learn it quickly.
- Do all this and still provide the means for people to create documents that will pass SGML validation tests, if so desired.

Despite the number of people involved and varying perspectives, the XML Working Group came up with a preliminary proposal in record time. After a preliminary draft was circulated for comments, Extensible Markup Langauge (XML) 1.0 was adopted as a W3C Recommendation on February 10, 1998. Unlike most of the XML books that were published prior to this one, this book is based on the final recommended specification, not a preliminary version.

Because its members were scattered all over the world, the XML Working Group used electronic communication—chiefly, e-mail and mailing lists—to perform its work. There seems to be something very powerful about this process. One would think it would dissolve in bickering. However, the Working Group participants had a lot of experience working in this environment and produced the XML specificaiton very efficiently. Another very successful example of Internet professional collaboration is the working group that created Linux, the remarkable Unix "clone" designed to run on Intel microprocessors.

The XML Standardization Process

The Cambridge, Mass.-based World Wide Web Consortium (W3C) is responsible for standardizing XML. The XML specification (*www.w3.org/XML*) actually encompasses a number of documents, not all of which have been finalized at this writing:

- **Extensible Markup Language (XML) 1.0** (W3C Recommendation, 10-February-1998). This is the core of the XML specification—in fact, it *is* XML, in the strict sense of XML as a subset of SGML. Version 1.0 is a W3C Recommendation, which means that it's completed and fixed.
- **XML Linking Language (XLink)** (W3C Working Draft, 3-March-1998). This document defines the hyperlink capabilities of XML. Defined in XML, it specifies the linking capabilities that enable XML to emulate all the hyperlinking capabilities of HTML; in addition, it incorporates more advanced hyperlinking capabilities that draw on advanced research in hypermedia. The current specification has the status of a working document, which means that it's reasonably standardized; still, changes could occur when the final Recommendation is published.
- **XML Pointer Language (XPointer)** (W3C Working Draft, 3-March-1998). This document is also concerned with XML's hyperlinking capabilities—specifically, linking to specific units of information within the destination document. This is something that HTML does only crudely by means of *fragment identifiers* (such as "#Smith") tacked on the the ends of URLs; as you'll see, XPointer provides very powerful tools for finding and linking to well-defined units of information in destination documents.

- **Namespaces in XML** (W3C Working Draft, 27-March-1998). Here's another brilliant idea from the XML Working Committee. With XML in widespread use, lots of people are going to create DTDs that provide elegant definitions for elements in specific content areas—commerce, birdwatching, whatever. But some people will want to create documents that combine content areas—consider, for instance, a commercial page on birdwatching! The namespace proposal provides a means to employ well–worked–out elements from a *variety* of DTDs and use them in your document. This will help build uniformity (for example, a <date> element that's widely reused will reduce the variation in the way people express dates) and eliminate a lot of unnecessary duplication of effort.
- **Document Object Model (DOM)** (W3C Working Draft, 16-April-1998). Right now, the leading browsers—Netscape Navigator and Microsoft Internet Explorer—contain "hooks" (called *application program interfaces,* or APIs) that make certain parts of HTML documents accessible to scripts and programs. There's some overlap, but there's a real need for a standard. The DOM specification provides a core set of hooks for both HTML and XML documents, and a set specifically designed for XML.
- **Cascading Style Sheets (CSS) Level 2** (W3C Recommendation 12-May-1998). This specification outlines a way to attach presentation (style) information to specific elements within HTML and XML documents.
- **Extensible Style Language (XSL)** (W3C Working Draft 18-August-1998). The least developed of all the specifications discussed in this book, XSL is currently a W3C Working Draft. Although this book

describes XSL, it focuses on CSS Level 2 as the recommended style sheet mechanism for XML documents.

You'll find extensive coverage of the XML language specification, XLink, XPointer, namespaces, and CSS Level 2 in this book. DOM isn't covered in detail because the topic is mainly of interest to programmers.

Please bear in mind that, at this writing, the Namespaces, XLink, and XPointer specifications have the status of Working Drafts, which mean that they aren't finalized. Although there's every reason to believe that they're close to completion, the final W3C Recommendation may introduce changes or additions, and the portions of this book that cover these topics may contain out-of-date information.

The XML Working Group's 10 Goals

As the XML Working Group met and clarified its goals, its members redefined its charge in the form of "Ten Commandments." The following sections discuss each of them and outline how the Working Group chose to solve these problems. As you read this section, you'll learn more about the rationale underlying XML's design; the next section highlights those features that I believe have truly revolutionary implications for Web publishing.

Make It Useful on the Internet

Although SGML can be used on the Web, its complexity causes a lot of problems, and they go beyond the fact that SGML doesn't support the Web protocols for hyperlinking to remote resources. The biggest problem is that SGML is far too complex to be useful on the Web. Web developers—many of whom are business people, not computer geniuses—aren't going to take the time to learn something as sophisticated and complex as SGML, and what's more, SGML is too complicated to be handled efficiently by simple browsers.

Making XML useful on the Web requires two things:

- Supporting Web protocols (including URLs, HTTP, ECMAScript, Java, and more).
- Making XML much, much simpler than SGML.

As you'll see, XML does both of these beautifully; it gives you Web operability plus just about everything that's worth preserving from SGML. The omitted SGML features are highly specialized and difficult to learn.

How much was thrown out? The latest SGML specification occupies 500 pages; the XML 1.0 specification takes just 40. You can truly say that XML gives you 80% of SGML's functionality for 20% of the effort.

Support a Variety of Applications

One of the lessons HTML teaches is that it's a bad idea to leave processing up to the people who create applications. If Company A makes a browser that ignores certain features that Company B likes, you've got a huge problem: lack of standards. XML isn't going to happen if this game repeats itself once XML appears on the Web.

The XML design committee chose to deal with this challenge by breaking the link between the XML standard and the proprietary implementations of XML created by profit-seeking software publishers. This is done by creating an intermediary-level program, called the *XML processor,* which *must* conform exactly to the XML standard. In fact, the entire XML 1.0 specification amounts to a set of rules that XML processors must follow if their publishers wish to describe their products as standards-conformant.

What is an XML processor? It's not a browser or an editor. The function of the XML processor is to read XML documents and map their structure. It does this for the benefit of an XML application, to which it provides the data.

By decoupling the XML processor and XML applications, the Working Group ensures that there will be a basic level of compatibility shared by all XML programs, and that anyone who creates an XML document can expect that any XML application will know what to do with it.

There's a problem with this approach, though. In order to get the XML processor and applications to talk to each other, there needs to be a standardized *application program interface (API)* that governs the communications between the two. Microsoft and other firms have proposed APIs, but as yet there's no W3C standard. This is the major roadblock holding back the development of XML-aware software at present. The Document Object Model (DOM) specification will resolve this problem.

Be Compatible with SGML

Many companies and organizations have already made significant investments in SGML. They don't want to throw everything out and start over! For this reason, the working group decided to make sure that any XML document could be read and be processed by SGML-aware software.

Note that XML's SGML compatibility doesn't necessarily work both ways. XML-aware software might not be able to process some SGML documents if these documents make use of SGML features that were omitted from the XML specification.

Make It Easy to Write XML Software

By making XML much less complex than SGML and throwing out little-used features, the Working Group ensures that companies won't have to spend millions developing XML-aware software.

Keep Optional Features to a Minimum

Over the years, the SGML standard accumulated far too many optional features, many of which were highly specialized and useless for most developers. With each added feature, the cost of developing testing and supporting SGML software increased.

Make XML Documents Human-Readable

This goal arises from experience with SGML. Although SGML allows certain shortcuts that reduce markup, they make SGML documents harder for humans to read. For example, there are situations in which elements can be omitted, but their existence is inferred by the processing software. For instance, HTML allows you to omit the HTML or BODY element entirely. XML documents should be written in such a way that their structure is immediately apparent. This avoids confusion and reduces the possibility of making mistakes.

The latter concern is particularly important where XML is concerned, because any markup mistakes will harm the

XML processor's ability to deduce the document's structure.

Prepare the Specification Quickly

Something like XML was bound to happen; the deficiencies of both SGML and HTML meant that something had to give. The question was, would the development of a simplified, Web-aware generalized markup language happen under the control of standards bodies, or would it be introduced as a proprietary standard of a profit-seeking software publisher? By taking the lead and getting the XML standard out quickly, the Working Group hoped to forestall proprietary development efforts and create a standard that will ultimately benefit everyone (including software publishers). The history of the computer industry clearly shows that the biggest markets (and biggest profits) arise where solid, well-controlled standards have emerged.

Make the XML Design Formal and Concise

One of SGML's major drawbacks is the amount of time it takes to understand the language's specification. Here, the XML Working Group decided to decrease the learning curve by expressing the XML language specification in a concise, formal language preferred by the programming community: *Extended Backus–Naur Format (EBNF).*

If you've never seen EBNF before, you'll find it to be totally incomprehensible. But it's actually not very difficult to learn how to read EBNF or, indeed, to write it. And that's just what you'll need to do if you choose to write your own DTDs, as Part Three of this book explains.

Make XML Documents Easy to Create

Experience shows that most people just aren't going to spend months learning something as complex as SGML; on the contrary, HTML's simplicity paved the way to its explosive growth. With SGML, the pain comes from developing the required DTDs—and there's no way around this.

To make XML documents easy to create, the Working Group threw out the requirement that an XML document must be associated with a DTD. You can create a simple XML document (called a *well–formed* document) just by using your own elements, as long as you follow the XML rules. The XML processor can infer its structure and make this structure available to applications.

XML liberates Web authors from the DTD straitjacket. This fact alone virtually guarantees that there's going to be an explosion of XML on the Web. Of course, a lot of this XML is going to be illogically designed and ineptly implemented, but who cares? As long as these documents are well–formed (in that they obey XML rules), XML processors can infer the (perhaps ineptly designed) structure and make the document available to XML-aware applications. This is analogous to the current situation on the Web; a lot of people have put up poorly designed HTML pages, but the Web's richness of content lies in the fact that so many people have done so. According to a recent research report, there are more than 225 million documents accessible via the Web!

In XML, the use of a DTD is optional. If your XML document is based on a DTD, it's called a *valid* XML document, because the XML processor can now examine the

DTD to see whether you've followed the DTD's rules when you coded your document.

So XML gives you the best of both worlds. I'll return to the well–formed vs. valid distinction later in this chapter; for now, just bear in mind that it's very likely to prove to be the key to XML's success.

Make Sure Markup Is Unambiguous

One of the biggest problems with SGML and HTML lies in the many "typing shortcuts" that enable coders to skip end tags. For example, in HTML, you can omit the end tag for the P, LI, HTML, BODY, and many other elements. This simplifies typing but can make the document's structure ambiguous.

As you'll learn in Part Three of this book, XML processors can't infer your document's structure unless your markup is absolutely nonambiguous. Perhaps the most brilliant thing about XML's design is the fact that it ensures nonambiguity even if you omit a DTD. In other words, XML will be as simple to use as HTML, but it enables people to create documents that have computer–discoverable structures.

Introducing the XML Language Specification

The first part of the XML specification, the one that defines the language from the XML processor's point of view, has been completed and published as a W3C recommendation. This section introduces XML 1.0, explains its differences from SGML, and points out its revolutionary capabilities for Web publishing.

XML isn't a radical departure from SGML. On the contrary, it's a *subset* of SGML. Essentially, the XML Working Group focused on SGML's most useful features (particularly for the Web environment) and left out the little–used, complex options that give people fits when they try to learn SGML. Added were hyperlinking capabilities and style sheets which I'll discuss later in this chapter in the sections that introduce XML-Link and XML-Style, also known as Extensible Style Language (XSL).

Rather than explaining in detail just how XML differs from SGML, let's approach XML from the standpoint of somebody experienced in Web publishing. You're wondering just what's so cool about XML that it's worth learning how to use it.

With respect to the XML markup language, XML offers three features so revolutionary that they are certain to change the nature of Web publishing: discoverable document structures, optional validity testing, and external file inclusion.

Discoverable Document Structure

As compared to HTML, the greatest advantage of XML lies in the fact that an XML processor can discover an XML document's structure, as long as the XML document is *well-formed* (follows the essential rules for writing XML, as explained in Chapter 9). An XML-aware browser will typically display two windows: one showing the document's tree structure and the other showing the text within the currently selected element. This greatly enhances document navigability, enables element-specific searching, and much more.

No Validation Straitjacket, Thank You

You can use XML to create new tags without having to define a DTD or subject your documents to validation. Still, you can write up an XML document in such a way that an SGML validating parser will be quite happy with it. The key to this amazing capability in XML is the distinction between *well-formed* and *valid* documents, which is introduced in this section.

In a well-formed XML document, you add your own elements, and you do so consistently using good XML coding practices. (You'll learn how to do this later in this book.) But there's no DTD. And since there's no DTD, there's no validation. That means, essentially, that you're not subjected to the whole intimidating process of having your document rejected if some of your elements don't contain the required subelements. Does this mean the elements you've added are meaningless? No. Your XML document is read by a program called an *XML processor,* which scans the document, analyzes the elements, and deduces the elements' tree structure.

Here's an example. Suppose you've created an element called APPENDIX, and you create a subelement called BIBLIOGRAPHY. Within BIBLIOGRAPHY, you include additional elements called CITATION. The XML Processor scans your document and infers that CITATION belongs within BIBLIOGRAPHY, and BIBLIOGRAPHY belongs within APPENDIX. Of course, if you stick one of these elements in the wrong place, you'll confuse the XML processor. But that's a lot better than finding out that your document's inaccessible because you made some minor coding mistake.

A *valid* XML document is just like a valid SGML document in that it's associated with a document type definition (DTD), and it's subjected to validation. To create a valid XML document, you could use an existing SGML or XML DTD, or you could learn to write your own DTD.

Making the Structure Unambiguous

As you learned in the previous chapter, a major limitation of HTML is that its syntax prevents authors from representing document structure without ambiguity. As a result, programs can't reliably describe the document's tree structure. In SGML, the tree structure can't be discovered unless authors create DTDs, which is a time-consuming and difficult task. Perhaps the most important thing about XML is that, as long as it's well-formed, an XML document *does* enable programs to detect the document's tree structure, even in the absence of a DTD.

How is this possible? You'll learn more about how this is achieved in Chapter 9, but here's one example. XML insists that there can be one and only one element at the top of the tree. This element is called the *document element*. Every XML document can include just *one* element—and one element only, at least at the top logical level. For example, the following isn't a well-formed XML document, because it contains four elements at the top level of the document tree:

```
<to>Alice</to>
<from>Bob</from>
<date>June 15, 1998</date>
<re>Vacation leave</re>
```

```
<body>You've got six weeks! Go for
it!</body>
```

If you try to put this illogical gunk into an XML processor, it will generate a fatal error and stop processing the document. That's right: In order to get processed at all, an XML document *must* be well-formed. This may sound like another version of the DTD validation straitjacket, but it's not at all difficult to write well-formed XML (once you get the hang of it). Now compare the following version of the same document (which, incidentally, is well-formed XML):

```
<doc-memo>
  <header>
    <to>Alice</to>
    <from>Bob</from>
    <date>June 15, 1998</date>
    <re>Vacation leave</re>
  </header>
  <body>
    <summary>You've got six weeks! Go
    for it!</summary>
  </body>
</doc-memo>
```

Here's the tree:

```
doc-memo
 |   header
 |     ├─  to
 |     ├─  from
 |     ├─  date
 |     └─  re
 └─  body
       └─  main-point
```

Even in the absence of a document type definition (DTD) that defines the structure of this memo document, an

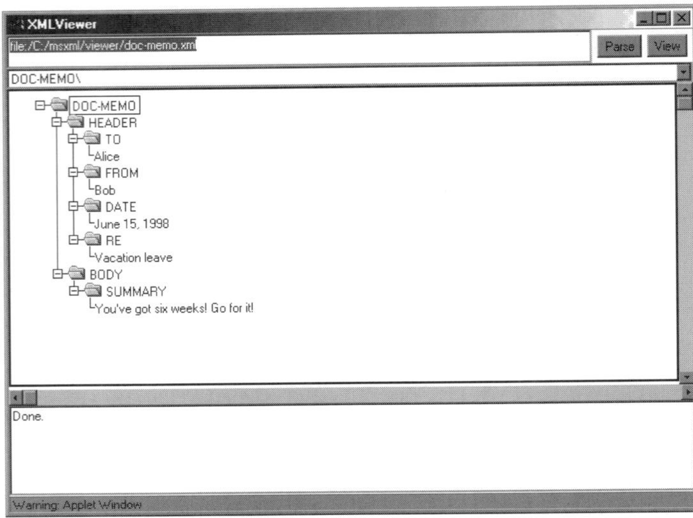

Figure 4.1 Memo document's tree structure detected and displayed.

XML-aware program can read this document, map the tree structure, and make the various document elements available for processing by an application. If you're skeptical, just take a look at Figure 4.1, which shows how the doc-memo example appears in msxml, a Microsoft XML processor.

Incorporating Files into XML Documents

In Chapter 3, you learned that one of HTML's deficiencies is the problem of document reusability. There's no convenient way to incorporate a portion of an existing document into a new one you're writing. All too often, documents of exceptional importance—such as legally sensitive sections of an employee handbook—are stuck within some huge HTML document that's loaded with all sorts of presentation gobbledygook. The passage can't be independently accessed by other pages or incorporated into other pages dynamically.

XML solves this problem by breaking the distinction between the physical document—files that contain text and possibly markup—and the *logical structure* of markup. An XML "document" isn't a single, physical file, as is the case in HTML. Rather, it's a *logical* structure, which might include more than one physical file. The logical structure is created by the document element—yes, the same one you saw in the previous section.

Now here's the really cool thing. Within the document element, you can include not only as many subordinate elements as you wish, but an unlimited number of physical files, as well. This is made possible by tremendously expanding the concept of an *entity,* which—in HTML—is little more than a shorthand expression for a non-ASCII character. In XML, the concept of entity is greatly broadened to include just about anything that can be stored on a computer, such as a physical file, a record in a database, or a remote URL somewhere out there on the Web.

For example, you could put together an anthology of poetry by including a bunch of entity references within the document element:

```
<anthology>
    &poem1;
    &poem2;
    &poem3;
</anthology>
```

With this greatly expanded concept of entities, markup can encompass more than one physical file, enabling

XML authors to incorporate existing documents and make them appear as if they were part of a single, master document. This becomes very powerful when you add the potential of networking to the picture. For example, you could create a book by farming out the chapters to individuals, who would each be responsible for maintaining their chapters and keeping them up to date. Your XML master document would bring them all together and make them appear as if they were a unified entity.

Introducing XML Linking

With HTML, you get just one type of link, basically: You click on a hyperlink, and the browser retrieves and displays the requested document. To be sure, you can define a target within a document when you link to a target within a resource, an HTML browser gets the entire resource, and it scrolls down to the target's location. But that's it.

Experience with hypertext shows that many other types of links are possible (and desirable). In creating the XLink and XPointer specifications, which together form the hypertext portion of the XML architecture, the Working Group drew from the experience of HyTime (an international hyperlinking standard) as well as the hyperlink capabilities defined by the Text Encoding Initiative (TEI). The result is a major expansion of link capabilities when you're using XML, including the following:

- **More options for link display.** You can specify that the linked resource is included *within* your document instead of appearing in a new window. This essentially allows people reading your document to expand it, if they wish, without leaving the context they're reading.

- **More control over traversal behavior.** In HTML, when the user clicks a link, the browser traverses it—that is, fetches the linked resource and displays it. In XML, you can make traversal automatic, if you wish.
- **Greater control over what's retrieved.** In HTML, a link retrieves the linked resource—the whole file. Often, this is inefficient and time-consuming. Suppose, for example, you just want to link to a term's definition. Why download the whole dictionary? With XML linking, you can link (and download) just the portion of the resource that you want.

There's more to XML linking—much more—but this brief introduction highlights the possibilities that will appeal immediately to Web publishers.

Introducing XSL

In principle, there's no reason you can't use the Cascading Style Sheets (CSS) standard to specify the presentation aspects of an XML document. In Part Five of this book, you'll do just that. I believe that many Web publishers will blend HTML with XML, and they'll use CSS to control presentation, largely because CSS is simple and easy to use.

But CSS's simplicity is its downfall. With CSS, there's no way you can format output to a printer with page numbering, for example. That's because CSS, useful as it is, simply isn't powerful enough.

As you learned in Chapter 2, the SGML community has been working on a powerful style sheet mechanism,

DSSSL. Like SGML, it's too complex and confusing for mere mortals, such as most of the people who publish on the Web.

That's exactly the impetus behind XSL, a user-friendly version of DSSSL for use with XML.

Here's a brief look at how XSL works. To display your XML document, an XSL-capable program takes the output from the XML processor (the document's tree structure) and combines this output with the style sheet's formatting specifications. The result is another tree structure, except that this one contains *flow objects*. In brief, a flow object is formatted output with specified charcteristics (such as font, font size, alignment, and line spacing). This output can be directed to the screen, a printer, or other output devices. If you're printing, XSL will enable users to get numbered pages and other nifty features. Unlike the HTML–CSS combination, XML–XSL promises to make it very easy to get printed output from the Internet in reasonably readable shape.

From Here

This chapter introduced XML. As you've learned, XML promises to revolutionize Web publishing by addressing the many deficiencies of HTML. With XML, you can create single, authoritative versions of files and incorporate them into an XML document without having to make a physical copy of the text. You can create your own elements without having to take the trouble to write a DTD. You can write hyperlinks that dynamically incorporate external resources into your document.

In Part Six of this book, you'll examine some of the vocabularies that have been created with XML.

5

XML Questions and Answers

The previous chapters have outlined the need for XML and introduced the major components of the XML specification. But I'm sure you still have lots of questions. You'll find the answers here.

When Will XML Hit the Web?

It already has. Microsoft hard-coded the Channel Definition Format (CDF), a "push" media tag set defined in XML, into Microsoft Internet Explorer 4.0.

XML will hit the Web big time when Netscape and Microsoft (and other browser publishers) release the next major versions of their browsers, which (it is believed) will fully support XML as well as HTML. When this happens, XML will hit the Web with explosive force.

To be sure, there are still a lot of unanswered questions. In order for XML processors to communicate with XML applications, there needs to be a standard application program interface (API). Microsoft has developed such an API and proposed it as a Web standard. As with any potential standard, there's a possibility of companies coming in with proprietary APIs or delay in publishing the standard. That could hold XML back. Happily, the World Wide Web Consortium (W3C) has jumped into the fray with its Document Object Model (DOM), currently a Working Draft. The DOM specification includes a special section on XML and outlines the means by which applications can directly address the tree structure of XML documents in a nonproprietary way.

Perhaps the biggest limitation at present is that only one portion of the XML specification has been finalized (at this writing)—the XML language itself. The XLink specification is further along, but the XML style specification (XSL) seems to be the laggard here. Microsoft has once again taken the lead here by developing and proposing XSL as a Web standard, which will probably make an appearance in Microsoft Internet Explorer 5.0. It's uncertain whether other browser publishers will support XSL until it's approved as a W3C recommendation, however, so here's another area that could slow the acceptance of XML. Of course, there's no reason you can't use Cascading Style Sheets (CSS) to control the presentation aspects of your Web documents; CSS is supported right now, and it's an approved standard.

What Does *Extensible* Mean?

The "X" in XML—short for eXtensible—refers to XML's ability to enable authors to create new elements suitable to their needs. Of course, that's always been possible with SGML, but it isn't possible with HTML. By bringing a simplified version of SGML to the Web, XML puts an end to the browser publisher's extensions games and enables Web authors to create customized structural markup schemes focused specifically on their needs.

Why Is XML Important?

For the same reasons that SGML is important: Organizations need a way to ensure the longevity and reusability of documents. To be sure, SGML has been slow to make inroads, largely because most people use word processing programs to create documents with an appealing appearance. But organizations are realizing that this is very costly. These documents aren't easily reused, and the knowledge that's in them is difficult to retrieve on a computer network.

One way to think of XML is not only that it's a user-friendly version of SGML, but even more, that it's a network-friendly version of SGML. I believe that the most powerful characteristics of XML will turn out to be XML's capability to incorporate network-accessible resources into the flow of an XML document, while at the same time enabling the authors of these resources to maintain them separately, on their own computers. This will enable organizations to distribute knowledge responsibilities throughout an enterprise, and yet maintain a centralized document that enables users to browse and search this structure as if it were a unified entity.

The key to this capacity lies in XML's greatly expanded concept of entities. An entity can be just about anything that's capable of being stored on a computer, such as a database record. XML may prove to be the ideal way to deliver database information on the Web.

What Is a Document Type Definition (DTD)?

A DTD is a series of declarations that define the elements of a markup language. You can write a DTD using SGML, but it's much easier to do so with XML, which omits many of the hard-to-learn peculiarities that have held SGML back. If you've ever looked at the HTML specification, you've seen a heavily annotated DTD, which contains *declarations* for elements and the attributes associated with elements. DTDs can be placed in separate documents, or within a document, or both (in which case the internal DTD takes precedence over the external one). To learn more about DTDs, see Chapter 10.

Must I Write My Own DTD?

As long as your XML documents are well-formed, you can create your own elements and make your structured documents available on the Web. An XML processor can analyze your document, display its tree structure, and enable XML-aware applications to browse this structure. However, DTDs have many advantages.

In practical terms, the most important advantage of a DTD lies in the use of multimedia. In order to include graphic images, sounds, and other external binary files within your XML pages, as is commonly done with HTML, the XML language specification states that you should include an internal DTD that declares these files as *entities*. For this reason alone, most XML authors will want to learn a little about writing DTDs. However, early XML processors did not enforce the use of a DTD to declare entities.

A DTD can make authoring more convenient. With a DTD, you essentially write rules that specify what type of content and which elements can be placed within a given element that you're defining. Already, you can obtain XML-aware editors, such as XML <Pro> (*www.vervet-logic.com*), which will read your DTD and then assist authors by informing them which elements are appropriate for a given context.

Get started by learning how to write well-formed XML. That's a prerequisite for any XML document, since an XML processor generates a fatal error if the document isn't well-formed. This is a rather stringent restriction, but it's needed so that XML documents can self-disclose their structure (even in the absence of a DTD). Once you've learned how to write well-formed XML, you'll have the makings of your own, new markup language. You can then go on to formalize that language by writing a DTD for it. If this sounds scary, rest assured: It's quite easy to write a DTD in XML, and Part Four teaches you everything you need to know.

Will HTML Go Away?

No! HTML is a huge success at providing a simple markup scheme for document display on the Web. With

Cascading Style Sheets (CSS), Web authors now have a simple, easily learned way to separate structure from presentation. And with XML, Web authors have new ways to enhance HTML's capabilities. I believe that HTML will continue to provide the baseline for Web publishing; XML will be employed to add functionality to the Web.

That's already happened, in fact. Microsoft used XML to write the specifications for the Channel Definition Format (CDF), a "push" media format that enables Web users to "subscribe" to Web pages. With subscriptions, a user can be notified when the page changes; the notification can occur via an icon in the user's favorite sites list or even the display of the updated page on the user's desktop. Currently, CDF requires a browser that's "hard wired" to read the CDF tags; Microsoft Internet Explorer version 4 contains only primitive XML support for this.

Another area in which XML will make an almost immediate impact lies in the area of META content description. Currently, it's very difficult to search the Web successfully, largely because Web documents do not contain sufficient information to enable their authors to describe the document's content. In Part Six, you'll learn about the efforts underway to use XML to define tags that Web authors can employ to define document content more richly.

How Can I Incorporate XML into HTML?

Although almost everyone agrees that Web authors will continue to create HTML documents and will want to incorporate XML as needed, there still isn't any official, standard way to blend HTML and XML in a single document. At a W3C meeting held shortly before this book's publication, the consensus emerged that HTML needs an <XML> element, one that would enable authors to incorporate XML markup within an HTML document. In order to do this, a new, standard version of HTML will be needed.

In the interim, browser publishers will make XML-aware browsers available, and they'll incorporate mechanisms that will enable you to include XML within your HTML documents. At this writing, a developer's preview edition of Microsoft Internet Explorer 5.0 supports a new, non-standard XML tag, <XML>, which enables Web authors to embed XML markup within HTML documents. Here's an example:

```
<XML>
    <lastname>Smith</lastname>
    <firstname>Xena</firstname>
</XML>
```

You can also use the XML tag's src attribute to refer to an external XML file, as in the following example:

```
<XML src="subscribers.xml">
```

As you'll learn in Part 5, you can use Cascading Style Sheets (CSS) to define the presentation of the XML tags you introduce within HTML documents. Internet Explorer 5.0 will display these tags using the formats you've specified.

Where Will XML Make Its Greatest Impact?

Initially, XML promises to make its greatest impact in specialized knowledge areas that HTML cannot support. For example, the earliest implementations of XML stem from chemistry (the Chemical Markup Language) and mathematics (Mathematical Markup Language). But I believe that XML will come into much more widespread use, for the simple reason that XML offers a level of functionality, efficiency, and economy that Web authors will find absolutely irresistible.

Do We Really Need All Those Fancy XML Links?

You bet. As you've already learned, XML greatly expands the simple hyperlinking capabilities of HTML. When a user clicks an HTML link, the browser displays the requested resource—the *entire* requested resource. If all that's desired is a portion of the requested resource, this is obviously time-consuming and inefficient. To be sure, you can link to a target in the linked resource, but the browser still downloads the entire resource and then scrolls to the target.

XLink offers a much richer set of hyperlinking tools. With XLink, you can do the following:

- **Embed the requested resource within the flow of elements in your document.** For example, you could write a link that tells the reader to click to display additional information about the subject—but this link does not take the reader away from the current page.
- **Replace the element containing the link with the requested resource.** For example, you could write a link that tells the reader to click to display a more technical version (or a less technical version) of the current text. Again, this happens without taking the reader away from the current document.

- **Retrieve a chunk of the requested resource.** With HTML targets, you go to a point in the requested resource. With XML, it's possible to define chunks of text within the requested resource. For example, you can pull a definition out of a glossary, an employee record out of a database, whatever you like, as long as it's data that can be identified by an ID or structural location.
- **Link to more than one resource.** With *extended links,* you can create a link to two or more resources. For example, suppose you write an extended link that tells the reader to click to display a series of related terms. These could be retrieved and embedded within the current document or displayed in a new window.

In terms of hyperlinking, the biggest XML gold mine for Web publishing lies in the use of *out-of-line links*. In HTML, all links are inline—that is, you have to put them within the body of the document. This makes HTML documents hard to read, but there's a more fundamental problem. Inline links are horribly expensive to maintain. (If you've ever maintained a large Web site, I'm sure you will agree with this statement.) When you move documents around, links might not work, and it's a huge pain to chase them all down and correct them.

With out-of-line links, it becomes possible to create a *single file* that contains the actual physical locations of all the links you want to use. An unofficial term for this is a *link farm*. Within your documents, you can insert inline links using shorthand names for the links, such as link-1 and link-2.

The concept of a link farm is analogous to a style sheet. In a style sheet, you group together in a single, easily maintained list all the styles you want to use in a document. If you create a style sheet in a separate document, you can use that style sheet to define a whole range of physically separate documents, each of which refers to the styles located in the style sheet. Here's where the tremendous efficiency and cost reduction of style sheets comes into play: Should you wish to change the appearance of all the documents linked to the style sheet, you just make one change, in one place, and bingo! All the documents appear differently.

In the same way, the link farm can serve as a central repository for all the links you want to use. If one of the links changes, you make the correction just once, and all the linked documents will reflect the change you've made.

If you're experienced with Web publishing, reading the previous paragraph is probably enough to get you started with XML right away!

But Isn't XML Difficult to Learn?

XML is no more difficult than HTML if you just want to create well-formed documents or hitchhike on somebody else's XML DTD. Most users will do just that.

But don't be afraid of writing your own DTD. It's actually quite easy and opens up a whole new world of XML functionality for you. Everything you need to know is contained in Part Four.

Is XML Compatible with SGML?

XML is a subset of SGML. This means that XML DTDs are fully compatible with existing SGML software. However, it doesn't necessarily work the other way. Because SGML contains features that were omitted from XML, an XML application might not be able to use an SGML DTD, if that DTD contains SGML components that aren't supported in XML.

From Here

This chapter addressed the questions you're most likely to ask about XML. In Part Three of this book, you'll learn how to write well-formed XML—and you'll be on your way to creating your own markup language.

Part Three

Writing Well-Formed XML

6

Understanding the Rules for Well-Formed Documents

Are you ready to try your hand at XML? The easiest way to begin lies in creating a *well-formed* document, which doesn't require a document type definition (DTD). It's a big job to create a DTD, as you'll discover in Part Four, so you'll want to carefully consider whether the well-formed document route meets your needs. In this chapter, you'll learn what goes into a well-formed XML document.

Even if you're planning to create a DTD, you should still read this chapter, because DTD-based documents must still meet the well-formedness criteria explained here.

Well-Formed vs. Valid Documents in XML

As previously mentioned, you can create two different types of documents in XML:

- **Well-formed documents.** A *well-formed* XML document obeys the rules for creating an XML document capable of withstanding scrutiny by an XML processor, but it doesn't necessarily have an associated document type definition (DTD).
- **Valid documents.** A *valid* document has an associated DTD. What's more, each element in the document must conform to the rules that the DTD defines. If the document fails to conform to these rules, it flunks the XML processor's validity test.

An XML document must be at least well-formed. If an XML processor finds that an XML document fails the well-formedness test, the processor generates a fatal error, and the document is ignored. In contrast, a valid XML document can fail the validity test, but this error isn't fatal; you'll probably see an error message, but the data are still available.

Why is well-formedness so important? Simple. It's the key to generating the *tree structure* that makes XML so useful. The well-formedness constraints are intended to avoid the situation created by HTML, in which it's impossible to verify a tree structure due to the ambiguity of HTML coding.

Rules for Well-Formed XML Documents

As you've just learned, the minimum requirement for an XML document is well-formedness. Thanks to the clarity and nonambiguity of its tags, a well-formed XML document displays a tree structure, even in the absence of a supporting DTD. What are the rules for well-formedness?

To understand these rules, you should begin by thinking of XML elements as if they were *containers* capable of holding something (like an orange juice carton). Now that you've got the container concept in mind, examine the following rules.

Use a Single Root Element

Every XML document must have one outer container, called the *root element*, which contains *all* the other elements.

In HTML, the root element is the optional HTML element, which encompasses the HEAD and BODY elements. In XML, you can name the root element anything you wish. It's a good idea to name the root element in such a way that it describes the data that the document will contain.

Suppose you're developing a site containing information benefitting owners of a particular brand and model of sailboat. One of the site's pages contains amusing stories about how people named their boats. For this page, you could develop a root element called boatnames. Within this root element, you would place all the other elements you create to store this information, as in the following example:

```
<boatnames>
  <boat>
    <name>Liquid Assets</name>
    <owner>Tim and Suzy Smith</owner>
    <hull-number>680</hull-number>
    <year>1988</year>
```

```
      <description>We know it's a popular
      name, but we had just cashed in a
      retirement account to buy this thing,
      and it seemed appropriate!</description>
    </boat>
  </boatnames>
```

Within the root element (boatnames), you would place several boat elements, each of which describes how a particular boat got its name.

Keep Nesting Order Clear

Within the root element, you can use as many additional elements as you wish. These may occur in sequence, as in the above example; within the boatnames root element, for example, you can have a whole series of boat elements. In addition, these subordinate-level elements can be nested, as long as you always nest them in the same logical order. What you *shouldn't* do is violate the nesting order by using the same element at two different levels in the nesting hierarchy. For example, in the boatnames example just mentioned, there's an unambiguous tree structure, as follows:

```
boatnames
  boat
    name
    owner
    hull-number
    year
    description
```

In other words, the boatnames element occurs at level 1 of the tree structure, while boat occurs at level 2, and the other elements occur at level 3. Were you to violate this structure in any way—for example, by using level 3 elements at level 2—you'd violate the logical order you've established, and the XML processor might not know how to display your document's tree structure. (Note, however, that using the same element name at different logical errors does not generate well-formedness errors, at least in the early XML processor software used for testing this book's examples.)

To put this point another way, you can say that the boat element is the *parent* of the following elements: name, owner, hull-number, year, and description. In turn, these contained elements are the *child* elements of their parent (boatnames). If you use any of the child elements, you should use them within their proper parent.

Don't Overlap Elements

In careless HTML coding, it's common to cross-thread (overlap) elements, as in the following example:

```
<H1><B>Title</H1></B>
```

Logically, the correct form is the following:

```
<H1><B>Title</B></H1>
```

In XML, cross-threading generates a well-formedness error, and it's fatal. Here's an example of illegal cross-threading:

```
<boat>
    <name>Latitude Adjustment
      <owner>Jim Hernandez</name>
    </owner>
    [ ... ]
```

Don't take this example to mean that you couldn't have some nesting elements within the name element—it's just that the nested elements shouldn't overlap. Here's an example of proper nesting:

```
<boatnames>
  <boat>
    <name>
      <owner-name>Speedy</owner-name>
      <nickname>Slowpoke</nickname>
    </name>
    [ ... ]
```

Here, the name element contains two children: owner-name and nickname. You use these *only* as children of the name element.

Why create a DTD? Here's a very good reason! With a DTD, you can write rules that prevent users from placing elements at the wrong level. XML editors can read these rules and help you avoid breaking them accidentally. When you create your document with an XML editor, the program will automatically tell you which elements are available at a given level, which helps to prevent well-formedness errors.

Be Sure Your Start and End Tags Match

Every element must have a start tag and an end tag, and these must match exactly. *Don't forget that XML is case-sensitive!* The capitalization pattern must be consistent. In addition, the end tag must have a forward slash. Here's a well-formed element:

```
<name>Juliana</name>
```

Here's one that violates the well-formedness rules:

```
<Name>Juliana</name>
```

Why? The tags' capitalization patterns aren't consistent.

To ensure that you don't accidentally make a capitalization error, get into the habit of writing all your XML elements in lower case only. If you're used to HTML, this habit requires unlearning an old one; although HTML elements aren't case-sensitive, HTML textbooks generally advise you to type the element names in uppercase letters so that it's easy to distinguish the tags from surrounding text.

Close Empty Elements with the Empty-Element Tag (/>)

Some elements are *empty*—that is, they contain no content. Here's an example:

```
<record id="125"/>
```

Note the forward slash (/) before the closing angle bracket. This is required to close the empty element properly. If you leave the slash out, you violate well-formedness rules because the XML processor will be looking for an end tag—and it won't find it.

If you're used to coding in HTML, note that this rule represents a major change from the way you code empty tags in HTML. In HTML, you don't use the forward slash to close an empty tag.

Always Surround Values with Quotation Marks

In XML, you can create elements that have *attributes*, which give you ways of providing additional information about the element. You provide this information by specifying a *value*. Here's an example:

```
<record id = "125" updated = "yes"/>
```

In HTML, it's a good practice to surround values with quotation marks. In XML, it's mandatory! You can use either single quotation marks (‘ and ’) or double ones (“ and ”). What you *can't* do is leave them out. If you omit quotation marks around a value, the XML processor generates a fatal error.

Understanding XML Document Structure

Now that you know the basic rules for creating well-formed documents, look more closely at the basic structure of an XML document. As you'll see, a well-formed XML document is properly known as a *document entity*, which for our purposes here is equivalent to the file that contains your document. Within this file, the XML code begins with a *prolog*, which specifies the version of XML that you're using. Optionally, you can include an *encoding declaration* if you'd like to write your document in a foreign language. The document continues with the *document element*, which contains all the other elements in your document; you'll need to make sure that you follow the rules for naming elements. Within the document, you'll find markup (such as element start and end tags) and *character data*, which is simply everything that isn't markup. The following sections explain these vital points in detail.

The Document Entity

From a physical standpoint, each XML document contains one overarching structure called the *document entity*. An *entity* is a storage unit. When we're talking about storing documents, we're talking about files, so you can define the document entity as a file. Normally, an XML document is stored in a single file, so the document entity and the file are one and the same. Note, though, that it's possible to incorporate additional files within an XML document—that's one of the things that makes XML so powerful compared to HTML—but there's still only one, overarching document entity (even though it contains more than one file). To keep things simple for now, just think of the document entity as a single file, the one you put your XML document in.

Do you have to do anything special to indicate that your document entity exists? No. It's obvious to the XML processor. You need to be concerned about the document entity concept only when you are incorporating additional files by means of external entities, which are discussed later in this book.

The XML Prolog and XML Declaration

The first component of an XML document, the *prolog*, contains two sections:

- **XML Declaration.** This tells human readers (and software) that the document is indeed an XML document and indicates the XML version. Although it's optional, you should always include the XML declaration, even if you're writing a well-formed document that doesn't have an associated DTD.
- **Document Type Declaration.** This tells the XML browser which DTD you're using (and where it's located). The use of a DTD declaration is optional if you're not using a DTD, but you must include it if you're writing a valid document. You'll learn more about the Document Type Declaration in Part Four of this book.

For well-formed documents that won't have an associated DTD, the only prolog component that you need to include is the XML declaration. For a well-formed, DTD-less document written in version 1.0 of XML, use the following:

```
<?XML version="1.0"? standalone="yes">
```

The standalone declaration tells the XML processor that there are no external declarations for this document—that is, no external DTD.

The Encoding Declaration

In the XML declaration, you may also include an *encoding declaration*, which tells the XML processor which character encoding you're using. This isn't really necessary for XML documents served on the Web, since servers tell browsers what type of encoding has been used; still, it's a good idea to include the declaration in case the server doesn't do this correctly. In addition, the encoding declaration enables an XML processor to read the document when no server is involved (in other words, when it's read directly from a disk drive).

By default, XML documents are assumed to be in ASCII code (UTM-8), consisting of the first 127 characters in the ASCII character set (and found on most U.S. keyboards). You may also use any of the more than 65,000 Unicode (ISO 10646) characters (see *www.unicode.org*). Unicode is a standard that brings together dozens of coded character sets in a huge 16-bit coding space; there's a 32-bit version in the works. If you use 16-bit Unicode characters, you must type a *numerical* character code (referring to the Unicode character set) and *escape* the code using an ampersand (&), a pound or hash mark sign (#), the letter *x* specifying that you're using a hexadecimal number, and semicolon (;), as in the following example:

```
&#xe9;
```

This produces a small letter e with an acute accent (é).

For a list of ISO 10646 character codes, see *charts.unicode.org/charts.html.*

If you're used to the HTML method for referencing character entities using an alphabetical name (such as &), bear in mind that XML requires you to declare all named entities at the beginning of your document. Worse, failure to do so generates a fatal error! The only exception to this rule lies in the use of predefined entities that are needed to escape the ampersand (&), the left (<) and right (>) angle brackets, and the single (') and double (") quote marks, which are frequently used in XML markup.

Should you wish to use some other character set, you need to identify the character set you're using by including an encoding declaration. Table 6.1 lists the character sets that are specifically supported by the XML specification (and should be supported by XML processors). Even if you declare another character set for your document, you can still use the Unicode hexadecimal codes for character entities, as just discussed.

Table 6.1 Supported Character Sets for XML Documents

Name	Description
ISO-8859-1	Western (Latin-1), including French, Spanish, Catalan, Galician, Basque, Portuguese, Italian, Albanian, Afrikaans, Dutch, German, Danish, Swedish, Norwegian, Finnish, Faroese, Icelandic, Irish, Scottish, and English).
ISO-8859-2	Central European (Latin 2), including Czech, Hungarian, Polish, Romanian, Croatian, Slovak, Slovene, and Serbian.

ISO-8859-3	Central European (Latin 3), including Galician and Maltese, and miscellaneous (Esperanto).
ISO-8859-4	Scandinavian/Baltic (Latin 4), including Estonian, Latvian, Lithuanian, Greenlandic, and Lappish. ISO-8859-1 can handle Swedish, Danish, and Norwegian.
ISO-8859-5	Cyrillic, including Russian, Bulgarian, Byelorussian, Macedonian, Serbian, and Ukrainian. Be aware that Russians prefer KOI8-R; see *www.nagual.pp.ru/~ache/koi8.html.*
ISO-8859-6	Arabic
ISO-8859-7	Greek
ISO-8859-8	Hebrew
ISO-8859-9	Turkish
ISO-8859-10	Lappish/Nordic/Eskimo
EUC-JP	Japanese (Unix systems)
Shift-JIS	Japanese (PCs and Macs)
ISO-2022-JP	Japanese (Internet mail/news), also called JIS
EUC-TW	Chinese. Note that GB-2312 is commonly used to represent mainland Chinese, while BIG5 is used to represent the Chinese used in Hong Kong and Taiwan.

You can use other character sets, but you must identify them using the codes established by the Internet Assigned Numbers Authority (IANA); for a list, see *ftp://ftp.isi.edu/in-notes/iana/assignments/character-sets*). Note that character set names are *not* case-sensitive, so you don't have to worry about capitalization.

To include an encoding declaration, add the declaration to the XML declaration as follows:

```
<?XML version="1.0"? encoding="ISO-8859-8">
```

The Document Element

As you learned earlier in this chapter, every XML document contains just one *document element*, which contains all the other elements you'll use. An XML document entity *must* begin and end with this element.

Rules for Naming Entities

You can name your document element anything you like, but be sure to follow the rules for creating names. (See Table 6.2.)

Table 6.2 Rules for Creating Valid Names

Position	Rule
First character	Must be a letter (excluding the letters "xml," capitalized or not), or an underscore.
Next characters	Must be a letter, a number, a hyphen, an underscore, or a period (full stop).

Note that you can't begin an element name with the letters "xml" in any combination of uppercase or lowercase.

According to these rules, the following names are *not* valid:

- xml-library (starts with "xml")
- 2new (starts with a number)
- .myname (starts with a period)

The Text

Within the XML document, you create *text*, a term that has a special meaning in XML. Text includes both *markup* and *character data*. Let's look at markup first.

Within the document entity, you can place *markup,* which includes the following:

- **start tags.** A start tag (such as <boat>) begins every nonempty element.
- **end tags.** An end tag (such as </boat>) closes every nonempty element.
- **empty element tags.** An empty element (such as <record = "125" /> must end with />. Note that you can't use empty elements unless you declare them.
- **entity references.** You refer to a named entity (such as &) by prefacing the name with an ampersand (&) and following it with a semicolon (;). Note that you can't use named entity references unless you declare them.
- **character references.** A reference to a hexadecimal Unicode character (such as é). Begin the reference with an ampersand (&) and a pound or hash sign (#); these are followed by the Unicode number and the closing semicolon.
- **comments.** You can place a comment anywhere by starting the comment with <!-- and ending the comment with -->. Don't put a double hyphen (--) within the comment text, lest you confuse the XML processor.
- **CDATA section delimiters.** These are used to "escape" blocks of text in which you want to display lots of characters that are used in XML markup, such as angle brackets and ampersands. To delimit this

text, start with the beginning CDATA delimiter ("<![CDATA[") and end with the closing delimiter ("]]>"). Here's an example: <![CDATA[Type <boat> followed by the boat's name.]]>.

- **document type declarations.** A DTD, whether contained in the same document or externally referenced.
- **processing instructions (PI).** This enables you to pass instructions on to an application; this is advanced stuff that's beyond the scope of this book.

What's left? Character data, which is simple to define. It's anything that isn't markup. The only restriction on character data lies in the need to "escape" angle brackets and the ampersand, as shown in Table 6.3.

Table 6.3 Escape Codes for Angle Brackets and Ampersand

Code	Character
<	< (less than)
>	> (greater than)
&	& (ampersand)

A Well-Formed Document: An Example

What does a well-formed document look like? Here's the boat names document, fleshed out with a couple more <boat> entries. There's an XML declaration, too. Note the <boatnames> element, which is the document element. Also, note how each of the contained elements is used at the proper nesting level. This is a well-formed document that passes muster when it's viewed by a parser. (See Figure 6.1.)

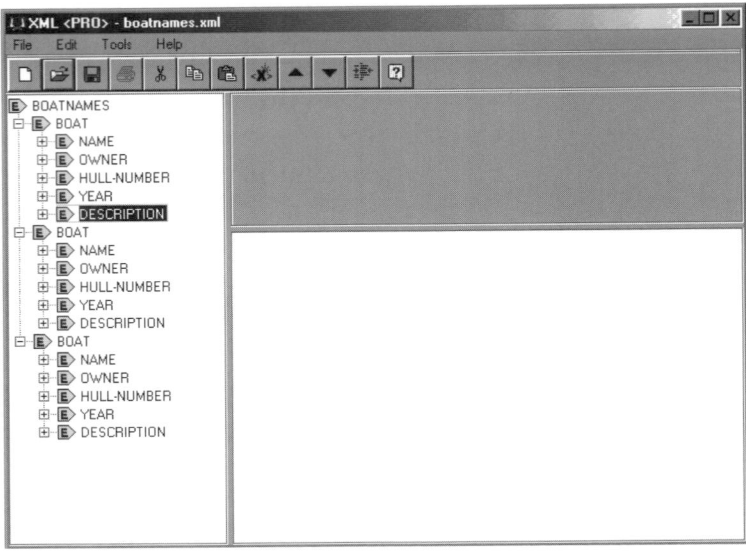

Figure 6.1 Well-formed XML document viewed by parser (XMLPro).

```
<?XML version="1.0"?>
<boatnames>
  <boat id="1">
    <name>Flipper</name>
    <owner>Liz and Frank Jones</owner>
    <hull-number>1354</hull-number>
    <year>1994</year>
    <description>Named after our
    favorite TV character!</description>
  </boat>

  <boat id="2">
    <name>Liquid Assets</name>
    <owner>Tim and Suzy Smith</owner>
    <hull-number>680</hull-number>
    <year>1988</year>
    <description>We know it's a popular
```

```
      name, but we had just cashed in a
      retirement account to buy this thing,
      and it seemed appropriate!</description>
    </boat>

    <boat id="3">
      <name>Obsession</name>
      <owner>Ronnie Kyung</owner>
      <hull-number>897</hull-number>
      <year>1991</year>
      <description>Pretty much sums it up.
      Owning one of these things isn't
      rational, is it???</description>
    </boat>

</boatnames>
```

From Here

Many Web authors will be quite content to create well-formed XML documents, which do not have DTDs. Despite not having a DTD, a well-formed document can generate a tree structure, which XML processors can pick up and pass on to browsers and custom applications. With a very modest investment in XML skills, Web authors can easily create rich structures for expressing data that's unique to their sites.

Understanding the rules for well-formed documents provides the first major step toward mastery of XML. In the next chapter, you learn how to write XML hyperlinks.

7

Linking with XLink and XPointer

If you believe that the Web defines the sum total of hyperlinking possibilities, you're going to get quite a surprise when you read this chapter. It introduces the XLink standard, the second of the several standards that will define the way XML works. (Note that the XLink standard was once called XLL, but this proved too difficult to pronounce. The official name is XLink.)

XLink is composed of two components: XLink proper (which governs how you place hyperlinks into your XML files) and XPointer (which spells out how you control what you're linking *to*). As you'll see, XLink introduces rich new ways of creating and maintaining hyperlinks.

Once you fully grasp what XLink can do, you'll surely agree that it's going to move the Web to a much higher level of functionality as a hypermedia system.

---

*Please bear in mind that this chapter is based on a working draft of the XLink and XPointer specifications, which have not yet been finalized by the World Wide Web Consortium. Some of the material in this chapter may not be accurate (at the level of specific details) once the final specification is approved; however, the general outlines of XLink and XPointer seem stable at this point. Watch out for changes in the spelling of key words! After you read this chapter, check the W3C site (*www.w3.org*) for the latest XLink and XPointer recommendations.*

What's Wrong with HTML Linking?

If XML is to generate a whole series of successors to HTML, it must provide facilities for *hyperlinking*: creating active connections between documents that enable people to navigate to new material. This is one of the major deficiencies of early SGML versions, which enabled linking (conceptualized as "cross-referencing") only within a single document. One of HTML's major innovations was to introduce the notion of hyperlinking and URLs, thus transforming the vast Internet into a hypermedia system of global proportions.

HTML linking is simple and effective, and XML could not succeed if it didn't incorporate HTML-like linking at a simple level (and it does). But HTML linking has a number of serious deficiencies. It does not really enable you to link to *information* in other documents. In addition, HTML hyperlinks are difficult and expensive to maintain, and they do not take advantage of rich new types of hyperlinking that have been developed in experimental systems. Let's look at these shortcomings one by one.

Problem 1: Inability to Link to Remote Information

In keeping with HTML's simplicity, its hyperlinking model enables only two types of links, and both of them require downloading the *entire* document that's referenced in the link. After you click, you wind up at the beginning of a new document or perhaps at a target place within the new document. You're familiar with these types of links—and you also know how inefficient they are. Often, you would like to link to only a small part of another document's text, but there's no way to do this. After you click an HTML hyperlink, your browser downloads the *entire* document—even if it's 900K long and you only want to read a portion of a paragraph!

So what are you linking to, really? Information? No! You're linking to a bunch of text.

With XML, a totally new possibility arises. When you structure your documents with XML, you create rich new ways of describing the information your documents contain—and what's more, making this information accessible to computers for processing purposes. Since XML documents are self-describing, as you learned in the last chapter, it now becomes possible to link to *information*, not just an ocean of text.

Here's an example to illustrate this point about linking to information in external, structured documents. In the previous chapter, the boat names document contains three <boat> elements, each with its own, unique ID. With XLink and XPointer, as you'll see, it's quite possible to write a link to just the contents of <boat id= "2">, and this link would retrieve *only* the following:

```
<boat id="2">
  <name>Liquid Assets</name>
  <owner id="Smith">Tim and Suzy
  Smith</owner>
  <hull-number>680</hull-number>
  <year>1988</year>
  <description>We know it's a popular
  name, but we had just cashed in a
  retirement account to buy this thing,
  and it seemed appropriate!</description>
</boat>
```

It's important to stress how radically this type of linking differs from HTML. In HTML, you can write a hyperlink that moves to a named target within the destination document, but you can do this *only* if the destination document's author has inserted this target. If such a target exists, the link simply takes you to the point where the target exists. The link isn't to any information that's readable by computers; it's just a physical location in an ocean of text. *With XLink and XPointer, it becomes possible for the first time to link to specific units of information in remote documents.*

Problem 2: Difficulty and Expense of Maintenance

As a Web author, you'll surely agree that maintaining hyperlinks is one of the least rewarding (and most time-consuming) jobs of keeping your Web site going. Part of the problem lies in the fact that all HTML links must be *inline*; that is, they must be placed within the document's text. When the time comes to update links, you've got a huge mess on your hands.

XML solves this problem by enabling you to write *out-of-line links*. Essentially, an out-of-line link is written apart from the document's text; in fact, you can even place the link in a separate document. The link specifies which parts of the source and destination document are to be linked, and the XML processor takes care of marking these parts so that users know they're linked. You'll see some examples of this later in this chapter, but for now, note a very important by-product of out-of-line links: They're *bidirectional*. After the XML processor searches for (and marks) the two link locations, the link exists in *both* directions—from the source document to the destination document, and from the destination document to the source document. Think of the time this saves over placing HTML-type hyperlinks in both places!

With out-of-line links, a wonderful new possibility emerges: You can create a single table, perhaps in a separate document, that contains *all* the links in your site. You don't have to fuss with putting the links into specific parts of the text; the XML processor does the work of finding these locations and marking them as links. And with a centralized list of links, the tedious job of maintaining hyperlinks suddenly becomes quite easy.

Out-of-line links transfer the work of inserting hyperlinks to computer programs—and that's where the work belongs. In your list of links, you specify that element such and such, with a given ID, should be linked to element such and such in another document. The software does the work of finding the relevant sections of the source and destination document, and making the links appear. Does that sound like heaven?

Problem 3: Lack of Richness

Although HTML introduced hyperlinking to the Internet community, it incorporated only the simplest type of hyperlink, a unidirectional link from the source to the destination document. But there are many more ways to link, as the authors of experimental hypermedia systems have discovered. For example, in the previous section, you learned how out-of-line links enable links that are inherently *bidirectional*, that is, links that appear *simultaneously* in both linked documents and enable the user to traverse the link from either direction. In XLink and XPointer, that's just the tip of the iceberg. Here are some more link types:

- **New ways to specify link behavior.** You can specify what a link does. The linked information can appear in a new window, replace the text that contains the link, or expand the text that contains the link. In addition, you can specify whether links are automatic or actuated by the user (as in HTML).
- **Multidirectional links.** You can write a list of related links that automatically appear in relevant sections of all the listed documents, so that the user has a choice of selecting two or more links in a given location. You can think of this as similar to a list of "see also" items at the end of a definition in a dictionary; it's up to you which way you want to go!
- **Creating outgoing links in somebody else's document.** With XLink, it's possible! Whether people are going to like this is quite another question!
- **Creating links in types of data (such as multimedia) that lack any built-in means of providing links.** You can do this in a limited way with HTML—it's what the IMG tag does—but XML takes this much further.

There's more to XLink and XPointer's capabilities, as this chapter explains. First, though, take a look at the way XML implements the valuable part of HTML, its capacity to implement simple, unidirectional links in a straightforward way.

Writing Simple HTML-Like Links

XLink is designed to be fully compatible with HTML, HTTP, and the Web. For this reason, XLink fully implements the simple, unidirectional linking capabilities of HTML, including linking to a target location within a document. (You do this by means of a *fragment identifier,* a pound or hash sign followed by a target name.) Fully supported are all the neat things about the Web's underlying protocols that have made the Web so popular and easy to use, such as Uniform Resource Identifiers (URIs), including absolute (URL) and relative links. Even at this level, though, XML introduces some wonderful innovations, as the following sections explain.

Any Element Can Become a Linking Element

There's one *huge* difference between a simple XML link and an HTML link. In HTML, you can create links only with certain elements (such as <A> and <IMG>). In XML, you can insert a link using *any* element. This is necessary in order to give XML authors the freedom they want; for example, you might want to create an element called <reference> and enable this element to display a bibliographic citation.

But how does the XML processor recognize which elements are linking elements? To create the link in a well-formed XML document that lacks a DTD, you must add two attributes to an element if you wish the XML processor to recognize that the element contains a simple (HTML-like) link:

- **xlink = "simple."** You can add this attribute to any element in your XML document. It asserts that the element should be considered a *linking element.*
- **href.** You use this attribute to specify the *locator* data, which tell the XML processor where the destination document can be found.

Here's an example of an Xlink that identifies an XML element as a linking element:

```
<boat xlink:form="simple" href="another-docu-
ment.xml">
  [ ... ]
</boat>
```

The example just given illustrates the use of a *relative URL,* in which the referenced document is assumed to be physically located in the same directory as the document containing the link.

Here's an example of an absolute URL:

```
<boat xlink:form="simple" href="http://www.
myserver.org/docs/another-document.xml">
  [ ... ]
</boat>
```

And here's an example of a link directed to a specific physical target within the destination document:

```
<boat xlink:form="simple" href="another-docu-
ment.xml#Smith">
```

```
    [ ... ]
  </boat>
```

One of several good reasons for learning how to write a DTD lies in simplifying the typing of links such as these; you can define an element so that the xlink attribute is a fixed property of the element, which enables you to skip typing it every time.

"We're Not in Kansas Anymore, Toto"

The preceeding example fully conforms to the HTML syntax for referencing targets, but it's actually much more powerful. In HTML linking, when you specify a target using a pound or hash sign (#) followed by a name, the link goes to a location that's physically inserted into the destination document using the <A> element with the name attribute (for example, <A name = "owner">). If the destination document doesn't contain the <A name> tag, the link just takes you to the beginning of the document and dumps you there.

In XML linking, the name that follows a pound or hash sign (such as "#Smith" in the example just given) is assumed to be an ID assigned to an element in the destination document, as in the following example:

```
<boat id="2">
  <name>Liquid Assets</name>
  <owner id="Smith">Tim and Suzy
  Smith</owner>
  [ ... ]
```

This example begins to illustrate the incredible power of the XPointer capabilities built into XLink. It doesn't matter if the destination document's author inserted a physical link destination using something like <A name>; as long as there are IDs, you can create a fragment identifier that jumps to this location.

XPointer gives you many more ways to specify just which information you want to retrieve from the destination document; you'll learn more about these ways later in this chapter. For now, it's worth noting that the fragment identifier syntax in XLink is designed to give the *appearance* of an HTML link to an <A name> target; in reality, it's a shorthand way of writing an XPointer link to a named element ID. There's much more to XPointer, but let's examine some ways to make these simple HTML-link hyperlinks do things that HTML can't do (or can do in only very limited contexts).

Specifying Link Behaviors

In HTML linking, you have no control over what the link does. It's actuated by the user, and it initiates a one-way transversal: from the source document to the destination document (or perhaps to an <A name> target within the destination document). That's it.

With XLink, you have much more control over how the link behaves. You can control where the retrieved data appear, and you can specify automatic as well as manual links.

Controlling Where the Linked Data Appear

Using the show attribute, you can specify where the linked material should appear:

- **show = "embed."** The retrieved information is inserted into the source document at the linking element's location.
- **show = "replace."** The retrieved information replaces the linking element's content in the same window.
- **show = "new."** The retrieved information appears in a new window.

Specifying How the Link Is Activated

With the actuate attribute, you can specify whether the link is manual or automatic:

- **actuate = "auto."** The link is activated automatically when the user opens the source document.
- **actuate = "user."** The user must activate the link manually (for example, by clicking on it).

Understanding How Link Behavior Controls Work

If these options sound a bit mysterious, relax; actually, you're familiar with them. In a very limited way, HTML implements them. For example, consider the following IMG tag in HTML:

```
<IMG src="picture.gif">
```

This is the same as the following, in XLink:

```
<picture xlink:form="simple"
href="picture.gif" show="embed"
actuate="auto">
```

See? The IMG element implements an automatic link that embeds the destination graphic into the source document, as if it were part of the source document.

What's so refreshing and exciting about XLink is its ability to give you control over the linking behavior of *any* element. This creates so many possibilities that we could spend the rest of the book talking about them!

Here's just one example, one that goes to the heart of the unfulfilled promise of SGML: information reusability.

Suppose you create a bibliography that contains the following citation (among others):

```
<citation id="Smith1999">
  <author-last>Smith</author-last>
  <author-first>Juanita</author-first>
  <pub-date>1999</pub-date>
  <title>Southern Memoir</title>
  <publisher>New Southern Voices</publisher>
  <pub-city>Charleston, S.C.</pub-city>
</citation>
```

You've created a style sheet that formats this citation very nicely, as in the following example:

```
Smith, Juanita. 1999. Southern Memoir.
Charleston, S.C.: New Southern Voices.
```

Now suppose you want to reference this citation in another context. Why retype it? Use the following Xlink instead:

```
<citation xlink:form="simple" href="bibliog-
raphy.xml#Smith1999" show="embed"
actuate="auto">
```

This inserts the citation into the source document automatically.

Later, you find out that you got some of the publication data wrong. It turns out that *Southern Memoir* was published by Magnolia Press, not New Southern Voices. What do you do? *You make the correction in one place and one place only—bibliography.xml—and the change is automatically reflected in every document that links to this citation.*

Creating Extended Links

The simple links just described fully implement the basics of HTML unidirectional linking, but with enhanced functionality that hints at the power of XLink. With *extended* links, that power becomes a reality.

In brief, an extended link breaks the connection between the *linking element* (the element that defines the link type and behavior) and the *locator element* (the element that specifies where the destination information should be found). As you'll see, this enables you to accomplish a number of wild and wonderful things, including *out-of-line links,* multidirectional links, and more. The following sections explain what you can do with extended links.

Creating Out-of-Line Links

Suppose your Web site has two documents: essay.xml and bibliography.xml. You would like to link elements within these two documents so that they point to each other. For example, you want the Smith 1999 citation in the bibliography to point to the place in essay.xml where you discuss Smith's work. Similarly, you want the place in essay.xml that discusses Smith to point to the Smith 1999 citation. With HTML (and with simple XML links) you would have to put inline links in both locations. (By default, simple links are inline links.) But there's an easier way. *You can create a single out-of-line link.*

To create the out-of-line link for any element in your document, you create one element to define the link type and behavior, and another to serve as the locator. (For convenience, you could call these elements extended-link and locator.) Here's an illustration:

```
<extended xlink:form="extended" show="new"
actuate="user">
  <locator xlink:form="locator"
  href="bibliography.xml#Smith1999">
  <locator xlink:form="locator"
  href="essay.xml#Smith1999">
</extended>
```

What does this do? When the user opens the document that contains this code, the XML browser opens the searches the two referenced documents (bibliography.xml and essay.xml), and marks as hyperlinks the elements with the ID Smith1999. (Just how XML browsers will mark extended links isn't certain; probably, you'll see an icon in the margin.)

An out-of-line link is inherently bidirectional; it automatically creates a link from the source document to the destination document, and a back-link from the destination document to the source document. Actually, the whole concept of "source" and "destination" documents becomes meaningless when you're talking about extended links. An extended link is a way of bringing two (or more) documents or portions of documents together so that they are linked to each other.

Creating Links within Someone Else's Document? Yes!

XLink's extended linking capabilities enable you to create a link within a document that you don't have the rights to modify. Yes, I'm serious. Consider the following code, inserted within your document, essay.xml:

```
<extended xlink:form="extended" show="new"
actuate="user">
  <locator xlink="locator"
  href="http://www.university.edu/~jones/
  bibliography.xml#Smith1999">
  <locator xlink:form="locator"
  href="essay.xml#Smith1999">
</extended>
```

Here, bibliography.xml isn't your document at all; it exists out there on somebody else's server, and you don't have any rights to modify the document. Even so, when somebody opens essay.xml, the XML browser will download bibliography.xml, find #Smith1999, and format this element as a hyperlink *back to your page*. My term for this is *virtual hyperlinking*, the rather remarkable act of inserting a hyperlink into somebody's document without so much as a by-your-leave from the document's author.

Before you start to panic thinking about how you're going to lose control of the links on your Web pages, bear in mind that these links are only apparent to people who open the specific XML page containing the <extended-link> code. In other words, Dr. Scholar at the Big University has created a very nice bibliography, but this bibliography contains a backlink to my humble essay *only* if somebody opens *my* essay first. Anyone else will see only the inline links that Dr. Scholar chose to place within bibliography.xml.

Linking Three or More Resources

And now for something really far out, at least from the HTML perspective. In the previous examples, you learned how XLink can create bidirectional links that appear automatically and simultaneously in two documents. You can do this for three or more documents, if you wish. Consider the following:

```
<extended xlink:form="extended" show="new"
actuate="user">
  <locator xlink:form="locator"
  href="http://www.university.edu/~jones/
  bibliography.xml#Smith1999">
  <locator xlink:form="locator" http://
  www.state-univ.edu/~carter/
  article.xml#Smith1999">
  <locator xlink:form="locator"
  href="essay.xml#Smith1999">
</extended-link>
```

This group places *three* locator elements within the extended-link group. So what happens? When the user downloads the document containing this code, the XML browser downloads the three referenced documents, and formats each of them so that it's obvious to the user that the Smith1999 elements are links. But what happens when the user clicks on one of these links?

Normally, when you click on a hyperlink, the browser takes you to the referenced document. With XML, as you've seen, you can alter this behavior so that the browser replaces or embeds the referenced information within the source document. But there's no question about which information is displayed, embedded, or replaced.

With three or more locators in an extended-link group, however, the browser will need to give the user some means to choose among the options. Most likely, this will be done by means of a pop-up menu.

Defining Extended Link Document Groups

As the preceding sections have suggested, extended links take XML into uncharted territory indeed. They break the connection between a document's underlying code and the hyperlinks that seem to appear within them. You've seen how you can make a "virtual" hyperlink appear in somebody else's document, even though you don't possess the rights to modify that document's code. Yet these "virtual" hyperlinks do not appear unless all the linked documents are downloaded to the user's computer and processed by the XML browser. To make it easy on XML browsers, you might wish to provide them with a list of documents that refer to each other in this "virtual" sense. You can do this with *extended link groups*.

An extended link group is simply a list of documents that contain information you've referenced by means of extended links. (These don't have to be documents on your server or under your control, necessarily!) The extended link group tells the browser to download all of them, search them for extended link references, and format the linked text accordingly so that the virtual hyperlinks appear.

Here's an example. Previously, you've seen extended links that involve three documents: bibliography.xml, essay.xml, and article.xml. Only one of them, essay.xml, is on your server. In order to make all the richness of your virtual links apparent to users, you create the following extended link group:

```
<group xlink:form="group" steps = "2">
  <document xlink:form="document"
  href="http://www.university.edu/~jones/
  bibliography.xml>
  <document xlink:form="document" http://
  www.state-univ.edu/~carter/
  article.xml">
  <document xlink:form="document"
  href="essay.xml">
</group>
```

What's going on here? This code tells the XML browser that there's a group of documents in which you've implemented virtual hyperlinks. These are listed within the document elements (bibliography.xml, article.xml, and essay.xml).

Note the steps = "2" attribute. This is an important safeguard against a very dirty trick. Consider this: Suppose I create an extended link group, which in turn references documents that contain an extended link group. These documents, in turn, contain extended link groups. Before this stops, the poor user might have inadvertently downloaded hundreds of megabytes of unwanted data! The steps = "2" attribute stops the downloading two steps away from the source document.

Specifying Link Content with XPointer

As you've already learned, the XPointer portion of the XLink specification provides powerful tools for specifying the content to be retrieved when a hyperlink is activated. What appears to be a simple implementation of the HTML fragment identifier (for example, "#Smith") turns out to be much more powerful than an HTML link to a named target:

- **You're linking to element IDs, not <A name> targets.** By default, XLink defines fragment identifiers as shorthand XPointer links to element IDs. For this reason, as previously mentioned, you can establish links to any elements bearing ID names in the destination document; in contrast to HTML, you do not need write permissions in order to establish a link to specific information.

- **You're linking to all the content within the identified element, not just a physical location in the destination document.** The powerful default ID-linking capabilities of XPointer demonstrate a point that this book has repeatedly stressed about XML, namely, that XML enables Web authors to transform *text* into *information* that is subject to computer retrieval and processing.

Impressive as they are, XPointer's default fragment identifier barely scratches the surface of XPointer's capabilities, which are summarized in this section—several chapters would be needed to fully explain everything that XPointer can do. And believe it or not, XPointer is itself a simplified version of a more complex ancestor, the Text Encoding Initiative's Extended Pointer syntax. My intention here is to emphasize the basic structure of the XPointer linking language and illustrate what I believe to be XPointer's must useful capabilities; just bear in mind that there's much more to the specification than this section can cover.

XPointer Language Essentials

As you've already learned, XPointer is a language for expressing fragment identifiers that are tacked onto the end of URLs by means of a *connector* (such as #). And as I've just stressed, an XPointer expression can precisely identify elements (and their content) within the tree structure of the destination document. Each XPointer expression contains one or more *location terms* that consist of a *keyword* and *arguments*. Here's a closer look at these terms:

- **Connector.** You can choose between "#" (pound or hash mark) and "|" (vertical bar character). If you use the "#" connector, the XML browser downloads the entire destination document, processes it, and identifies the fragment. If you use the "|" connector, you leave the retrieval technique up to the application. (Some might be able to retrieve the requested information *without* downloading the entire destination document.)
- **Location terms.** These follow the connector, and use the syntax keyword(argument). For example, to locate an element with the ID "Smith1999," you use the location term id(Smith1999).
- **Keywords.** The keyword specifies how XPointer locates the requested information. You can choose between keywords that find *absolute locations* (such as elements named with a unique ID) or keywords that look for *relative locations* (such as the third element down from the first <boat> element).

Note that the location term used in this chapter's examples—the one that looks like an HTML fragment identifier (#Smith1999)—is actually a shorthand expression for #id(Smith1999). This shortcut was deliberately introduced because of its similarity to HTML's fragment identifiers.

As you'll see later in this section, you can combine more than one location term in a single XPointer expression. (When you do so, you separate the location terms by typing a period.) Because you can use more than one location term, it's important to understand that the *first* location term establishes the basic point of reference for locating the desired information. For example, suppose you want to write an XPointer that would go to the element with the ID "Smith1999," and locate the ninth citation element that follows. Here's how you'd write the XPointer:

```
id(Smith1999).following(9,citation)
```

This XPointer combines an absolute location term (the first one) with a relative location term. Let's look at absolute location terms first, and for good reason: They're the safest to use. They're not likely to change if the document's author adds some material. In contrast, you're risking a dead or inaccurate link if you point to the ninth citation after Smith 1999. What happens if the author adds or deletes citations between Smith 1999 and the one that used to be nine citation elements down?

Linking to Absolute Locations

Absolute location terms establish links to fixed locations within the destination document, such as an element with a unique ID. If you have no control over the destination document, an ID link is far and away the best type of link to establish; it's not likely to change if the document's author inserts or rearranges the document's text.

To create a link to an element with a unique ID, use the following:

```
id(name)
```

where *name* is the element's ID. Remember the shortcut: You can skip the keyword and parentheses, and just type the ID name.

Linking to an Absolute Location within the Same Document

To create a link to an element within the source document (an internal link), use the origin keyword as the first location term, and specify additional location terms as needed:

```
origin().id(references)
```

Note that the origin() keyword includes empty parentheses; these are necessary to distinguish the keyword from a named ID. When you use the origin keyword, the search begins from the locator's position within the document and proceeds toward the end of the file. This search would begin at the locator and look for the element with the ID named "references."

If you're linking to an HTML document that has named targets (created with <A name>), you can use the html keyword, as in the following example:

```
html(Smith1999)
```

Table 7.1 sums up the absolute location keywords that you can use with XPointer.

Table 7.1 XPointer Absolute Location Keywords

Name	Description
root()	Establishes that the root element of the destination document is the starting place for locating

	the desired information. This is the default unless you specify another absolute location keyword: origin(), id, or html.
origin()	Points to a location within the *source* document. This is used for linking to locations within the same document that contains the hyperlink.
id	Specifies a named element ID within the destination document.
html	Creates a link to an HTML document's <A name> target.

Linking to Relative Locations

In contrast to absolute locations, a relative location isn't fixed by a named ID. Instead, it's determined by a series of location steps. For example, a street address (such as 11219 Culver Park Drive) is like an absolute location. Resembling a relative location are directions such as the following: "When you get into town, take a right at the first stop light, and you'll pass three stop signs. At the third stop sign, turn left. Our house is the ninth one on the right."

Like the direction example just given, relative location XPointers require a starting point; if you don't supply one, it's assumed that you want to start at the root element of the destination document. To specify another starting point, you can use an absolute location, as in the following example:

```
id(Smith1999).following(2, citation)
```

This XPointer begins at the element with the ID "Smith1999," and jumps to the second citation element after the one with the ID "Smith1999."

Relative Location Term Syntax

With relative locations, you specify a keyword, followed by parentheses. Within the parentheses, you specify the following:

- **All or instance.** If you specify "all," the XPointer finds all the locations that match your conditions. If you specify an instance by means of a positive number, the XPointer skips down to the *n*th item that you specify. If you specify a negative number, the XPointer counts up from the last item.
- **Optionally, the type of node you're looking for.** Here, the term *node* refers to an element, a processing instruction (PI), a comment, some grouped text, or some grouped CDATA. If you type a name (such as "citation"), XPointer counts only those elements with the name you specify. If you leave the name out, XPointer counts all the elements it finds.

Use a comma to separate the node type, if you decide to specify it. Here's an example:

```
following(2, citation)
```

This expression looks for the second citation element that follows the beginning element.

If you leave the node type out, XPointer assumes you're looking for any element. Consider the following:

```
following(2)
```

This XPointer looks for the second element after the beginning one.

Relative Location Keywords

Table 7.2 sums up the relative location keywords you can use.

To understand the various relative location keywords listed in Table 7.2, it's important to conceptualize the beginning point as a container (rather than a physical location). This helps to clarify the differences among the various options. For instance, the child keyword locates a node that's nested below the beginning container in the document's tree structure, while the following keyword locates a node that comes *after* the beginning container.

Table 7.2 XPointer Relative Location Keywords

Name	Description
child	An element that is *nested below* the link's beginning container
descendant	Content of any node type that's nested *within* the link's beginning container
following	A node that appears *after* the link's beginning container
ancestor	An element that *contains* the link's beginning point of reference—or, to put it another way, the element that contains the beginning container
preceding	An element that *precedes* the link's beginning container
psibling	A node that shares the same parent as the beginning container and appears prior to the beginning container
fsibling	A node that shares the same parent as the beginning container and appears after the beginning container

Should You Use Relative Location Terms?

XPointer's relative location terms give you many possibilities, but it's important to remember that they're hazardous to use. If the document's author inserts or deletes some material, they may fail to work correctly or may locate the wrong item. For most Web linking purposes, it's best to stick with absolute locators, unless you have no other choice. If you must use relative locators, it's best to specify named elements—or, as the next section suggests, search for matching text.

Creating a Link That Searches for Text

If you want to link to somebody else's document that doesn't have element IDs, perhaps the safest relative link is one that matches text you specify. To create this kind of XPointer, you use the string keyword, as in the following example:

```
root().string(1, "Smith 1999")
```

This XPointer begins at the document's root element and finds the first instance of text that matches "Smith 1999."

Text searches are case-sensitive. If you search for "smith 1999" and the destination document contains "Smith 1999," the link won't produce the results you want.

Relative Linking Horizons

This section has barely scratched the surface of XPointer's relative location possibilities. In addition to the capabilities I've already mentioned, you can match elements with specified attributes (such as emphasis= "yes" in the following element: <major-heading emphasis = “yes”>) and even search for text in the destination document.

From Here

This chapter outlined the working draft of the XLink and XPointer recommendations; please bear in mind that some of the details discussed here (such as the names of keywords) could change when the final recommendation is published. In particular, watch out for the xlink:form keyword.

At this point, you've learned everything you need to know to create a suite of well-formed XML documents, place them on the Web, and take advantage of XML's advanced capabilities. The next chapter provides an extended example that illustrates XML's attractive possibilities for everyday Web publishing tasks.

8

Well-Formed XML in Action: An Example

In this chapter, you'll see an extended example of XML's possibilities for Web publishing. Emphasized here are ways that simple, well-formed XML (including XLinks) can solve some of the most vexing problems of Web site design. You'll work through a complete site development process, focusing on a small business's Web publishing plan.

Please remember that some of the details of XML are not yet finalized, including XLinks. The code in this chapter may need revision once the World Wide Web Consortium finalizes its XML recommendations.

HTML's Shortcomings for Site Design

Although HTML is a wonderful tool for creating Web sites, it's far from ideal when you want to present structured information and keep your readers focused.

The Problem

Let's say you own a small but sophisticated wine shop in a major metropolitan area. Your challenge: To stay in business, you need to get people to buy wine from your store instead of the supermarket, and you'd like to see whether the Web can help.

Here's the problem. You know your customers won't spend more per bottle, on average, than they'd spend at the supermarket. To compete effectively with supermarket wine prices, you need to create interest in little-known, bargain wines that offer very good quality and very good value. (One of the fun things about wine is that it's quite easy to find such wines; every year, there are dozens of little-known wines sold for $12 or less that are superior to wines that cost 10 times that much.) In addition, you've learned that your customers are often somewhat embarrassed to come into your store because they don't know how to pronounce wine names and terms. What's more, they don't know how to describe the taste they're after, which compounds their embarrassment.

Your goal: Get out your message while contributing something of genuine value to the Internet. And while you're at it, help your customers feel more comfortable about coming into your store.

The Web Publishing Plan

So you come up with a neat plan for a Web site that's intended to promote your business (and genuinely contribute to the growing store of wine lore on the Internet).

You'll feature 25 inexpensive but wonderful wines at a time, with updates every week or two: The Top 25 Best Wine Values Page. You're hoping to use the Web's hyperlinking capabilities to help people learn what all those strange wine-tasting terms mean, and you're planning to include a pronunciation guide that enables people to learn how to pronounce wine names and terms. In addition, you hope to link each wine to a recipe so that your customers can learn how to pair wine with food in a creative way, one that goes beyond the dictum, "red with meat, white with fish."

After working with some local Web consultants, you come up with a great-looking HTML site. The site's welcome page features a link to your Top 25 Best Wine Values and introduces locals to your shop and its location.

On the Top 25 Best Wine Values page, each wine is described with extensive tasting notes, including numerical scores from wine-tasting magazines, the current price, and a Bargain Index factor computed from the score and price (with 10 representing the ultimate bargain, a wine that scores 100 points for $10). Terms (especially tasting terms) are linked to a glossary page, which incorporates a pronunciation guide. Each wine's description closes with a link to a recipe.

Here are a couple of these (fictitious) entries (note that the underlined terms represent hyperlinks):

White Wines

Chardonnays

1996 Vistamount Barossa Valley Chardonnay. Australia. Reminiscent of a white Burgandy, this delicious Chard doesn't hit you in the face with oak and butter; you'll taste tropical fruit that stays light and refreshing on the smooth finish. Try it with Couscous Shrimp. Bargain Index: 8.8 (88 pts/$10)

1996 Pine Forest Chardonnay (Reserve Label). California. A wonderfully complex, buttery Chardonnay with just the right amount of oak; the wine explodes on your palette with pear and pineapple, deepening to fig and date. The long, delicious finish leaves you refreshed. A stunner. Try it with Steamed Cod. Bargain Index: 7.5 (91 pts/$12)

What's Wrong with the HTML Version of This Site?

By HTML standards, this Web page is going to be quite good. But it has all of HTML's limitations, including the following:

- **The links are informative but distracting.** To find out how to pronounce or define a term, users can click on the hyperlink. But they're taken away from the heart of your site, the descriptions of your top 25 wines. Will they come back?
- **The links don't function well.** They take readers to a named place within a much larger document (the glossary or recipes), which contains a great deal of information that isn't relevant to the reader's interests.

- **The data is a mass of undifferentiated text.** In order to place your reviews into a growing archive and make them searchable in a meaningful way, you'll have to spend a lot of money on a custom HTML-to-database gateway.
- **Navigation isn't easy.** You've organized your reviews by varietal (Chardonnay, Cabernet Sauvignon, Sangiovese, Zinfandel, etc.), and they're alphabetized this way. Readers interested in Zinfandel have to page down through a lot of material in which they're not interested. Will they give up and quit? Of course, you could put up a bunch of different pages, one for each varietal—but will they get lost navigating through all these pages and quit in frustration?

Most of these problems can be solved to some extent by means of extensive JavaScript and Java programming, server-side scripts, and other time-consuming, expensive fixes. But XML can solve them with considerably less effort and expense.

Why XML Offers a Better Solution

XML provides tools that enable a superior implementation of this site's underlying design. With XML, you can

- **Use embedded links to keep readers focused.** When readers click on a tasting term or recipe, the link text appears within the source document. As you'll learn in Part Five, you can use CSS Level 2's fixed positioning capabilities to make the link text appear in a column next to the source location—and absolutely no programming is required to do this.
- **Link to precise units of content.** A hyperlink to a two-sentence definition does not force the download

of a lengthy document, which then scrolls to a named location. The definition document has already been downloaded—it's included in a group that's downloaded automatically at the start of the session—and the link retrieves just the text that's needed.

- **Develop elements that identify your unique content.** To facilitate data retrieval by means of easily constructed Java applets, you can code your data so that every significant fact in your reviews becomes accessible to computer processing, including search and retrieval.
- **Facilitate navigation by means of a tree structure.** XML browsers will display this site's tree structure in one window, and the document text in another. This will enable readers to browse the Top 25 Bargain Wines by navigating a collapsible tree. For example, at the top-most level, the tree can show just "Whites," "Reds," and "Rosés." If you click on "Reds," you see "Cabernet Sauvignon," "Syrah," "Zinfandel," "Sangiovese," etc. A further click reveals the individual entries, which appear in the text window.

Combining HTML and XML

Although XML provides superior tools for the Top 25 Bargain Wine list, there's no need to abandon HTML completely. Combined with CSS Level 2 style sheets, HTML code provides excellent tools for the site's home page and information pages, which don't really need XML's data-structuring power.

In order to include your XML within a site that begins with an HTML welcome page, the simplest and best way is to provide links from the welcome page to the XML documents. Here's an example of an HTML link to an XML document:

```
<A href="top25.xml>The top 25 wine bar-
gains!</A>
```

Alternatively, with some browsers, you may be able to include the XML content as an *object* within the HTML. (An object is a unit of data that requires a special application to process it.) You will probably be able to use HTML's OBJECT element to do this, as in the following example:

```
<OBJECT data = "top25.xml" type = "text/x-
xml">

Your browser does not support embedded XML
documents.

</OBJECT>
```

There's a drawback to the OBJECT method: Netscape Navigator version 3.0 doesn't support the OBJECT element, so there's no way—even with a plug-in or Java program—that this browser could recognize your XML.

And there's a better method on the drawing boards. Currently, the World Wide Web Consortium (W3C) plans to recommend the inclusion of an XML element in the next version of HTML. This element would enable you to embed XML code within an HTML document, as in the following example:

```
<HTML>
  <HEAD>
    <TITLE>Top 25 Wine Bargains</TITLE>
  </HEAD>
  <BODY>
```

```
    <H1>The Top 25 Wine Bargains</H1>
    <XML>
      [XML markup goes here]
    </XML>
  </BODY>
</HTML>
```

One problem with this approach: The code might show up in some older browsers. A not-so-satisfactory way around this problem would be to enclose the XML element within SCRIPT tags, as in the following example:

```
<SCRIPT language="xml">
  <XML>
    [XML markup goes here]
  </XML>
</SCRIPT>
```

This would effectively hide the XML markup from non-XML-aware browsers, without interfering with the ability of the XML processor to detect and validate the XML code. The only problem with this approach is that it's illogical; XML isn't a scripting language!

This discussion illustrates (once again) the basic point that there are many details that must be worked out before XML can be implemented on the Web.

Please remember that, at this writing, there are no XML-capable browsers, and it's anyone's guess just how XML inclusion will be handled. Although the OBJECT technique just described will represent one possible means of including XML data into an HTML document, some browser publishers may choose to implement XML inclusion differently.

Planning the Site

You've decided to use HTML for the site's welcome and information pages. What's at issue now is the XML portion of your site. What's the ideal way to divide up the material?

As you learned in Chapter 6, a well-formed XML document has one and only one document element, a named element that describes and subsumes all the document's content. For this site's purposes, it makes very good sense (as I'll explain in a moment) to create four separate XML documents, each with its own, descriptive document element, as Table 8.1 shows.

Table 8.1 Site Development Plan: XML Documents

Name	Description
top25	The current list of the top 25 bargain wines, organized by wine type (red, white, rosé), varietal, and bargain index score.
taste-terms	The glossary of tasting terms (and the pronunciation guide), organized alphabetically.
wine-terms	The glossary of wine terms.
recipes	The database of recipes, organized by the type of wine that complements them.

Why not put all of this data into one structured document? There are two reasons to divide up the documents this way:

- **Facilitating navigation.** Remember that XML-aware browsers will display the document's tree structure in a separate window or panel (see Figure 8.1) and

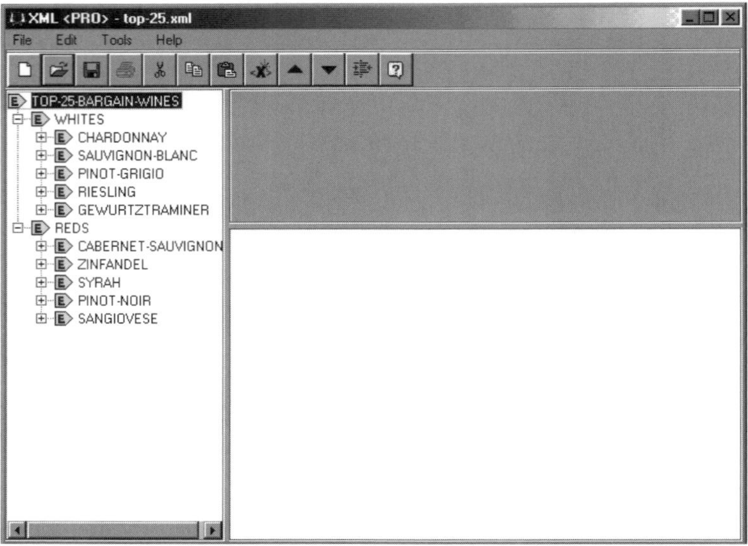

Figure 8.1 Tree structure displayed by XML software (XML Pro)

enable users to browse a document by expanding or collapsing element names within the document tree. The tree structure's organization should be easy to understand at a glance. Keeping the content unified helps the reader to see instantly what's available and how it's organized.

- **Facilitating maintenance.** This site will be easier to maintain if the various types of content are stored in separate, easily edited documents.

Analyzing Your Data

With HTML, you'd be ready to code at this point. With XML, you've still got some work to do: analyzing your data to determine how you should name and organize your elements.

Envision the Tree Structure

Remember that XML-aware browsers will display your document's tree structure in a separate window, and users will be able to browse your document's content by expanding and collapsing element names. Keep the names simple, and organize them in a way that invites exploration and discovery.

Here's a good plan for the overall organization of the document's tree structure:

```
<?XML version="1.0">
<top-25-bargain-wines>
  <whites>
    <chardonnay>
    </chardonnay>
    <sauvignon-blanc>
    </sauvignon-blanc>
    <pinot-grigio>
    </pinot-grigio>
    <riesling>
    </riesling>
    <gewurztraminer>
    </gewurztraminer>
  </whites>
  <reds>
    <cabernet-sauvignon>
    </cabernet-sauvignon>
    <zinfandel>
    </zinfandel>
    <syrah>
    </syrah>
    <pinot-noir>
    </pinot-noir>
    <sangiovese>
    </sangiovese>
```

```
    </reds>
</top-25-bargain-wines>
```

You could have more elements here or fewer. In fact, one benefit of writing well-formed XML lies in the ease of adding elements; if you wrote a DTD, you'd need to modify the DTD should you decide to create a new element for a new type of wine.

There isn't a law that says you must organize elements alphabetically. You can use any method of organization that suits your needs. This tree structure is organized using a most-important to least-important plan of attack; for example, Chardonnay is the white wine most customers ask about.

Refine the Tree Structure

Within each of the wine varietal categories (such as Chardonnay or Sangiovese), it makes good sense to break down the entries by wine-growing region or country (such as France, Australia, or California) and then by year, as in the following example:

```
<top-25-bargain-wines>
  <whites>
    <chardonnay>
      <California>
      </California>
      <Australia>
      </Australia>
    </chardonnay>
```

Break Your Data Down into Meaningful Components

Now take a closer look at the wine bargain entries themselves. Here's another example:

Bargain Index: 7.5 (91 pts/$12)
1995 Tuolumne Vista Sangiovese **(Private Reserve).** California. You won't mistake it for Chianti, but you won't care after you discover the black cherry aromas and taste the rich black fruit with cedar highlights. Try it with Pork Risotto.

These entries have an underlying structure, although it isn't a rigid one. Here's a plan for naming the components of this structure:

```
<wine>
  <year>
  </year>
  <name>
  </name>
  <region>
  </region>
  <tasting-notes>
  </tasting-notes>
  <recipe-recommendation>
  </recipe-recommendation>
  <bargain-index>
  </bargain-index>
</wine>
```

The following shows how a completed entry looks:

```
<wine>
  <year>
    1996
  </year>
  <name>
    Tuolumne Vista Sangiovese (Private
    Reserve).
  </name>
  <region>
    California.
  </region>
  <tasting-notes>
```

```
    You won't mistake it for Chianti, but
    you won't care after you discover the
    <taste-term xlink type="simple"
    show="embed" href="taste-terms.xml#black
    cherry">black cherry</taste-term> aromas
    and taste the rich <taste-term xlink
    type="simple" show="embed" href="taste-
    terms.xml#black fruit">black
    fruit</taste-term> with <taste-term
    xlink type="simple" show="embed"
    href="taste-terms.xml#cedar">
    cedar</taste-term> highlights.
  </tasting-notes>
  <recipe-recommendation>
    Try it with <recipe xlink type="simple"
    show="embed" href="recipe.xml#pork-
    risotto">pork risotto</recipe>.
  </recipe-recommendation>
  <bargain-index>
    Bargain Index: 7.5 (91 pts./$12)
  </bargain-index>
</wine>
```

Creating Supporting Documents

The Bargain Wines page is the highlight of this XML application, but it needs three supporting documents for tasting terms (including the pronunciation guide), wine terms, and recipes. Each should be placed in its own, separate document, with a document element that describes the document's content.

To create the supporting documents, you would use the same development method used for the Bargain Wines page:

- **Envision the tree structure.** Name the document element, and decide how you'd like the nested elements to appear within the document's tree structure.
- **Refine the tree structure.** Create elements that name and store the data you'd like the document to contain.
- **Break the data down into meaningful components.** Consider whether you'd like to break down the data within elements into further components. Doing so would enable you to set up sophisticated searching and other applications, should you wish to do so.

The following shows what one of the entries in the tasting terms document looks like:

```
<taste-terms>
  <term id="cedar">
    <term-name>Cedar</term-name>
    <definition>
      A delicious taste associated with the
      fragrant wood found in cedar chests
      and those little blocks you can buy to
      freshen your closet. A hallmark of
      an exceptionally good Cabernet
      Sauvignon.
    </definition>
  </term/>
</taste-terms>
```

Testing Your Work

Is your XML really well-formed? You'll find out when you open your XML document with a program that uses an XML processor. According to the XML specification, violation of the rules for well-formedness generates a fatal error—which means that the XML processor stops processing your file at the point where the error was detected. You'll see an error message informing you what's wrong, if the program is able to interpret the error correctly.

Remember, to avoid common mistakes,

- Use a single root element.
- Don't violate the nesting order.
- Don't overlap elements.
- Be sure your start and end tags match.
- Close empty elements with the empty-element tag.
- Always surround values with quotation marks.

For a review of these rules, see Chapter 6.

From Here

In this chapter and the previous one, you've learned all you need to know to create well-formed XML documents and place them on the Web in a way that takes full advantage of XML's superior linking capabilities.

But what about presentation? Unless you're writing documents that will serve as fodder for applications (such as a CDF file), you will surely want to use style sheets to give your XML document an attractive appearance. In Part Four, you'll learn how to use Cascading Style Sheets (CSS) to control the presentation of XML documents, and you'll also find an introduction to XSL, the XML style sheet language.

And what about DTDs? Should you decide that a DTD is needed for your XML documents, you *can* learn how to write one. Thanks to XML's simplicity, the task of writing an XML DTD isn't as daunting as writing a DTD with

SGML. As you'll see, writing your own DTDs is a very good idea, because XML editors can automatically detect your DTD's rules and tell you which elements and attributes you can use in a given context.

9

Using an XML Editor

Because you're experienced with HTML, you know that there are good grounds for using an HTML-savvy editor rather than trying to type tags yourself. HTML editors enable you to enter elements and attributes by choosing them from a menu; the editor adds the markup symbols automatically. In addition, the editor performs validation checks to make sure you've entered everything correctly.

With XML, there's an additional motivation for using an editor: The XML 1.0 specification demands that every XML document meet the requirements for well-formedness—and if the document violates these requirements, the processor stops dead in its tracks! In contrast, HTML processors try to display the document even if the code contains serious errors. (For this reason, very few Web authors run their documents through HTML validators; but every XML author *must* do so.) An XML editor helps you make sure that your code is well-formed.

This chapter introduces XML <Pro>, an early XML editing tool created by Vervet Logic (*www.vervet.com*). You can use XML <Pro> to create well-formed or valid XML documents. Here, you'll learn how you can use XML <Pro> to create a simple well-formed XML document. By the time you read this book, many more XML editors will be available. My purpose here is to illustrate how XML editors work by looking at a pioneering product. Future editors are likely to work in much the same way.

Introducing XML Pro

XML <Pro> is a visual XML editor. Like the best HTML editors, the program features a visual interface that makes the task of choosing and inserting elements easy. But we're talking about XML here, not HTML. In contrast to an HTML editor, XML <Pro> incorporates an XML processor, which enables the program to detect and display the tree structure of any well-formed or valid XML document. In Figure 9.1, for example, you see the tree structure of the Top 25 Wine Bargains page.

You can use XML <Pro> to edit existing XML documents or create new ones. Either way, the program enables you to define elements, display them in a list, and insert them into your document. You don't have to worry about the syntax—XML <Pro> takes care of that automatically. The program's Element and Attribute wizards walk you through the process of adding new elements to your document.

With XML <Pro>, you can work with well-formed or valid documents; the program enables you to associate any document with a DTD. (In this chapter, you'll explore XML <Pro>'s features for creating well-formed XML.)

Based on the W3C's XML 1.0 recommendation, XML <Pro> provides a sound basis for beginning your exploration of XML coding. Bear in mind, though, that the version of XML <Pro> featured in this chapter (1.0) does not incorporate XML linking and pointing features, which are not yet standardized.

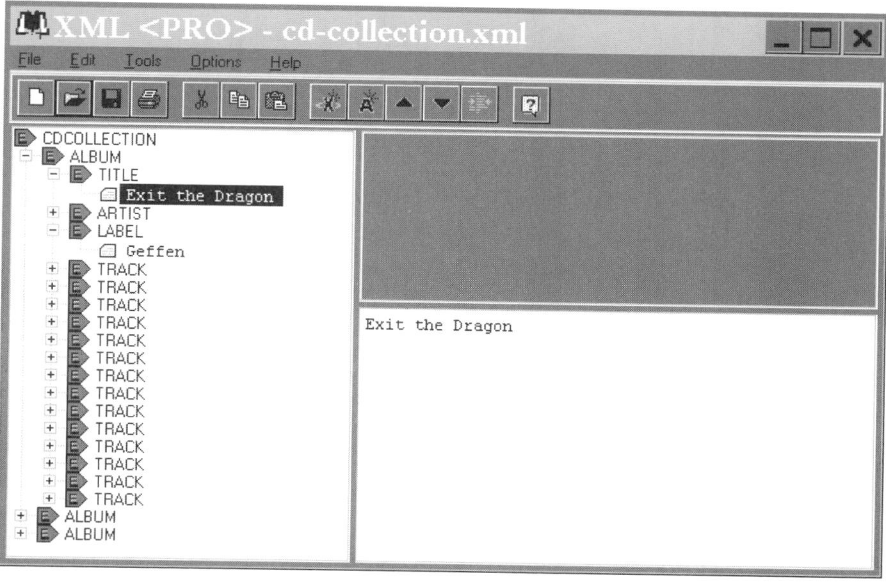

Figure 9.1 The XML <Pro> window.

Exploring the XML <Pro> Window

The XML <Pro> window, shown in Figure 9.2, features the following areas:

- **Menu and toolbar.** The menu bar provides access to all of XML <Pro>'s commands. From the toolbar, you can choose the most frequently accessed commands.
- **Document tree view.** On the left, you see the elements you're working with. You can collapse and expand the list of elements by clicking the element icons.
- **Attribute pane.** On the top right, you see the attributes that have been defined for the selected element.

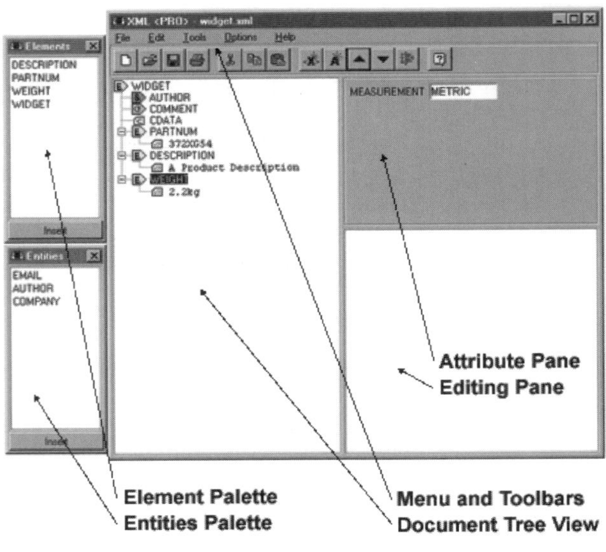

Figure 9.2 Components of the XMLPro window.

- **Editing.** On the lower right, you see the content of the selected element. You can add content to an element by typing it here.
- **Elements palette.** This window automatically lists all the elements that the document contains. You can insert elements into your document by choosing them from this palette.
- **Entities palette.** This window automatically lists all the entities that the document contains, such as codes for foreign-language characters. You can insert entities into your document by choosing them from this palette.

The XML <Pro> Toolbar

From the toolbar, you can choose the most frequently accessed commands. Table 9.1 explains the tools in the order they appear on the toolbar (left to right).

Table 9.1 XML <Pro> Toolbar

Tool	Description
New	Creates a new XML document. When you create the document, you specify a name for the root element.
Open	Opens an existing XML document. The document must be well-formed, or you will see an error message and the document will not open.
Save	Saves the current file.
Print	Saves the file with a different name or different location.
Cut	Deletes the selected text from the editing window and places a copy of the text on the Clipboard.
Copy	Copies the selected text to the Clipboard.

Paste	Inserts the current Clipboard contents at the cursor's location.
Element Wizard	Displays the Element Wizard, which you can use to create, modify, or delete elements.
Attribute Wizard	Displays the Attribute Wizard, which enables you to create, modify, or delete attribute types for existing elements.
Move Up	Moves the selected item up in the document structure.
Move Down	Moves the selected item down in the document structure.
Validate	Validates the current document using the associated DTD, if there is one.
Help	Accesses the XML <Pro> help page.

Creating a New XML Document

To begin creating your document, choose New from the File menu, or just click the New button. You'll see the Root Element Name dialog box, shown in Figure 9.3.

For this exercise, you'll create a simple XML document intended to store information about your favorite mystery novels. Here's the document design:

```
<fave-mysteries>
  <mystery-novel>
    <author></author>
    <title></title>
    <date></date>
    <publisher></publisher>
    <review></review>
```

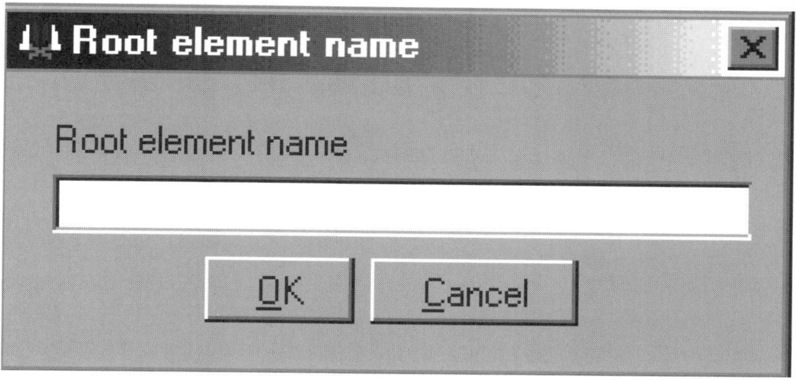

Figure 9.3 To start a new XML document, enter the root element name.

```
        </mystery-novel>
    </fave-mysteries>
```

Now type the root element name (fave-mysteries) in the text box, and click OK. XML <Pro> creates a new XML document. You see the new element in the document tree view, as shown in Figure 9.4.

From the Tools menu, choose View XML. You'll see the following XML code, which XML <Pro> has created:

```
<XML? version="1.0" encoding="UTF-8"?>
<fave-mysteries/>
```

As you can see, XML <Pro> created the root element as if it were an empty element (with a closing slash mark). Why? Simple: It *is* an empty element, at least for now. When you add content to this element, the program will transform the fave-mysteries element accordingly.

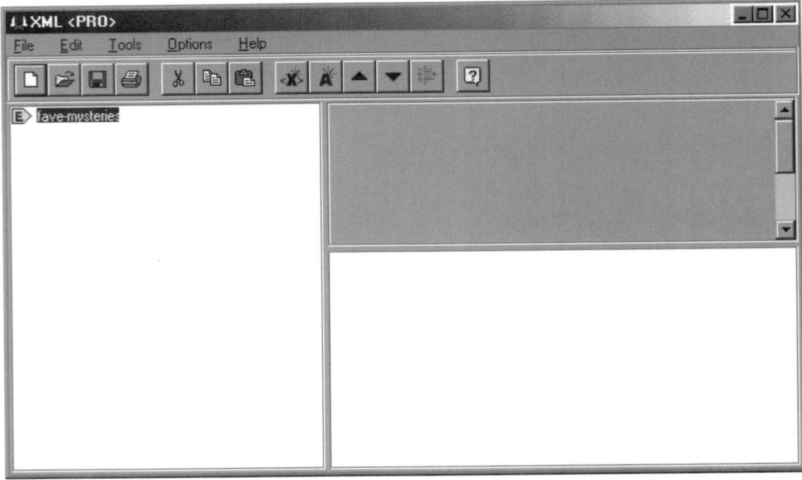

Figure 9.4 New document (with root element).

Creating Elements

Now add the rest of the elements at the second level (author, date, and review). To do so, click the Element Wizard tool on the toolbar. You'll see the Element Wizard, shown in Figure 9.5.

In the New Element Name box, type **mystery-novel**, and click Add. Repeat this procedure to add the author, date, and review elements. Click Close to return to the main window.

If you notice you've made a typing mistake only after you click Add, select the element. Click Remove to delete the element from the list. Type the element name again, and check your typing before you click Add.

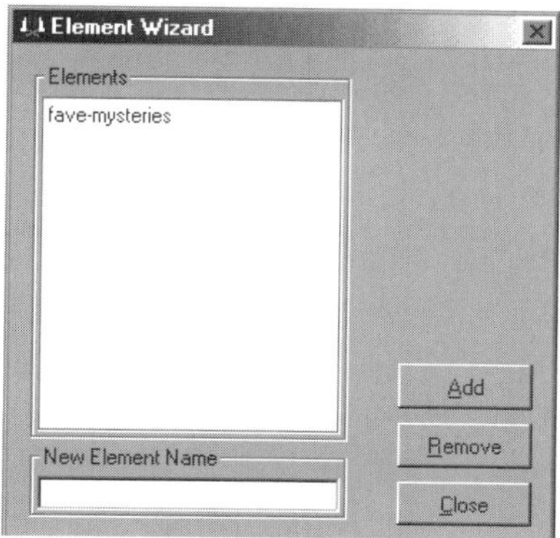

Figure 9.5 The Element Wizard enables you to create child elements.

Inserting Elements

After creating new elements, you see them in the Element Palette, a window that opens automatically when you start XML <Pro>. (If you do not see this window, click the Options menu, and choose Show Element Palette.)

To insert elements into your document, select the parent element in the Document Tree View. (Here, the parent element is the root element, fave-mysteries.) In the 0, select the first element you want to add (author), and click the Insert button. Select the parent element again, select the second element (date), and click Insert. Continue until you've added all the new elements to your document.

If you inadvertently add an element at the wrong level, it's probably because you forgot to select the parent element first. Select the element that you inserted at the wrong level, right-click the element, and choose Delete from the pop-up menu. Select the parent element, and repeat the insertion.

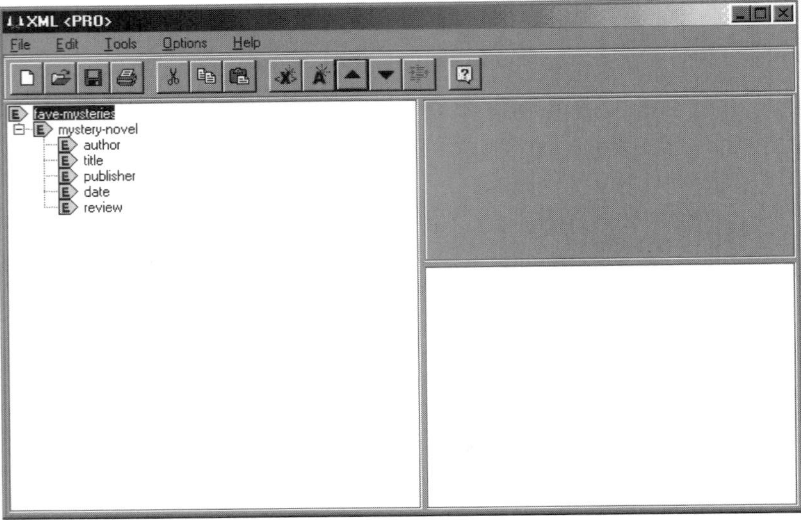

Figure 9.6 Child elements added to root element.

When you've finished adding child elements to the fave-mysteries element, your document should look like the one shown in Figure 9.6.

If you entered the child elements in the wrong order, select a child element, and click the up or down button. Continue moving elements until you've got them in the right order (author, date, review).

Adding Attributes

You've created one complete child element (mystery-novel), which contains three child elements of its own. At this point, you may wish to add attributes to the elements you've created.

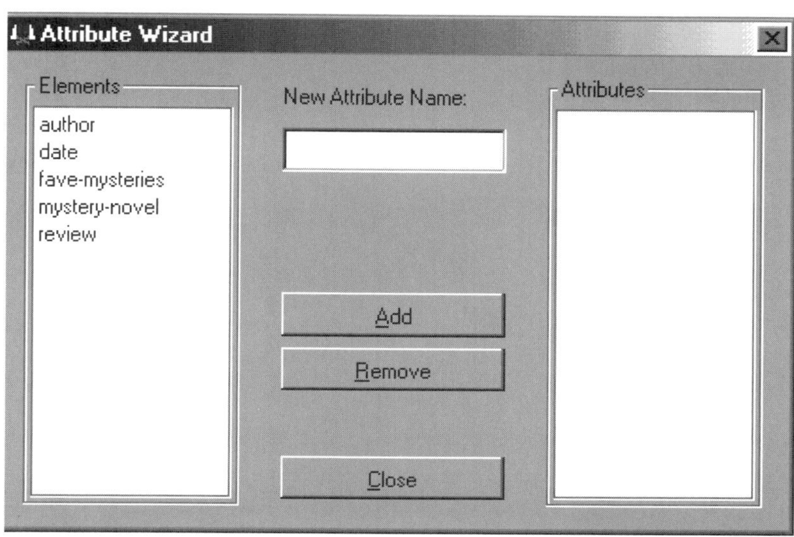

Figure 9.7 Attribute Wizard.

Two useful attributes to add are the following:

- **id.** This attribute enables processing software to identify the element's content uniquely.
- **title.** This attribute, strongly endorsed in the W3C XML recommendation, enhances your document's accessibility for readers with special needs.

To add attributes, click the Attribute Wizard tool on the toolbar. You'll see the Attribute Wizard, shown in Figure 9.7. In the Elements pane, select the element that you want to modify. (Try adding attributes to the mystery-novel element.) In the New Attribute Name panel, type the attribute name, and click Add. You can add more attributes, if you wish. When you're finished adding attributes to this element, click another element name or click Close to exit the Attribute Wizard.

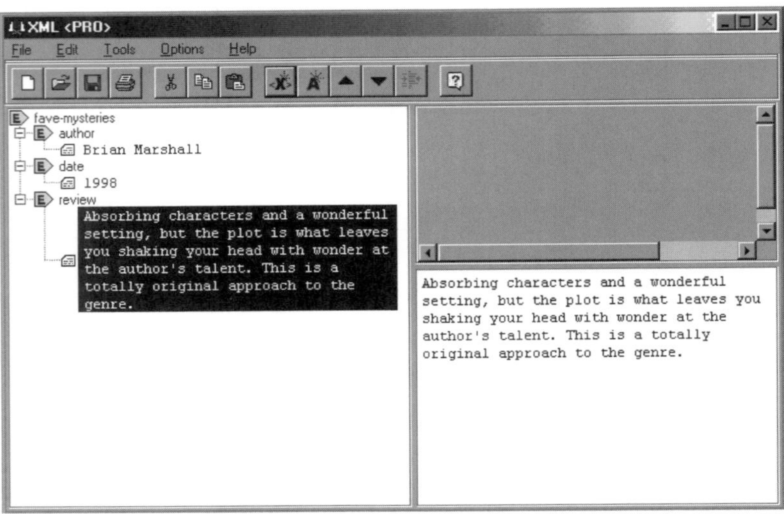

Figure 9.8 Attribute text boxes in the attributes view.

After adding attributes, the attribute view shows text boxes for the attributes, as shown in Figure 9.8. These text boxes expand to accommodate the text you type.

Adding Content to an Element

Now you're ready to add content to the child elements. This content will be character data (PCDATA). To add PCDATA content to an element, right-click element name, and choose Add PCDATA. After you've added the PCDATA sections to your document, you see them in the document tree view.

Adding Text to Your Document

To add text to your document, select one of the PCDATA sections, and type text in the editing pane. (You'll see the

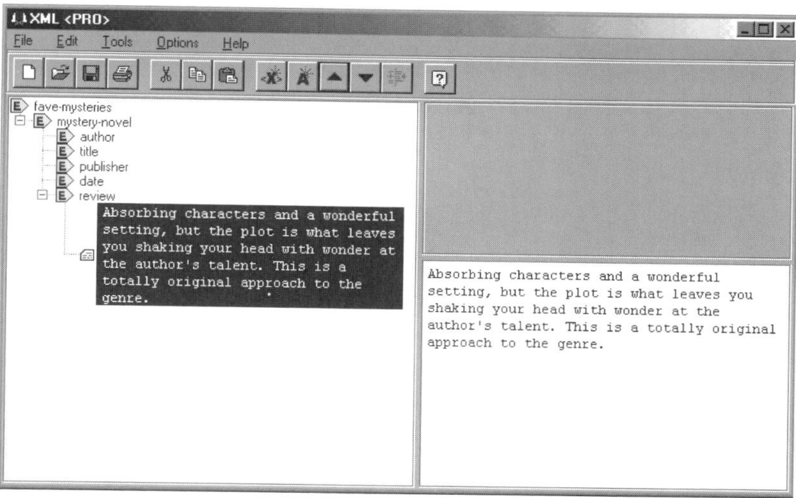

Figure 9.9 Text added to PCDATA section.

text in the Document Tree View as well.) Figure 9.9 shows how the document looks afer adding text.

Additional XML <Pro> Features

This chapter has covered the fundamentals of XML <Pro> for creating well-formed documents. In addition to the features mentioned, XML <Pro> can also do the following:

- **Comments.** You can enter an XML comment at any time by rightclicking the editing pane and choosing Add Comment from the pop-up menu.
- **CDATA.** In addition to PCDATA, XML <Pro> enables you to add CDATA sections to any element.

(CDATA consists of text that is expressly considered to be other than markup.)

Checking Your XML Syntax

Is your XML well-formed? One way to tell: Save your XML <Pro> file and try reopening it with XML <Pro>. If the code isn't well-formed, XML <Pro> won't open it. (XML <Pro> contains a conforming XML processor, which means that any errors in well-formedness cause processing to halt.) To find and fix the error, you'll need to open the XML document with a text editor.

Here's another way to check your XML syntax: Upload your XML file to your Web publishing directory and access the RWUF? syntax checker (*www.xml.com/xml/pub/tools/ruwf/check.html*). Type in the URL of your XML file. If there are syntax errors, you will see a detailed error message.

From Here

Once you've defined the basic element structure, you can add additional data. However, you will soon run into a shortcoming of XML <Pro>: You can enter the mystery-novel element by choosing it from the Element Palette, but doing so does not enter this element's child elements (author, title, date, publisher, and review). Each time you insert a mystery-novel element, you must add the child elements manually.

Why is this so? There is no DTD. As a result, XML <Pro> can't judge whether a given element should contain certain child elements.

The more you work with well-formed documents, the more you'll realize that there's a good argument for creating DTDs. As you will learn in Part Four of this book, it's not very difficult to create simple DTDs for Web publishing purposes.

Part Four

Creating Document Type Definitions (DTDs)

10

Introducing Document Type Definitions (DTDs)

A *document type definition (DTD)* is a computer-readable text file that defines a markup language for a particular type of document, such as a poem, a novel, or an electronic business form.

Should you try writing a DTD? It's a big job. Requiring extensive knowledge and experience, professional DTD production isn't a task that Web authors should take on lightly; for example, several years of collaborative work went into creating the Text Encoding Initiative's TEILite DTD, which is designed for marking up works of literature. Most of the people who use XML will make use of

DTDs such as TEILite, recently reissued in XML, that were developed by others. As many who've attempted to write DTDs have found, the problem of defining elements to capture text structure appears simple on the surface, but in fact is a very complex task in which problems arise immediately. Many organizations have spent a great deal of money developing DTDs, only to find out that they contain some underlying design flaw that renders them close to useless for their intended objective.

Still, the basics of DTD creation are not that difficult to learn, and you may conclude that it's worth attempting the task for simple vocabularies that you've created in order to capture some very specific type of information—something that's unique to your site. (If someone else has already created a DTD for the information you want to mark up, it's best to use this DTD—or supplement it slightly by means of an internal DTD subset, as you'll learn in this chapter.)

In the pages to follow, you'll learn to judge when you might want to create a DTD (and when to leave it to others), and you'll find a general, conceptual overview of what goes into a DTD. In subsequent chapters, you'll learn the specifics of what goes into a DTD—and you'll start creating your own DTDs to give structure to your documents.

Using an Existing DTD

Do you really need to create your own DTD? It's much easier to use an existing DTD, for the simple reason that somebody else has gone to all the trouble of figuring out how to mark up a certain type of document structure. But there's a deeper reason. Using an existing DTD furthers one of XML's underlying aims, namely, to create pools of structured information on the Internet.

Is this really such a big deal? Yes—it's what XML is all about. In contrast to SGML, XML is designed to facilitate publication of information on the Web. However, if people encode their information with divergent vocabularies, the information is less widely accessible. In a search, for example, it might not be possible for a search engine to tell whether your fave-mystery element is the same thing as someone else's top-mystery element. If you discover that somebody has already worked out a well-thought-through DTD for encoding information about mystery novels, using this DTD enables you to contribute your information to a growing pool of structured data about favorite mystery novels, rather than isolating your data in an idiosyncratic vocabulary.

One proposal that seeks to address this problem defines XML namespaces, which provide a means for authors to incorporate elements defined in two or more DTDs. For example, if somebody else has already defined the <author> element satisfactorily, you could use the namespace syntax to refer to this element, rather than creating it on your own. Elsewhere in your document, you could refer to another DTD's <publisher> element, if you felt that element met your needs. The namespace syntax is discussed in Chapter 15.

Perhaps you're creating your DTD for your organization's internal use only, and you don't care whether it's in synch with the way other people mark up similar documents. But be sure to take a long-range view. What if your company merges with another firm that uses a different DTD? You might not think you want to share your data now. But the situation may change!

In general, it's best to avoid reinventing the wheel, if at all possible. Before creating your own DTD, try to find out whether somebody else has beaten you to it.

Finding DTDs

At this writing, there's no single, central clearinghouse for XML DTDs. (Since there's a clear need, expect somebody to start one soon.) However, you'll find several Web pages that provide links to existing XML vocabularies and DTDs:

- **Robin Cover's XML Applications and Industry Initiatives List** (*www.sil.org/sgml/xml.html#applications*). Comprehensive and frequently updated.
- **James Tauber's XML Info** (*www.jtauber.com/xml*). Tauber's "Application Profile and Document Types" page provides links to the better-known XML DTDs.
- **Finetuning.com's XML Applications** (*www.finetuning.com/xmlapps.html*).

More such Web pages will surely appear in the future. You can also try searching for DTDs using a search service such as AltaVista. A search for a poetry DTD revealed David Megginson's poem.dtd (*www.cen.com/ng-html/xml/examples/poem.dtd.txt*).

Working with an Existing DTD

If you're able to locate an existing DTD that's right for your data, you can use it to mark up your data. Until you've learned how to read DTDs, it's best to leave this task to an XML editor. An XML editor can show you precisely which elements and attributes are available within

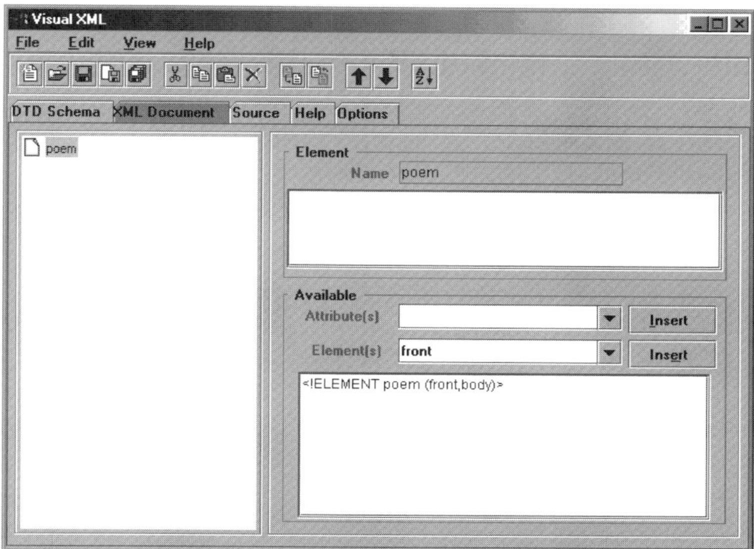

Figure 10.1 Visual XML editor displaying available elements.

a given context; you can insert them by choosing them from a menu.

In Figure 10.1, for example, you see the appearance of Visual XML after loading Dave Megginson's poem.dtd. Currently selected is the root element (poem). At the bottom right, you see the elements that are available as child elements of the root element. There are two: front and body.

To create a marked-up poem using the poem DTD, you choose the front element. This element enables you to enter the title, author, and revision-history. The DTD requires that you enter the title first; if you try to enter any of the other elements at this level before the title element, you won't be able to do so.

Why Create a DTD?

You've looked into existing DTDs, and you can't find one that captures all the nuances of your data. Should you create your own? Or to put the question another way, is it worth the trouble to create your own DTD, rather than just creating well-formed XML documents with an impromptu tag set? You may prefer to go the DTD route for any of the following reasons:

- **To ensure that your documents conform to a given structure.** When you create a DTD, you can ensure that authors will use certain required elements, enter them in the correct order, and supply the correct data. In the fave-mysteries example, you can ensure that every mystery-novel element contains all of its child elements (author, title, date, publisher, and review) and, what is more, that all of these child elements are entered in precisely that order.
- **To provide visual XML editors with information needed to guide authors.** When you link an XML document to a DTD, visual XML editors can analyze the current context and tell authors which elements and content types are available.
- **To enable the use of entities.** In XML documents, you can't use *entities* unless they're declared in a DTD. This means that you can't use sounds, pictures, or any other external files—unless you create a DTD. (This rule doesn't apply to any of the entities describing Unicode characters.)
- **To enable others to make use of the vocabulary you've created.** You've gone to all the work to create your vocabulary. Why not capture it in a form that others can use?

DTD Locations

You can locate a DTD within an XML file, although it's generally best to place the DTD in its own, separate location, where it's available for use by two more XML documents. (Remember, DTDs are machine-readable.)

To link an XML document with an external DTD, you use a *document type declaration*, such as the one you've probably noticed at the beginning of HTML documents:

```
<!DOCTYPE HTML PUBLIC "-//W3C//DTD HTML
4.0//EN" "http://www.w3.org/TR/REC-
html40/strict.dtd">
```

You'll learn more about document type declarations in a moment. For now, examine the various possibilities for locating DTDs.

When most HTML authors think of a DTD, they think of an external, separate document (such as the HTML DTD maintained by the W3C). But you can also place a DTD within an XML document. What's more, you can use an external DTD and supplement it with an internal one.

External DTDs

An external DTD is called an *external DTD subset*. Physically, an external DTD exists in a text file (with the extension *.dtd), which is housed on a computer somewhere. Some external DTDs are private, while others are available (by means of the Internet) to the public.

Internal DTDs

You may have noticed that external DTDs are called external DTD *subsets*. The reason for calling them subsets lies in the fact that the external DTD can be supplemented by means of an *internal DTD subset*. In the internal DTD, you can include additional components of a DTD within a document that's linked to an external DTD. The internal DTD subset takes precedence over the external one, but note that it's an error to try to declare the same element in both places.

In the internal DTD subset, you can include *additional* elements that aren't included in the external DTD. However, it's rarely a good idea to start adding a bunch of extra elements within the internal DTD, because the internal DTD information won't be available to other documents.

So what's an internal DTD good for? Plenty. With XML, you must declare all the entities you plan to use, and you must do so within the document's internal DTD subset. This includes graphics, character entities, shorthand expressions, and files. In most cases, then, you'll have an external DTD that defines your document's basic structure and lists all the elements you want to use; your internal DTD subset will list the entities your document contains.

Standalone DTDs

Sometimes you may wish to include the entire DTD within the XML document. (For Internet publishing, this has an important advantage: the XML browser doesn't have to go somewhere else to find the external DTD.) This type of DTD is called a *standalone DTD*. If you place your

DTD within your XML document, you should use the standalone DTD declaration, which goes into the XML declaration, as follows:

```
<?xml version="1.0" standalone="yes"?>
```

This says, "There's no external DTD at all." If you leave the standalone DTD declaration out, the value "no" is assumed—which means there *might* be an external DTD. To tell the XML processor which DTD you're using (and where it's located), you use the document type declaration, as the following section explains.

Document Type Declarations

Every *valid XML document* includes a document type declaration right after the XML declaration, such as the following:

```
<?xml version="1.0"?>
<!DOCTYPE poem SYSTEM "poem.dtd">
```

The document type declaration indicates the following:

- **Name of the document type (poem).** Here, it's "poem." This is actually a shorthand expression (in SGML parlance, a *parameter entity reference*) for the file that contains the DTD.
- **DTD location (SYSTEM).** It's located on the same computer as the XML document, and intended for local use only. For DTDs accessible on the Internet, you use PUBLIC.
- **File location.** Here, it's "poem.dtd," indicating that the DTD is physically located in the same directory

as the XML file. For public documents, you can use a URL.

The document type declaration says, in effect, "Here's a set of tags for coding a certain type of document, and here's where the DTD can be found." Here's an example of a document type declaration that refers to a (fictitious) public DTD:

```
<?XML version="1.0"?>
<!DOCTYPE RED-BOOK PUBLIC "-//W3C//DTD HTML
4.0//EN" "http://www.rivendell.org/bilbo/red-
book.dtd">
```

What's in a name? Whenever you're specifying a name—for such components as a document type, an element, an attribute, an ID—you can use any combination of alphanumeric characters and the following punctuation marks: period (.), hyphen (-), underscore (_), and colon (:).

DTD Components

This section introduces the basic components of a document type definition (DTD). You won't find very much DTD code here; this section introduces the general concepts. Subsequent chapters go back over this information in more detail and show you how to create these components in your own DTDs.

Element Type Declarations

A DTD's core lies in *element type declarations*, which name the document type's elements and specify rules concerning how they can be used. An element type definition consists of two parts:

- **Element name.** A string of connected characters, such as <stanza> or <part-number>. The name must be unique (not used by any other element).
- **Content specification.** A *content model* that describes what the element can contain. *Empty elements* contain only data, expressed in attributes (such as <record-number id="357">). Most elements contain one or more *child elements*. For example, <stanza> may contain <line>. You can also specify that the element can contain *mixed content*, which can include character data (PCDATA) as well as elements.

In the content model, you have an opportunity to guide authors. If the model allows more than one element, you can specify how much latitude authors have in using these elements. You can let them choose any of them; you can require one or more of them; and you can, if you wish, specify the sequence in which elements must be used. Called *occurrence indicators*, these rules are examined more closely in the next chapter. There's much more to say about element type declarations; they're the subject of Chapter 11. For now, let's move on to examine the other components of a DTD.

Much of the thought and creativity that goes into writing DTDs lies in choosing the appropriate occurrence indicators for your elements. In the Poem DTD, for example, it makes good sense to require authors to enter the bibliographical information (such as <title> and <author>) in a specified sequence. This ensures that all the documents created with this DTD will have the same type of information in the same place. But there's a trade-off here. If your rules are overly rigid, authors will feel constrained and may not wish to use the DTD. The bottom line is this: Can you justify the constraints you impose?

Attribute List Declarations

Attributes describe options for an element. Some of these are very important or even indispensable, while others are less often used. In HTML, for example, the IMG element enables you to position a picture inline. It includes the all-important src attribute, which enables you to specify the picture file's URL. It also includes the important alt attribute, which displays alternative text that is displayed when the browser is unable to display graphics. Less often used (but valuable) is the float attribute, which enables you to position the picture to the left or the right of the window, with text flowing around it.

When you compose a document, you specify the attributes within the start tag, as in the following, familiar HTML example:

```
<IMG src="sailboat.gif" float="left">
```

This tag inserts the file "sailboat.gif" and floats the picture to the left of the window.

You declare attributes with an *attribute list declaration.* Separate from the element type declaration, the attribute list declaration enables you to specify one or more attributes for a given element (which must be defined somewhere else in the DTD).

For every attribute, you specify three types of information:

- **Attribute name.** A string of connected characters, such as <stanza> or <part-number>. The name doesn't have to be unique—you can use it in other elements—but within a given element, you can't have two attributes with the same name.

- **Attribute type.** There are three types of attributes: *string attributes* containing CDATA, *tokenized attributes* containing one of a list of reserved words (such as ID and IDREF), and *enumerated attributes,* consisting of a list of possible values.
- **Default value.** Here, you specify one of the following: #FIXED (you specify a value as the default), #REQUIRED (you leave up to the author which value to use, but the author must specify some value), or #IMPLIED (the attribute doesn't have to appear, and the processing application is free to determine which value to use).

You'll learn more about writing attribute list declarations in Chapter 12.

Entity Declarations

As previously noted, you can't use any *entity* in an XML document without declaring it in the DTD. This includes picture files, sounds, movies, and external files that you want incorporated into your XML document. Since it would be very cumbersome to do this in an external DTD meant to be used by two or more documents, it's best to declare entities within a document's internal DTD subset.

In your entity declarations, you can define the following types of entities:

- **Internal entities.** An *internal entity* is used only within the document. Typically, internal entities are ways of cutting down repetitive typing tasks. For example, you could define an internal entity "&w3c;" that is automatically expanded to "World Wide Web Consortium."

- **External entities.** An *external entity* is generally a file of some sort, such as a picture, a sound, or another section of the current document. External entities are of two kinds: *text* or *binary*. A text entity contains character data, and it's considered to be part of the XML document itself. A binary entity contains data that the XML processor can't parse by itself. In order to use this data, you provide a *notation*, which tells the processor what type of data you're referring to (such as a JPEG or GIF graphic file).
- **Parameter entities.** A *parameter entity* is like an internal entity in that it's a typing shortcut. The difference is that it's used only within the DTD. Typically, parameter entities are used to refer to lengthy attribute value declarations, which you'd otherwise have to type over and over, every time you define a new element that uses the attribute.

That's just an overview of entity declarations. You'll learn the specifics in Chapter 13.

Notation Declarations

As you've just learned, you include a *notation* when you declare external data entities. The notation tells the application what type of data the file contains.

If you refer to external binary entities in your DTD, you must supplement your notations by including a *notation declaration*. In theory, the declaration tells the application where to find out more information about the type of data you're using and possibly where to find a *helper application* that can display the data. (A helper application is a program that the XML application starts when it encounters a certain type of data that it can't display on its own.) In practical terms, the notation declaration sets up a name for a certain type of external binary data (called NDATA), such as "gif" or "jpg." Once you have declared such names by means of a notation declaration, you may use these names when you declare external binary entities and when you supply entity names as values for attributes. You learn more about notation declarations in Chapter 13.

Don't let the term notation *confuse you. It really is a notation—a note about a certain type of external data.*

Conditional Sections

In an external DTD, you can create *conditional sections*. Such sections might include elements that are useful only for specialized applications of the DTD. For example, in a DTD that defines elements for literary genres, you might include a conditional section containing elements useful for marking up poetry. These elements wouldn't be needed by somebody who's marking up a play.

To mark a conditional section, you enclose its elements within a parameter entity that's set to the value "IGNORE." To include a conditional section, you put a parameter entity declaration in your internal DTD, with the value reset to "INCLUDE." Conditional sections are discussed in Chapter 14.

Processing Instructions (PI)

The last of the DTD components, processing instructions (PI), enable DTD authors to include instructions for applications. PIs begin with <? and end with ?>.You've already seen PIs; they're used to create the XML and DTD declarations, both of which give applications information they need.

Understanding Validation

As you've learned, every XML document must be well-formed. If the document violates the rules of well-formedness, then the XML processor generates a fatal error and stops processing the document.

What about errors in implementing a DTD, such as using an element where it's not supposed to be used—or using one twice when it's supposed to be used only once? As long as such errors do not violate well-formedness rules (and often they don't), they generate errors when a validating XML processor checks the document against the DTD. Unlike well-formedness errors, validation errors aren't fatal. The XML processor will generate error messages, but this doesn't stop the processor from trying to read and use the data that the document contains.

Although validation errors usually aren't fatal, you should always run your DTD-based documents through a validating processor before putting the document to use. If there are errors, find them and fix them.

From Here

This chapter introduces DTDs and explains that they can be located externally (in a separate document) or internally (within an XML document) or in a combination of external and internal subsets. With XML, you should generally create an external DTD and use the internal DTD subset for the required entity declarations, without which you can't include any internal or external entities (including sounds and pictures). You learned about the basic components of DTDs: the document type declaration, element type declarations, attribute type declarations, entity declarations, conditional sections, and processing instructions.

The following chapters explain the specifics of including these components in your DTDs, beginning with the most important of all: elements.

11

Creating Element Type Definitions

Ready to start writing a DTD? The basic building block of any DTD is the element type definition introduced in Chapter 10. In element type definitions, you specify the elements that authors will use to create XML documents using your DTD. As you'll see in this chapter, creating a DTD gives you an opportunity to decide whether to require certain elements or to insist that they're used in a certain order. A carefully crafted DTD can give authors needed guidance, ensuring that they provide all the vital information and that they use elements correctly.

Planning Your Document's Tree Structure

Before you try writing element definitions, you need a clear notion of your document's tree structure. Why? As you'll learn in this chapter, element type definitions—the basic building blocks of your DTD—enable you to specify this structure so that it's obvious to an XML processor. What's more, you can even *require* authors to follow certain rules about which elements can go where and how many times they can be used. Unless you know what you're aiming for, you won't be able to write meaningful element type definitions.

Here's an example of a tree structure (it's adapted from the example used in a previous chapter):

```
<fave>
  <novel>
    <author></author>
    <title></title>
    <date></date>
    <publisher></publisher>
    <review>
      <summary></summary>
      <paragraph></paragraph>
    </review>
  </novel>
</fave>
```

This XML document contains information about favorite mystery novels. Even though only one novel element is present in the above example, it can contain information about more than one mystery. Within each novel element, you find certain child elements, and one of these has additional child elements. In your DTD, you use *content models* to specify which elements go where.

Understanding Content Models

As you learned in Chapter 10, an element type definition includes the name of the element and the content specification, which (in XML) is either EMPTY (no content) or a *content model.* For example, here is an element type definition with a content model included:

```
<!ELEMENT paragraph (#PCDATA | bold | ital-
ic)*>
```

This element type definition creates an element <para> and specifies that it contain PCDATA (document text) as well as either of the following child elements: bold or italic. However, none of these is required; you could enter <paragraph></paragraph> without causing the XML processor to generate a validation error.

In DTDs, reserved words—such as ELEMENT and PCDATA—must be capitalized.

You need to know two things to read and write content models like this:

- How to understand what the items within parentheses mean.
- What certain symbols (such as *) that come after items mean.

The next sections explain both of these points.

Items within Parentheses

In a content model, you often see a group of items within parentheses. Sometimes they're separated by bar characters (|) and other times by commas. Table 11.1 explains that these lists are of two kinds:

- **Lists of alternatives (options).** Authors can choose any of the items in the list in no particular order. You use bar characters to separate items in a list of alternatives.
- **A sequence.** Authors must insert the items in the order listed. You use commas to separate items in a sequential list.

Table 11.1 Understanding Options in Parentheses

Symbol	Description
parentheses	Surround a list of items `(bold | italic)`
comma	Separates items that must occur in order `(title, author, date)`
bar character	Separates items in a list of options `(couplet | quatrain | sestet)`

Symbols That Follow Items

The symbols that come after items (or lists of items) add further information to the content model. These *postfix symbols* are summed up in Table 11.2. You can apply one of these to a single item:

```
publisher?
```

This means, "You don't have to include this element, but if you do, it should occur only once."

You can also apply one of these symbols to a group of items within parentheses. When you do, the symbol affects every item within the parentheses. Here's an example:

```
(author, title, date)+
```

This says, "You must include all of these at least once."

Table 11.2 Understanding Postfix Symbols

Symbol	Description
no symbol	**Required and nonrepeatable.** The item *must* occur once and only once. `title`
?	**Optional and nonrepeatable.** The item may occur zero or one time, but not more than one time. `author?`
*	**Optional and repeatable.** The item occurs zero or more times—as many times as the author wants. `bold*`
+	**Required and repeatable.** The item occurs one or more times, but must occur at least once. `title+`

Content Model Examples

In this section, you'll find lots of examples that illustrate how parentheses and postfix symbols are used to create *occurrence indicators*, which specify how authors can use elements in a conforming document.

List of Optional Child Elements

When you're starting your DTD, you begin by defining the basic elements. More than likely, these element definitions will contain a list of child elements. Here's an element definition for the novel element (from the fave document discussed in Chapter 9):

```
<!ELEMENT novel (author | title | date |
publisher | review )?>
```

Note that there's a ? after the closing parenthesis. All of these items are optional and repeatable. So this content model says, "The fave element can contain any of the following child elements. The child elements can occur in any order, and you can omit any of them. You can use any of them as many times as you wish." Is this really desirable? An author could write a valid document like this:

```
<fave>
  <novel>
    <review>Unintentionally
    hilarious.</review>
    <author>John Smith</author>
    <title>Three Sheets to the Wind</title>
    <publisher>Sea Press (original)
    </publisher>
    <publisher>Old Stuff Made New
    (reprint)</publisher>
  </novel>
</fave>
```

Note that the various child elements are out of order. One (date) is missing entirely, while another is used more than once—there are two publishers. All of this is quite valid, given the content model's lack of restrictions. You've given the author quite a lot of freedom to use these elements as the author pleases, and it makes sense here, seemingly: This entry is apparently about a mystery novel, published years ago, that has reappeared in a reprint edition. The question is, will the result be useful?

Maybe so. Suppose you've created a Web site in which you're asking people to submit reviews, and the results go into an XML database that's read by a Java application for display purposes. So the order in which elements appear doesn't really matter; the Java software will put them in the right order. As for the missing dates, they'd be nice to have, but you'd rather get flawed submissions than no submissions at all.

Elsewhere, this latitude might not be acceptable. Consider the following:

```
<!ELEMENT prescription (patient | date |
pharmaceutical | dose | frequency |
refill)?>
```

More than likely, you wouldn't want doctors writing prescriptions that didn't specify the patient's name or dosage!

List of Required Child Elements

If you would like to require at least one instance of each child element, just omit the symbol at the end of the list, as in the following example:

```
<!ELEMENT fave (author | title | date | pub-
lisher | review )>
```

This says, "Within the fave element, you must include all of the listed child elements exactly one time (and one time only)." If you would like to require authors to use all the child elements, but you would like to give them the freedom to use a child element more than once, use the plus sign (+), as in the following:

```
<!ELEMENT fave (author | title | date | pub-
lisher | review )+>
```

This says, "Within the fave element, you must include all of the listed child elements *at least* once. You can use any of these elements two or more times, if you wish."

Note that the postfix symbol appears at the end of the parentheses. This means that the symbol applies to every item within the parentheses.

Required Sequence of Child Elements

What about the order in which authors type the data? If you would like to specify the sequence in which the child elements are listed, use commas, as in the following:

```
<!ELEMENT fave (author , title , date , pub-
lisher , review )+>
```

This says, "Within the fave element, you must include all of the listed child elements at least once, and they must occur in this order."

It's tempting to impose a straitjacket on authors by requiring elements and specifying order, but remember that this makes the DTD much more tedious to use, and authors may resent it. And if they resent the DTD, they won't use it. For example, suppose I want to contribute a review of a mystery novel, and I know the author and title, but I don't know the publisher or date. Do you still want me to contribute my review? I'll bet you do, so it's a bad idea to require the additional information (although it would be nice to have it). In short: There's a trade-off between the amount of control you want to impose and authors' acceptance of the DTD. Require elements and specify sequence only when you feel it is absolutely necessary.

List with Varying Specifications

By attaching the postfix symbols to additional items instead of the end parentheses, you can create content models in which some of the child elements are optional, while others are required. Here's an example:

```
<!ELEMENT novel (author | title | date? |
publisher? | review+ )>
```

This says, "Within the fave element, you must include the author, title, and review, but you can omit the date and publisher if you like."

Using Nested Parentheses

You've looked at some basic examples. Now you'll learn how to create much more complex and interesting content models by using nested parentheses. In brief, nested parentheses enable you to combine content and sequence requirements in all kinds of interesting ways.

Here's an example that uses parentheses:

```
<!ELEMENT novel (author+, title, date, pub-
lisher?, (review (summary, paragraph+)))>
```

This says, "Within the novel element, you must include at least one author, which must be followed by exactly one title and date. After these, you may include one or more publishers. Following is one required review, which begins with a single, required summary and continues with at least one paragraph."

Elements Containing Text

If you're creating an element containing text, you indicate this content in the following way:

```
<!ELEMENT summary (#PCDATA)>
```

Remember to capitalize reserved words (here, ELEMENT and PCDATA).

You can also write *mixed content models*, which combine PCDATA with child elements. However, you must follow XML's rules if you wish to do this:

- #PCDATA always comes first.
- The child elements must be listed as a list of alternatives.
- The list must close with an asterisk (meaning that all the items are optional and can be repeated).

Here's an example of a valid element with mixed content:

```
<!ELEMENT summary (#PCDATA | bold | ital-
ic)*>
```

Why the restrictions? They're not present in SGML. The reasons for restricting mixed content in XML are too technical to go into here, but here's the short version: Experience with SGML demonstrates that it's dangerous to write mixed content elements in any other way because the processor might not be able to tell how to process the PCDATA. SGML authors are strongly cautioned to write mixed content elements this way; the authors of XML felt that it would be wise to require authors to do so.

What about CDATA? Simple: You can't use CDATA as the content model for an element. As you'll see in the next chapter, you *must* use CDATA as an attribute value when users supply the value in the form of text. So here's a simple mnemonic: "PCDATA for element content, CDATA for attribute values."

Remember: An element with mixed content must be expressed as a list of nonrequired alternatives.

Empty Elements

Sometimes you may wish to use an empty element, one that doesn't have any content. Typically, empty elements are used to store data by means of attribute/value pairs. In HTML, for example, the IMG element stores data about a graphic's location.

To create an empty element, you type the word EMPTY after the element name, as in the following example:

```
<!ELEMENT img EMPTY>
```

The ANY Content Model

In addition to the content models already discussed, you can also define an element with the ANY keyword, as in the following example:

```
<!ELEMENT annotation ANY>
```

This element can contain any other element as well as PCDATA, without any restriction whatsoever. It gives authors free rein. Inherently, it's a *mixed content* element.

Defining the Root Element

You might be surprised to find that there's no way to mark the root element—but that isn't a problem. Although XML does not provide a means to identify the root element within the DTD, the XML processor should be able to identify it from the content models—at least in theory.

Judging from early attempts to implement XML applications, it might not be so easy to determine which element is the root one, especially if the DTD contains errors. At least one XML application (XML <Pro>) insists that the root element name match the DOCTYPE; in other words, if your DOCTYPE is fave, your root element must be fave. This seems like a very wise policy, and I recommend that you follow it when you create your DTDs.

Including XLinks

As you learned in Chapter 7, you can include XLink capabilities in *any* XML element. (This stands in contrast to HTML, in which linking is restricted to certain elements, so this idea takes some getting used to.) In order to incorporate XLink capabilities in your DTDs, you define linking attributes, which you can attach to any of your DTD's elements. The next chapter explains how.

An Example

The following examples show what a completed DTD looks like in external and internal DTDs, and how you'd reference the DTD in an XML document.

Creating an External DTD Subset

To create an external DTD, just type the elements in a plain text file, and save the document with the extension *.dtd. Here's the fave DTD:

```
<!ELEMENT fave (novel)*>
<!ELEMENT novel (author+, title, date,
publisher?, review)>
<!ELEMENT author (#PCDATA)*>
<!ELEMENT title (#PCDATA)*>
<!ELEMENT date (#PCDATA)*>
<!ELEMENT publisher (#PCDATA)*>
<!ELEMENT review (summary, paragraph+)>
<!ELEMENT summary (#PCDATA)*>
<!ELEMENT paragraph (#PCDATA)*>
```

Referencing the DTD in an XML Document

Here's a valid XML document based on the above DTD:

```
<?XML version="1.0"?>
<!DOCTYPE fave SYSTEM "fave.dtd">
<fave>
  <novel>
    <author>David Williams</author>
    <title>The Northern Neck Mystery</title>
    <date>1999</date>
    <publisher>Riverneck Press</publisher>
    <review>
      <summary>Great characters, lousy
      plot</summary>
      <paragraph>A first novel, and it
      shows.</paragraph>
    </review>
  </novel>
</fave>
```

Creating an Internal DTD Subset

If you wish, you can include the DTD, or a copy of the DTD, within the XML document as an internal subset. To do so, you include the DTD within the document type definition, enclosed by brackets, as in the following example:

```
<?XML version="1.0"?>
<!DOCTYPE fave SYSTEM "fave.dtd"

    [

<!ELEMENT fave (novel)*>
<!ELEMENT novel (author+, title, date,
publisher?, review)>
<!ELEMENT author (#PCDATA)*>
<!ELEMENT title (#PCDATA)*>
<!ELEMENT date (#PCDATA)*>
<!ELEMENT publisher (#PCDATA)*>
<!ELEMENT review (summary, paragraph+)>
<!ELEMENT summary (#PCDATA)*>
<!ELEMENT paragraph (#PCDATA)*>

    ]>

<fave>
  <novel>
    <author>David Williams</author>
    <title>The Northern Neck Mystery</title>
    <date>1999</date>
    <publisher>Riverneck Press</publisher>
    <review>
      <summary>Great characters, lousy
      plot</summary>
      <paragraph>A first novel, and it
      shows.</paragraph>
    </review>
  </novel>
</fave>
```

What's Missing?

Since you're familiar with HTML, you have probably looked at the HTML DTD. If so, you may have noticed that the HTML element definitions look a little different from XML DTDs. That's because the HTML DTD is written in SGML, not XML. There are two major differences between SGML and XML elements:

- **Start tag and end tag specifications.** Each HTML element specifies whether the start tag and end tag are required or optional. In XML, you do not specify whether an end tag is optional or required; it's *always* required, unless you're writing an empty element. This rule helps ensure that XML processors won't encounter difficulties trying to figure out a document's structure.
- **Inline and block elements.** In HTML, each element type definition indicates whether the element is an inline element (an element that can be nested within character data) or a block element (an element that cannot be nested within character data or within any inline elements). In XML, this distinction is implicit in the document's tree structure; if you define a paragraph element that can accept PCDATA as well as <bold> and <italic>, you have implicitly defined <bold> and <italic> as inline elements. However, it's wise to make this explicit by means of style sheets, as you'll learn in Part Five of this book.

From Here

Once you've learned how to create element type definitions, you know how to create the core of a DTD. In the next chapter, you learn how to broaden your knowledge by creating attribute lists.

12

Creating Attribute Lists

As you know from your work with HTML, attributes add to an element's functionality in important ways—and some are indispensable. For example, the A (hyperlink) element is meaningless without the href attribute, which specifies the link's destination. In XML, too, attributes can enhance your DTD's effectiveness. With XML, though, it's up to you to decide which attributes to include.

Lest that task seem overwhelming, remember that most attributes deal with obvious matters, such as the names of source files for graphics and sound. And remember, too, that XML strictly enforces the distinction between structure and presentation that HTML had so much difficulty enforcing; you won't create any attributes dealing with presentation. (In Part Five, you'll learn how to use style sheets to assign presentation styles to your elements.)

Looking at Attribute List Declarations

An attribute list declaration can occur anywhere within the DTD; it doesn't have to be positioned near the element type definition of the element it modifies. Although you can define an element's attributes by using more than one attribute list declaration, it's good form to put all the attributes for a given element in one list.

Here's what an attribute list declaration looks like:

```
<!ATTLIST author
id ID #IMPLIED
role (author | compiler | editor ) #REQUIRED
date CDATA #IMPLIED>
```

This declaration specifies the name of the element (author) and lists the attributes that are being defined (id, role, and date). Following the attribute names are attribute type specifications, which the next section explains, and default values (such as #IMPLIED), which a subsequent section explains.

Attribute Types

You can define three types of attributes: *string types, tokenized types, enumerated types,* and *enumerated notation types.*

String Types

In a *string type* attribute, the attributes value consists of CDATA—character data that can contain any punctuation marks (except the left angle bracket [<]). This enables authors to type virtually any kind of character when they supply the value for an attribute, without worrying about using a character that's reserved for XML. Here's an example:

```
<!ATTLIST author
role CDATA #IMPLIED
```

To supply a value for this attribute, an author could type just about anything, as in the following example:

```
<author role="editor of a collection of
Fawn's essays">John Smith</author>
```

Tokenized Types

In a *tokenized type* attribute, you use one of a list of reserved words, each of which signifies a function that the XML processor is programmed to understand. Table 12.1 lists the tokenized types and illustrates their use.

Table 12.1 Tokenized Types

Type	Description

ID	A unique identifier for a particular instance of an element. Similar to the ID attribute in HTML 4.0, this token is always used with an attribute of the same name, as in the following example:
	`<!ATTLIST paragraph`
	`id ID #IMPLIED>`
	In the document, an author would supply a unique ID name (alphanumeric characters), as in

the following:

```
<paragraph id="A129">
```

IDREF This is a pointer to another ID in the same document. Resembling an <A name> target in HTML, this cross-referencing capability resembles a hyperlink. When applications encounter an IDREF, they could display an icon that would enable the reader to access the cross-referenced information. Here's an example:

```
<!ATTLIST paragraph
xref IDREF #IMPLIED>
```

In the document, an author supplies a reference to a unique ID elsewhere in the document, as in the following example:

```
<paragraph xref="A129">
```

IDREFS This token enables the document's author to list more than one IDREF (separated by spaces):

```
<!ATTLIST paragraph
xref IDREFS #IMPLIED>
```

NMTOKEN This token indicates that the supplied attribute value must conform to XML regulations concerning names (any alphanumeric characters plus a few punctuation symbols). Here's an example:

```
<!ATTLIST paragraph
tone NMTOKEN #IMPLIED>
```

Here's how an author could supply a value for this:

```
<paragraph tone="nasty">
```

NMTOKENS This token enables the document's author to list more than one NMTOKEN (separated by spaces) for a given attribute:

```
<!ATTLIST paragraph
tone NMTOKENS #IMPLIED>
```

ENTITY This token stipulates that the attribute's value must be an external binary entity (NDATA):

```
<!ATTLIST img
src ENTITY #REQUIRED>
```

ENTITIES This token enables the author to enter more than one external binary entity in a list separated by spaces:

```
<!ATTLIST img
src ENTITY #REQUIRED>
```

Like other reserved words, tokenized type names must be supplied in capital letters.

Enumerated Types

Sometimes, it makes very good sense to restrict an author's latitude when it comes to supplying values for attributes. For example, suppose you ask mystery novel reviewers to sum up their reviews by choosing one of the following: pageturner, good, average, boring, dreadful. You could then group reviews by these criteria.

To define an attribute with enumerated options, you supply an option list that includes the option names, as in the following example:

```
<!ATTLIST review
snaptake (pageturner | good | average |
boring | dreadful) #REQUIRED>
```

Avoid using the same option names for other attributes in the same attribute list—you might cause a parsing error if your DTD is read by an SGML processor.

Enumerated Notation Types

If you create notation declarations in your DTD, you can specify a list of notation options. (A notation declaration specifies a certain type of external binary entity, such as a graphics file format.) Here's an example of an enumerated list of notation types:

```
<!ATTLIST img
format (gif | jpeg | png) #REQUIRED>
```

Specifying Default Values

As you have seen from this chapter's examples, you can use the default specifications shown in Table 12.2.

Table 12.2 Specifying Default Values for Attributes

Keyword	Description

#FIXED	Specifies a fixed, default value for the attribute. Authors can't change this value.
	`<!ATTLIST img format ENTITY #FIXED "gif">`
	If you're specifying a default value for an enumerated type, you can specify the value by enclosing it in quotes after the list:
	`<!ATTLIST author role (author | editor | compiler) "author">`

#IMPLIED	Does not specify a default value, and authors don't have to supply one. If there's nothing supplied, the application is free to decide how to handle the attribute.
	`<!ATTLIST paragraph`
	`role CDATA #IMPLIED>`

#REQUIRED	There's no default value specified, but users *must* supply a value. Failure to supply a value will generate a validation error.
	`<!ATTLIST img`
	`src ENTITY #REQUIRED>`

Note that the default value reserved words (FIXED, IMPLIED, and REQUIRED) must be typed in capital letters.

Preserving White Space

In HTML, the PRE element preserves all the white space that the document's author types. If you would like to create an element that preserves white space in the way that PRE does, you use the special xml:space attribute, whose only possible values are "default" (uses the application's white-space method) and "preserve" (preserves the author's white-space entries). Here's an example:

```
<!ATTLIST freetext
xml:space (default | preserve) "preserve">
```

If you don't declare this attribute and specify the "preserve" value, the application will handle white space the way it's programmed. (For XML browsers, this will probably mean that the browser will ignore extraneous white space, just as HTML browsers do.)

Specifying a Language

If you would like to create an element to handle foreign languages, you can add a language attribute by using the special xml:lang attribute, as in the following example:

```
<!ATTLIST chateau
xml:lang NMTOKEN "fr">
```

Note that this declaration requires the NMTOKEN attribute type.

Creating Attributes for XLinking

As you learned in Chapter 7, you can add XLink capabilities to any of the elements you create. You do so by adding link attributes. In this section, you learn how to add linking capabilities to the elements in your DTD.

Advantages of DTD-Defined Link Attributes

In a well-formed XML document, you can add these attributes and supply data for them, but the process is tedious because you must define the defaults every time you do so. For example, in the following example, you must include *xlink="simple"* every time you want to insert a link using the boat element:

```
<boat xlink="simple" href="another-
document.xml">
  [ ... ]
</boat>
```

If you define this element so that *xlink="simple"* is a fixed default value of the boat element, you don't need to define the attribute every time you insert a link. Here's the element definition:

```
<!ELEMENT boat (#PCDATA)*>
```

To add attributes that give this element linking capability, you need to add linking attribute components listed in Table 12.3. Note that these are the default names for these components; you can't change them without remapping them, as described subsequently.

Table 12.3 Default Components for Linking Attributes

Name	Description
xlink:form	Default attribute for specifying the link type. Default values are "simple," "extended," "locator," "group," and "document." `xlink:form (simple | extended | locator | group | document) "simple"`
href	URL of link destination, expressed as CDATA. You should require this attribute; the link won't work without it. `href CDATA #REQUIRED`
inline	Indicates whether the link's content is marked in the document as clickable hyperlink text. Possible value are "true" (the default) and "false." You use "false" for out-of-line (extended) links. `inline (true | false) "true"`
role	The role of the link, containing author-supplied text of some sort (for example, "criticism" or "commentary"). Judging the light usage of similar attributes in HTML, most authors will probably omit this. `role CDATA #IMPLIED`

show	Determines display of linked resource; possible values are "embed," "replace," and "new." The current XLink specification leaves the default up to the application, but it will probably be "replace" in most XML browsers (as it is in HTML). You should fix a default value if you want to be sure. `show (embed | replace | new) "replace"`
actuate	Controls how the link is activated. Possible values are "auto" (automatic display) and "user" (user-initiated display). The default is left up to browsers, but it will probably be "user" (as it is in HTML). `actuate (auto | user ) "user"`
content-role	Role of the linked resource in the link. `content-role CDATA #IMPLIED`
content-title	Title of the linked resource. `content-title CDATA #IMPLIED`

Here's the attribute list for a simple XLink for the boat element:

```
<!ATTLIST boat
xlink:form CDATA #FIXED "simple"
href CDATA #required
show (embed | replace | new) "replace"
content-title CDATA #implied>
```

Specifying Link Behaviors

You can add link behaviors (see Chapter 7) to your attribute list.

Here's an example that lets authors choose how to display the link by means of the show attribute's three options:

```
<!ATTLIST citation
xlink:form CDATA #FIXED "simple"
href CDATA #required
title CDATA #implied
show (embed | replace | new)>
```

Emulating HTML's <A> Tag

Chances are that you—and anyone else authoring documents with your DTD—will be familiar with HTML's hyperlinking capabilities. It makes abundant good sense to include an XML version of the <A> tag in every DTD you create. Here's the element type declaration:

```
<!ELEMENT a xml:link #CDATA #FIXED "simple">
```

And here's the attribute list:

```
<!ATTLIST citation
xlink:form CDATA #FIXED "simple"
href CDATA #required
content-title CDATA #implied
show (embed | replace | new) "replace"
actuate (auto | user ) "user">
```

Note that this attribute list creates a simple link that requires a URL. The retrieved document replaces the link source, and it's activated at the user's discretion.

Emulating HTML's <IMG> Tag

Similarly, you'll probably want to include an img element in your DTD, one that emulates the HTML element of the same name.

Here's the element type declaration:

```
<!ELEMENT img EMPTY>
```

And here's the attribute list that emulates the IMG element:

```
<!ATTLIST img
xlink:form CDATA #FIXED "simple"
href CDATA #REQUIRED
show (embed | replace | new) "embed"
actuate (auto | user) "auto">
```

Note the fixed setting of the show and actuate options; this is how the HTML element operates.

Creating Extended Links

Chapter 7 discussed XLink's extended link capabilities and introduced two elements, extended and locator, which can be used to create extended links. Here's an example from a well-formed document:

```
<extended xml:link="extended" show="replace"
actuate="user">
  <locator xml:link="locator"
  href="bibliography.xml#Smith1999">
  <locator xml:link="locator"
  href="essay.xml#Smith1999">
</extended>
```

Here are sample element definitions for the extended link elements in this example:

```
<!ELEMENT extended (locator+)>
<!ELEMENT locator EMPTY>
```

Note that the extended element must contain at least one locator element, and the locator element is empty.

And here are the attribute definitions:

```
<!ATTLIST extended
xlink:form CDATA #FIXED "extended"
inline (true | false ) "true"
show (embed | replace | new) "replace"
actuate (auto | user) #FIXED "user">

<!ATTLIST locator
xlink:form CDATA #FIXED "locator"
href CDATA #REQUIRED>
```

To create an extended link group, you need to define two elements, group and document:

```
<!ELEMENT group (document)*>
<!ELEMENT document EMPTY>
```

Here are the attribute lists for these two elements. Note the required default values for the xml:link attributes:

```
<!ATTLIST group
xlink:form CDATA #FIXED "group"
steps CDATA #IMPLIED
href CDATA #REQUIRED>

<!ATTLIST document
xlink:form CDATA #FIXED "document"
```

```
href CDATA #REQUIRED>
```

Creating the Attribute List

For each element, group all the attributes together into a list, as in the following example:

```
<!ATTLIST img
id ID #IMPLIED
title CDATA #IMPLIED
xlink:form CDATA #FIXED "simple"
href CDATA #REQUIRED
show (embed | replace | new) "embed"
actuate (auto | user) "auto"
format NOTATION (gif | jpeg | png) #IMPLIED>
```

If several of your attributes contain the same list of enumerated options, you can use a parameter entity instead of typing them over and over again. For more information, see the next chapter.

From Here

In this chapter, you learned how to define attributes for your document's elements. In the next chapter, you'll learn how to declare entities. As you'll see, this is an essential skill not only for DTD authors, but for authors of XML documents as well.

13

Declaring Entities and Notations

In XML, the term *entity* refers to a number of things that don't seem (at first glance) to have much in common, encompassing internal entities (such as abbreviations that the display software can automatically expand), external binary entities (such as graphics files), and *parameter entities* (abbreviations useful within DTDs only). Diverse as they are, all these types of entities share one thing in common: You must declare them in your DTD.

This chapter shows you how to declare entities and, in so doing, take advantage of advanced XML capabilities, such as creating a single *logical document* that consists of two or more physical files. Also covered in this chapter are notation declarations, which tell applications what kind of data you're using when you refer to external binary entities.

Where to Declare Entities and Notations

You must declare entities and notations in your DTD. But which DTD? As you learned in Chapter 10, you can create an *external DTD subset*, a separate file that two or more XML documents can reference, as well as an *internal DTD subset,* which is included at the beginning of an XML document (and affects only that document). Where should you place your entity and notation declarations? As the following sections explain, it all depends on what you're declaring.

Declarations in the External DTD Subset

If you create an external DTD, you should declare any entities that you believe might prove useful for all or most of the documents created with that DTD. For example, suppose you're creating a DTD for a company with a lengthy name (Rappahannock River Marine Services, Inc.). Anyone creating a document would appreciate being able to type "rrms" instead of the company's lengthy name! An abbreviation as generally useful as this one belongs in the external DTD. This chapter turns to the specifics of declaring entities in a subsequent section, but here's what this entity looks like:

```
<!ENTITY rrms "Rappahannock River Marine Ser-
vices, Inc.">
```

Another example: the GIF file (an external binary entity) containing the company's logo:

```
<!ENTITY logo SYSTEM "logo.gif" NDATA gif>
```

The same goes for notations: If they're useful for more than one document, put them in the external DTD subset. As you learned in Chapter 10, *notations* are used to declare a certain type of external binary data (NDATA), such as a JPEG or GIF file. You should include all the general types within your external DTD, as in the following:

```
<!NOTATION jpeg PUBLIC>
<!NOTATION gif PUBLIC>
<!NOTATION wav PUBLIC>
```

After you have declared these NDATA types, you may use the data type names (such as "jpeg" or "wav") in attributes that have the ENTITY or ENTITIES name tokens. (See Chapter 15.) You may also use these data type names in your entity declarations.

What happens if you don't declare external binary data types? Your document gets a validation error. That's not a fatal error—it doesn't stop the processor from reading your document—but it might prevent the application from displaying the data properly.

Declarations in the Internal DTD Subset

What about the internal DTD? The internal DTD subset is the place to put any entities that are useful for the current XML document only. Examples include graphics files that are referenced only in the current document, such as the following reference to a graphics file:

```
<!ENTITY featured-pic SYSTEM "featured-
pic.jpg" NDATA jpg>
```

Should you ever declare notations in an internal DTD subset? If you're creating an XML document with a standalone DTD, as described in Chapter 10, that's the only place such declarations can go. If you're basing your documents on an external DTD, you would declare notations in the internal DTD only if this particular XML document contained some special type of data that isn't used in any other document of the same type.

Creating an Internal DTD Subset

Because most XML authors will create internal DTD subsets for one purpose only (namely, declaring document-specific entities), it's worthwhile to review the procedure for incorporating an internal DTD within an XML document. You insert the internal DTD within the document type declaration, as in the following example:

```
<?XML version="1.0"?>
<!DOCTYPE newsletter SYSTEM "newsletter.dtd"

    [

<!ENTITY featured-pic SYSTEM "featured-
pic.jpg" NDATA jpg>

    ]>
```

Don't forget to enclose the internal DTD subset within brackets, as shown here, and be sure to include the closing angle bracket.

Declaring Internal Entities

Internal entities provide a means of creating shorthand expressions, such as abbreviation for Rappahannock River Marine Services, Inc. Within your XML document, you can type the abbreviation instead of typing the lengthy phrase:

```
<paragraph>%rrms; announces special prices on
rigging gear for the new boating
season.</paragraph>
```

Note that you precede the abbreviation with a percentage symbol (%) and follow it with a semicolon.

If you've created attributes that accept CDATA, you can use your entity there as well:

```
<heading1 title="%rrms;">
```

To declare internal entities, you create an *entity declaration* that includes the abbreviation followed by the expanded text:

```
<!ENTITY rrms "Rappahannock River Marine Ser-
vices">
```

Declaring External Entities

External entities include text files or files containing binary data. If the entity is a text file, the XML processor *parses* (reads and processes) the file, so text files are also called *parsed entities.* If the entity is a binary file (an *unparsed entity)*, you need to make this clear so that the poor XML processor doesn't try to parse it.

External Parsed Entities (Text Files)

To declare an external text file, you create a name for the entity, indicate that it's directly available somewhere on the computer network by using the SYSTEM keyword, and indicate the file's actual location. Here's a simple example, one that refers to a text file in the same directory as the referring document:

```
<!ENTITY part1 SYSTEM "part1.xml">
```

To provide more information about the document's location, you can use any valid URL:

```
<!ENTITY homepage SYSTEM "http://www.riven-
dell.org/bilbo/home.xml">
```

As you'll learn later in this chapter, you can insert an external parsed entity anywhere in an XML document by inserting the entity symbols (a percentage sign, the entity name, and a semicolon). In this way, you can create a logical XML document that includes references to any number of external files, as in the following example:

```
<?XML version="1.0"?>
<fave>
%review1;
%review2;
%review3;
</fave>
```

Compared to HTML, this is a particularly useful and powerful feature of XML, and we'll examine it more closely later in this chapter.

External Unparsed Entities (Binary Files)

To declare an external binary file, you follow the same procedure: Create a name for the entity, indicate that it's directly available somewhere on the computer network by using the SYSTEM keyword, and indicate the file's actual location using a URL. In addition, you add the keyword NDATA, followed by the type of notation data that you've declared in your notation declaration:

```
<!ENTITY logo SYSTEM "logo.jpg" NDATA jpg>
```

Where can you refer to external unparsed entities? In one place only: attributes that can take the ENTITY or ENTITIES data types. For more information on these data types, see Chapter 12.

Declaring Notations

If you declare external unparsed entities, you must include a notation declaration. When you declare the notation, you create a name for a particular type of external data. You may then use this name in your DTD (when you declare external binary entities) and in your XML documents (when you supply values for tokenized attributes). If you wish, you can include the name of a helper application that knows how to read the data. Here's what a notation declaration looks like:

```
<!NOTATION jpg SYSTEM "paint.exe">
```

You can leave out the helper application name, if you like:

```
<!NOTATION jpg SYSTEM>
```

Note that the XML specification requires validating processors to issue a validation error if the keyword SYSTEM is used without a specific file; this is the only permitted exception.

Creating Parameter Entities

Parameter entities closely resemble the internal entities discussed earlier in this chapter: They're abbreviations for lengthy phrases that you don't really want to retype. The difference lies in where they operate. You use internal entities within XML documents. In contrast, you use parameter entities within DTDs.

Why do you need a shorthand expression within DTDs? Not just to cut down on typing. Using parameter entities reduces the chance of a typing error that might injure your DTD's functionality. Here are two places within your DTD that parameter entities may come in very handy indeed: content models and attribute lists.

Parameter Entities for Content Models

When you create element definitions, you may find that many elements have the same content models. For example, when you create mixed content elements that accept character data, they'll probably look something like this:

```
<!ELEMENT paragraph (#CDATA | bold | ital-
ic)*>
```

You will probably create several elements that have the same content model, one that enables the author to type character data and to use the bold or italic elements. Why not create a shorthand expression for this content model? Here's how:

```
<!ENTITY % text "#CDATA | bold | italic">
```

This parameter entity defines a shorthand expression (%text;) that you can enter in place of the content model in any element definition. Here's how you can use it:

```
<!ELEMENT paragraph %text;>
```

This is the same as typing:

```
<!ELEMENT paragraph (#CDATA | bold | ital-
ic)>
```

How does the XML processor tell the difference between a parameter entity and an internal entity? The difference lies in just one character: the percentage sign, followed by a space, in the entity declaration. (Note the percentage sign: <!ENTITY % text ...>. Don't forget to include the percentage sign within the parameter entity declaration! If you leave it out, you'll create an internal entity for use within your XML documents—it won't work within your DTD.)

Parameter Entities for Attribute Lists

Parameter entities come in very handy for attribute lists. For example, suppose you want to create a core attribute list that's used in every attribute list you create:

```
id ID #IMPLIED
title CDATA #IMPLIED
```

Instead of typing this repeatedly (and possibly making mistakes), you can create a parameter entity that includes them and inserts them in your attribute lists. Here's the entity declaration:

```
<!ENTITY % core
"id ID #IMPLIED
title CDATA #IMPLIED">
```

Don't forget the percentage sign and quotation marks!

Here's how you use this entity:

```
<!ATTLIST paragraph
%core;>
```

Creating Logical Documents

As this chapter earlier suggested, you can create a single, *logical* XML document that spans two or more *physical* files, in the form of parsed external entities. However, you need to follow a basic rule: Elements must begin and end in the same entity.

What this means, practically speaking, is that the first physical file must contain the document element (and all required declarations), as in the following example:

```
<?XML version="1.0"?>
<!DOCTYPE fave SYSTEM "fave.dtd"

[

<!ENTITY review1 SYSTEM "review1.xml">
<!ENTITY review2 SYSTEM "review2.xml">
<!ENTITY review3 SYSTEM "review3.xml">

]>
```

```
<fave>
%review1;
%review2;
%review3;
</fave>
```

Similarly, elements used within the entities (review1, review2, and review3) must begin and end within the file. For the fave DTD, this necessitates that each entity consist of one complete <novel> element. The file review1.xml could contain the following:

```
<novel>
  <author>David Williams</author>
  <title>The Northern Neck Mystery</title>
  <date>1999</date>
  <publisher>Riverneck Press</publisher>
  <review>
    <summary>Great characters, lousy
    plot</summary>
    <paragraph>A first novel, and it
    shows.</paragraph>
  </review>
</novel>
```

Parsed external files shouldn't contain anything other than text and markup; you don't need to include an XML or document type declaration.

From Here

This chapter described entity declarations, which are required if you want to incorporate shorthand expressions (including parameter entities) or any external text or binary data in your XML documents. You learned how and where to declare entities, and also how to declare notations for external binary data. In the next chapter, you learn how to organize your DTDs for maximum ease of use and maintenance.

14

Designing Useful DTDs

In the previous chapters, you've learned how to construct the components of a DTD: element type declarations, attribute lists, entity declarations, and notation declarations. In this chapter, you learn how to put these all together—and what's more, how to do so in a way that ensures that all the effort you've expended won't go to waste.

Framing Your Objectives

In order to create a useful DTD, you need to think through your goals:

- **Who is going to use this DTD?** If you're the only user, you don't need to worry so much about explaining how it works and using readable, understandable names for elements and attributes. If other authors will use it, you've got to work to do in order to make your DTD understandable and usable.
- **What type of document are you trying to capture?** Consider all the documents you're working with now, and divide them into categories (such as "progress reports," "proposals," and "memos"). Are you sure you've properly categorized them? Take a look at lots of real-life examples.
- **Identify all the possible structural components of your document type.** Once again, it's helpful to look at lots of examples. If you fail to include an element that authors expect, they will resent the DTD and will resist using it.

It's not worth putting a lot of work into a DTD until you've thought through what you're trying to accomplish. You may discover only too late that you have to throw everything out and start over.

One of the nice things about XML is that you can start with a well-formed version of the vocabulary you're trying to create. You can then try it out to see how it works in practice—without having made a major investment in DTD production.

Understanding DTD Design Trade-offs

Here's a basic design maxim: No single best way to design something exists. Instead, every design choice involves a trade-off. In DTD design, you must deal with three trade-off issues, which are discussed in this section.

Description vs. Prescription

If you're trying to describe what authors are currently doing, they'll find it easy to learn how to use your DTD—but you'll miss opportunities to lend structure and discipline to your documents.

- **Description.** If you simply want to describe the way authors currently create documents, you will try to capture the structures they're using, and make elements for them. Authors—including yourself, if you both design the DTD and use it—will find the DTD intuitive and easy to use.
- **Prescription.** Here, you want to *change* the way things are currently done. You want to alter current practices, introduce new elements, and take advantage of cool new XML possibilities. But you're going to make the learning curve steeper. If other authors beside you will use your DTD, they may not care for the additional work you're asking them to do.

Complexity vs. Ease of Use

Keep it simple! It's tempting to create a DTD that includes dozens or even hundreds of elements, enough to capture every last nuance of document structures. But remember the lesson of HTML. Although the current version of HTML has more than 75 elements, most HTML authors use only one or two dozen. You will be wise to follow HTML's example!

If you would prefer to create a more complex DTD that can cover a range of documents, consider including conditional sections that enable authors to learn just a portion of the elements you've created. You'll learn how in a subsequent section.

Guidance vs. Flexibility

As you've learned, visual XML editors can guide authors through the process of document construction, informing them which elements are available in a given context. However, guidance comes at the cost of reduced flexibility.

The fewer the choices, the easier it is to use the DTD. In the fave-mysteries DTD, for example, there's only one choice available in the <fave> context: <novel>, which enables the author to create an entry for a new review. If you set up the <novel> child elements in a prescribed order, there will continue to be only one element option available, until the entire record is completed.

But here's the trade-off. The more sharply you restrict choice, the less freedom you give authors to capture novel document structures. The fave-mysteries DTD is very close to the rigidity of a data entry form in a database program. It's not very flexible and doesn't enable authors to play with the structure in novel ways.

It's Your Call

How do you resolve these issues? It all depends on the context and what you're trying to accomplish. Admittedly the fave-mysteries DTD is quite rigid in the way it forces authors to supply data in a fixed format—but I need the data supplied in just that way. At the other extreme, HTML provides authors so much freedom that they can create just about anything. That's fine for the Web, but it might not be appropriate for an in-house application.

Making Your DTD User-Friendly

DTDs are designed to be readable and usable by humans as well as computers, but often it seems that the humans get the short end of the stick. There's no way around knowing a little about DTD notation—the question marks, asterisks, parentheses, and plus signs—and the basic syntax of the various declarations. Even so, you can take a few simple steps to make your DTD easier to read, as described in this section.

Comments

You can place comments in your DTD to explain what the various components do, or to add tips for use. To create comments within your DTD, you use the same syntax used to insert comments in XML documents:

```
<!-- here is a comment -->
```

Note that there are a few rules to follow when inserting comments in your XML DTD:

- You can't place comments *within* declarations, such as element type declarations or attribute lists. Note that the HTML DTD does this—but the HTML DTD is written in SGML, which allows comments all over the place. To avoid parsing errors, XML places restrictions on comment location.
- Don't nest comments within comments.
- Make sure you haven't put any spaces within the comment delimiters.

Element Names

In the early days of SGML, computer memory was limited, and SGML limited element names to eight characters. Early SGML DTDs tended to use element names (such as EM or P) that were difficult to remember and didn't provide a clue to their proper use.

Those days are gone, and with them the requirement to use short element names. Of course, it's easier to type short element names, but that's not an issue if you're creating documents with an HTML editor.

Make your names as descriptive as possible:

- author, not au
- company, not co
- citation, not cite

Attribute Options

Here's one way to make your DTD *much* easier to use. Look through your attributes, and consider supplying your authors with an enumerated series of options rather than "CDATA."

Consider this attribute:

```
<!ATTLIST author
role #CDATA #IMPLIED>
```

What are you supposed to supply? It could be anything, ranging from one character to the entire text of *Hamlet*. Provide some guidance! Compare this revision:

```
<!ATTLIST author
role (author | editor | compiler) #IMPLIED>
```

To make things even easier, supply a default value:

```
<!ATTLIST author
role (author | editor | compiler) "author">
```

Organizing Your DTD

You can get away with a sloppily organized DTD, but you'll find it difficult to read and maintain. Here are some tips for organizing your DTD so that it is easy to understand and modify:

- **Use parameter entities liberally.** They make your DTD much less cluttered and more legible. They also make it much easier to add extra elements and attributes that incorporate previously used declarations.
- **Declare parameter entities first.** They're a necessary precondition for understanding what follows.
- **Declare elements in the order in which they appear in a typical document.** Authors will be looking for element-related information in this order.
- **Keep attribute lists separate from the element type declarations.** Again, this makes your DTD easier to read, maintain, and expand.
- **Group all of an element's attributes in a single attribute list.** XML permits you to create more than one attribute list for an element, but it's illogical and inefficient to do so. And it could cause errors: An author might find only one of the lists for an element and fail to detect other, needed attributes.

Including Conditional Sections

If you've decided to create a lengthy DTD with more than a few dozen elements, chances are that you've decided to do so in order to deal with two or more document types or subtypes. If so, consider using *conditional sections*, which enable authors to switch on only those portions of the DTD that they need to use. This enables them to avoid having to learn a lot of elements that they will never use.

Introducing Conditional Sections

To create conditional sections in an external DTD subset, you surround some of the markup declarations with a parameter entity that's set to "IGNORE." To switch the section on, an author can redefine the parameter entity in the XML document's internal DTD subset. As you might remember, anything that's redefined in the internal DTD subset overrides the declarations in the external DTD, so the conditional section is included.

Creating the Parameter Entities

Suppose you've created a DTD for your company's memos and letters. You create several elements that are used in both. Then you have two conditional sections: one for memos and one for letters. To create the conditional sections, you need two parameter entities, defined as follows:

```
<!ENTITY % include-memo "IGNORE">
<!ENTITY % include-letter "IGNORE">
```

Marking the Conditional Sections

After the parameter entities are set up, you can mark the conditional sections, as in the following example:

```
<![%include-memo; [

<-- memo elements go here -->

]>
```

Note that the memo elements (indicated by an XML comment) are enclosed within brackets, and the entire memo element section is included within the conditional section's distinctive syntax.

To mark the letter elements, you surround them in the same way, but use the letter parameter entity you created:

```
<![%include-letter; [

<-- letter elements go here -->

]>
```

From Here

In this chapter, you learned how to plan your DTD, find your way among the various trade-offs of DTD design, and organize your DTD for easy use and maintenance. Should you wish to create more complex DTDs, this chapter also demonstrated how to create conditional sections, which authors can switch on or off as they please.

In the next chapter, you'll explore the W3C's namespace proposal, which will (when finalized) enable XML authors to incorporate elements drawn from two or more Internet-accessible DTDs. As you'll learn in the next chapter, this capability may greatly reduce—or even eliminate—the work you'd otherwise have to do to produce a high-quality DTD.

15

Using Elements from Two or More DTDs

Thus far, you've explored document type definitions (DTDs) with an SGML model in mind: There's one DTD (and one only) for each type of document. In this chapter, you'll learn why this model isn't entirely satisfactory (especially for XML's purposes) and what's being done about it. Specifically, you'll learn about the W3C's Namespaces proposal—still a Working Draft at this book's writing—that will enable XML authors to use elements drawn from two or more DTDs.

This chapter's focus shifts away from DTDs and back to the process of authoring XML documents; you'll learn how to incorporate elements into your documents that draw from multiple DTDs. This doesn't mean that your documents don't need at least an internal DTD subset, which is still required should you wish to use entities. But it does raise the possibility that you could greatly reduce the amount of work that goes into creating your own external DTD subset—and you might even be able to avoid this work altogether.

Please remember that this chapter is based on a Working Draft and isn't yet finalized. Check the W3C's home page (www.w3.org) to find out whether the proposal has achieved the status of a W3C Recommendation, and check carefully to see whether the final version contains any changes from the material discussed in this chapter.

Understanding the Need for a Namespace Mechanism

Why should XML authors be able to draw elements from two or more DTDs? There are at least two good reasons, as explained in the following sections.

Avoiding Reinventing the Wheel

It's a lot of work to create DTDs, as I'm sure you'll agree after reading the previous chapters. Worse, you must often duplicate the learning process that others have already gone through.

For example, consider adding elements for a bibliography. The task sounds simple enough—until you take a closer look. A bibliography is composed of dozens of different types of items (books, magazine articles, archival journal articles, personal communications, e-mail messages, etc.), each of which must be arranged in accordance with a particular discipline's style manual. Creating a DTD capable of handling a bibliography in a professional manner is an enormous task, one that requires considerable expertise and a good chunk of time—several weeks, at the minimum. To be sure, you could create a simple <citation> element and type the reference as character data, but you've given away the benefit of using XML in the first place: namely, the possibility of separating out items such as <author>, <date>, <journal>, <publisher>, <place>, and <keyword>. You would save a lot of work by being able to incorporate fully worked out elements from some existing DTD, even if you didn't want the rest of the elements that DTD offered.

Enhancing Information Retrievability

Reinventing the wheel is not only a lot of work; it also raises the possibility that you'll inadvertently reduce information retrievability by giving your element a name that differs from others' usage.

Suppose you create an element for the date of a document's last modification. One author might call this element <last-mod>, while another calls it <date-last>. This isn't necessarily a problem when you're creating a DTD for use on a nonpublic network. On the Internet, however, the use of divergent names for similar elements reduces information retrievability. Suppose, for example, I want to search for the latest review of my favorite mystery novel, and I tell my XML-aware search software to search the <last-mod> element. If someone has placed this information in an element that employs another name, the software may not find it.

Toward an Online Community of Shared Elements

To solve the problems of reinventing the wheel and ensuring element name consistency, the W3C's Namespace proposal calls for a mechanism that will enable XML authors to draw on elements from existing, well-designed DTDs—as many DTDs as authors wish. The mechanism is called *XML namespaces.*

Introducing the XML Namespace Mechanism

The XML namespace mechanism enables authors to use elements that have already been defined in Internet-accessible DTDs. As the following sections explain, this mechanism draws on XML's *qualified name* syntax. In order to use namespaces in your documents, you need to declare the source DTDs in a special namespace declaration. You incorporate the elements into your XML document using a special syntax.

Qualified Names

Throughout this book, you may have occasionally noticed an XML name that includes a colon, such as xlink:form or xml:lang. These names conform to the XML language specification's *qualified names* syntax, which combines two valid XML names separated by a colon. (Valid XML names must begin with an alphabetical character, and can subsequently include letters, numbers, periods, hyphens, and underscores.)

The namespace mechanism makes use of qualified names. In brief, instead of typing an element name in your XML documents, you type a qualified name, in which the first part is an abbreviation for the DTD you're using, and the second name is the element name. Here are a couple of examples:

```
tei-lite:stanza
html:table
```

Notice that the DTD abbreviations (tei-lite and html) do not include any information about the Internet location of these DTDs. They can't, because the restrictions placed on qualified names prevent you from including URLs (with all their nonstandard characters). That's why you must include a *namespace declaration.*

Namespace Declarations

To tell the XML processor where you're getting your elements, you must insert one or more *namespace declarations* into the *prolog* of your XML document—specifically, after the XML declaration and before the document type declaration. Essentially, the namespace declaration is a *processing instruction* (PI), the content of which is passed on to the application (as it should be, since the application may have to retrieve the DTD in order to display the data correctly). Here's an example of an XML prolog that contains two namespace declarations (with fictitious URLs):

```
<?XML version="1.0"?>
<?xml:namespace
ns="http://www.literature.org/"
src="http://www.literature.org/dtds/poem.dtd"
prefix="poem"?>
<?xml:namespace
ns="http://www.bibliography.org/"
```

```
src="http://www.bibliography.org/resources/
bibliography.dtd" prefix="biblio"?>
```

Table 15.1 lists the components that go into a valid namespace declaration. All are required except the source definition (src).

Table 15.1 Components of a Valid Namespace Declaration

Name	Description
PI	The processing instruction that declares the namespace. `<?xml:namespace`
name	Name or URL specifying source of the elements. This portion of the declaration is used to give *credit* for the utilized elements and to *identify* the schema that's being used, but applications aren't supposed to use this specification to *retrieve* the DTD for processing. `ns="http://www.myserver.com"`
source	URL specifying location of source DTD for processing purposes. `src="http://www.myserver.com/ poem.dtd"`
prefix	Abbreviation for this DTD that you'll use in your document. `prefix="billing"`

Why isn't the source definition required? Isn't the whole point of the namespace proposal to enable retrieval of elements from network-accessible DTDs? Yes, but the namespace proposal isn't limited to this. Applications could be hard-wired to recognize a variety of alternative schemas, for example, so they wouldn't need to retrieve any information from the network. For such applications, it's enough to specify the name; you don't need the source. If you do specify the source, the application can retrieve the information, but that's up to the application.

Note that you can't include a fragment identifier (such as #author) in the source definition.

Using Qualified Names in Your XML Documents

Once you've inserted the namespace declaration, you're ready to insert qualified names in your document in place of the element names you would normally use. As this section explains, you can also make use of attributes defined in the source DTD.

Using Qualified Names

To insert a qualified name into your document, you must use the prefix and colon in the end tag as well as the start tag. Note the following example:

```
<biblio:author>Marshall</biblio:author>
```

Using Attributes

If the source DTD defines attributes for the elements you are using, you can include these in your XML document. For clarity, you can use the prefix, but it's not necessary; if you use an attribute within an element that has a qualified name, applications will assume you're using the source DTD's attribute list. In the following example, the attribute *lifespan* is assumed to come from *www.bibliography.org*'s DTD:

```
<biblio:author lifespan="1928-1982">MacDon-
ald</biblio:author>
```

You can use empty elements, too. Just be sure to close them properly, as with any empty element:

```
<biblio:status cataloged="yes"/>
```

Understanding Universal Names

Doesn't the use of a prefix destroy one of the purposes of the namespace proposal—specifically, creating pools of information that are all marked with the same element names? After all, I could choose any prefix I want for the tags I'm borrowing from *www.bibliography.org*; I could choose *biblio, bibliography*, or something completely unrelated! So my document would have a bunch of tags with one prefix, while somebody else's has another, even though we draw from the same DTD.

Universal names prevent this variation from occurring. The prefixes you use aren't really of any importance, save as a convenience to you (and also as a means of staying within the XML language's syntax restrictions). When applications process an XML document that contains a namespace declaration, they are supposed to remove the prefix from the element names, and place the namespace definition's name in its place. This results in a *universal name*, such as the following:

```
http://www.bibliography.org/:author
```

Because every author's usage of this organization's elements resolve to this universal name, search software can group and retrieve them.

From Here

With this chapter, you come to the end of Part Four. In Part Five, you turn to the subject of presentation—a very important matter, since the XML specification says absolutely nothing about how the elements you've defined should be presented for display purposes.

Part Five

Assigning Styles to XML Elements

16

Introducing Cascading Style Sheets (CSS)

If you're interested in XML more as a means of *displaying* structured data rather than storing it for use by applications, you'll need to learn how to control your elements' presentation with *style sheets*. In brief, a style sheet is a document (or portion of a document) that contains (essentially) a list of the elements you have defined, along with style specifications for each element. The specifications can govern such matters as line spacing, margins, fonts, and much more.

Despite all the attention given to XSL, it's clear that CSS—the Cascading Style Sheet specification maintained by the World Wide Web Consortium—will provide XML authors with the tools they need to display structured data. XSL is more advanced, and it can do things that CSS can't do, but CSS has several major advantages—not the least of which is that browser publishers have already developed CSS processors that they can easily incorporate into XML browsers. Accordingly, Part Five of this book stresses CSS; you'll get a look at XSL at the end of Part Five. In this chapter, you learn the fundamentals of CSS.

Understanding the Need for Style Sheets

With HTML, you don't need to do anything to get at least minimal presentation. Almost all HTML elements are either *block elements* (displayed as distinct paragraphs) or *inline elements,* which can be inserted within block elements without causing a paragraph break. And HTML browsers are programmed to assign basic presentation formats to most of these elements.

With XML, your document has no presentation whatsoever, save that an XML processor will delete extraneous spaces (a process called *normalization*). But that's it. Your work will look like the document shown in Figure 16.1. And there's no other way it *can* look. In contrast to HTML, XML does not give authors any means to differentiate between block and inline elements.

So XML is indeed very serious about the distinction between structure and presentation. Admittedly, this distinction cannot be absolute; even XML normalizes character data to the extent of stripping out extraneous whitespace. But the question is, how do you bring presentation back without blurring this distinction?

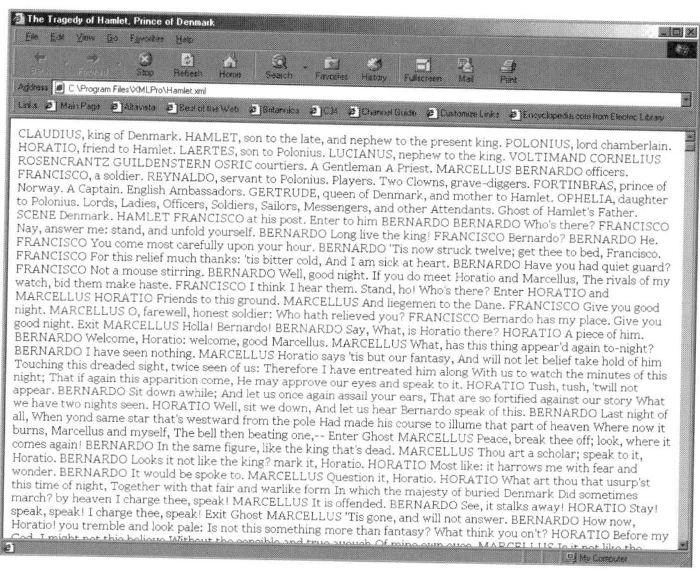

Figure 16.1 XML has no provisions for element display!

That's where style sheets come in. Ideally, a style sheet is entirely separate from the markup document, so the presentation code doesn't get in the way of the structural markup. With style sheet languages such as CSS and XSL, you can create external style sheets that house all of a document's presentation coding—there's no presentation-related markup in the XML document at all, save for a reference to the external style sheet's name and location. Your XML document remains uncluttered. The document looks beautiful on-screen (or, as you'll see, on paper). Yet, in your XML document, all you see is your document's structure. And that's the way it should be.

Keeping the styles in a separate document has another huge advantage: If you link two or more documents to the same style sheet, you can make major presentation changes to all the linked documents just by making a tiny change in the underlying style sheet.

You'll surely appreciate the advantages of external style sheets if you've ever tried to maintain a multidocument HTML-based Web site. In such sites, typically, the presentation is embedded in dozens or even hundreds of documents—and you must manually update every one of them should you wish to change your presentation styles.

Introducing CSS

The Cascading Style Sheets (CSS) style language is maintained by the World Wide Web Consortium (W3C) and as of this writing is in its Level 2 specification.

CSS Is Ideal for the Display of Structured Data

Why stress CSS in this book? Several good reasons exist:

- **CSS is easy to learn and use.** You can start writing your CSS style sheet within a few minutes of beginning study of CSS. XSL, in contrast, is more difficult to learn.
- **CSS is a W3C Recommendation.** At this writing, XSL exists only as a proposal to W3C and lacks any official status. Given the number of problems to be solved before the XSL standard can be completed, it might be some time before XSL is usable. In contrast, CSS is a finished product and, in fact, has just been released in a Level 2 specification.
- **CSS is well supported.** The major HTML browsers already support the CSS Level 1 specification (and partially support Level 2); full Level 2 support should be forthcoming in the next generation of browsers.

- **CSS handles most of what XML authors want to do.** If you're interested in XML as a means of displaying data rather than storing data for use by applications, CSS will interest you far more than XSL, which is essentially a programming language for rewriting XML documents on the fly.

There are certain things that CSS can't do, but these will prove of more interest to those who see XML as a way of storing data for use by applications. If your interests lean toward the display of structured data, CSS will prove far more interesting.

A Quick Look at CSS

Here's an example to show how easy it is to learn and use CSS. Let's suppose your XML document includes the following markup:

```
<title>The Tragedy of Hamlet, Prince of Den-
mark</title>
```

In a separate text file named with the extension .css, you type a *selector* (an element name) followed by a *declaration* (a style property and its corresponding value). Together, a selector and declaration form a *rule:*

```
title    {    display: block;
              font-family: Verdana, sans-
              serif;
              font-size: 18pt;
              text-align: center;
              margin-top: 6pt;
              margin-bottom: 12pt;
         }
```

Here, the selector is "title" (the name of the XML element), and the declaration consists of seven properties and their associated values.

Once you've linked the XML document to the style sheet containing this rule, the title will look like this:

The Tragedy of Hamlet, Prince of Denmark

That's how simple CSS is. There's more to learn, of course, but you've seen the essentials. To assign presentation styles to your XML elements, you create rules consisting of selectors and declarations. Selectors are simply the names of the elements in your XML document, and the declarations consist of various style properties and the values you've chosen for them.

Linking XML Documents to Style Sheets

At this writing, no formal recommendation exists for linking XML documents to external style sheets; the relevant W3C document is only a Note (unofficial and intended for discussion only). However, the following technique is likely to be implemented by the first wave of XML-savvy browsers, and will probably become an official recommendation as it comes into general use.

The W3C note ("Note-xml-stylesheet-19980405") recommends associating an XML document with an external style sheet by means of a processing instruction (PI), as in the following example:

```
<?xml:stylesheet
href="http://www.style.org/midnight.css" type
= "text/css"?>
```

Note that the href and type attributes are required. For href, you can use any valid URL, including a relative link to a file on your local system (e.g., href = "midnight.css").

Please be aware that the W3C may alter this technique, or scrap it in favor of some other mechanism, when a final recommendation is made. Check the W3C home page (www.w3.org) *before linking your XML document to a style sheet.*

If you're planning to display XML-tagged text within an HTML document, the following technique was implemented in a developer's preview release of Microsoft Internet Explorer 5.0. It makes use of the XML namespace proposal (see Chapter 15) in order to expose the content of XML tags to Microsoft's XML processor.

```
<html>
<head>
<XML:namespace prefix = "mytags">
<style>
@namespace mytags {
    example {font-family: Verdana}
                    }
</style>
</head>
<body>
<p>This is HTML text</p>
<mytags:example>This is XML
text.</mytags:example>
```

```
</body>
</html>
```

In the fifth line, @namespace is an example of a CSS "at-rule," which enables CSS authors to send a command to the browser. This command tells Internet Explorer to display the tags associated with the namespace's prefix.

Understanding CSS Syntax

CSS processors simply ignore any rule that contains a syntax error, so you must be sure to check your work carefully. Follow these simple rules to make sure your CSS rules work properly:

- **Case sensitivity.** CSS is case-insensitive, except for those components that CSS can't control. For example, XML element names are case-sensitive, so be sure to type your element names using the same capitalization pattern you used in your XML document.
- **Blocks.** Declarations are enclosed within curly braces. These can be nested, and you can place parentheses and brackets within them, but be sure to use an even number of each.
- **Semicolons.** If a declaration block contains more than one declaration, you must separate them using semicolons.
- **Properties.** Property names (such as "font-weight") are not case-sensitive, but be sure to type them correctly. In a declaration, they're followed by a colon and a value.
- **Quotation marks.** Don't use quotation marks around values.
- **Values.** With CSS, much of the learning process involves figuring out which values you can use. Some

values require whole numbers, others require lengths (in pixels, inches, centimeters, and other measurements), percentages, URLs, colors, and more. See Table 16.1 for a summary of the most commonly used value types.

- **White space.** Within the style sheet, white space is ignored. You can use white space to make your style sheet more usable.

Table 16.1 Value Types (Selected) for CSS Properties

Type	Description
integer	One or more numbers from 0 to 9. For some properties, you can specify positive (+) or negative (-) values, as in the following example: `margin-left: -18pt;`
em	Length: same as the font-size of the font used in the current context.
ex	Length: the x-height of the font used in the current context.
px	Length: abbreviation for pixel or pixels.
in	Length: abbreviation for inch or inches.
cm	Length: abbreviation for centimeter or centimeters.
mm	Length: abbreviation for millimeter or millimeters.
pt	Length: abbreviation for printer's points (1/72 inch).
pc	Length: Abbreviation for pica (12 points).
%	Percentage. Some properties allow positive or negative percentages, which refer to a percentage increase or decrease in whatever value this

	property has inherited. The following decreases the inherited font-size by 50%: `font-size: -50%`

url	An Internet location. Note the peculiar syntax:
	
	`list-style:`
	`url(http://www.style.org/ball.gif)`

color	Color model expressed in RGB, using any of the following formats:
	
	`color: white`
	`color: #FFFFFF`
	`color: rgb(255,255,255)`
	`color: rgb(100%, 100%, 100%)`

Understanding Inheritance

CSS is designed so that container elements pass on their properties to contained ones. In HTML, for example, the BODY element contains all other display elements. Block elements such as P and BLOCKQUOTE, in turn, contain inline elements (such as EM and ADDRESS).

How will this work in XML? Since the CSS specification requires the CSS processor to construct a document tree, inheritance should follow the tree structure. For example, the fave-mysteries document type includes a root element, fave, that contains every other element you can use. If you assign styles to fave, all of fave's child elements will inherit these styles. For example, suppose you create the following rule:

```
fave      { font-family: Helvetica;
            font-size: 12pt;
            color: blue;
          }
```

This rule will affect all of the elements in the entire document, since all of them are descendants of fave.

Note a couple of exceptions:

- **If you choose conflicting styles for child elements, the child element styles take precedence.** Suppose, for example, I choose black for the author element's text color. The author element is a descendent fave element, so it inherits the blue color—but not after I override it.
- **Not all elements are inheritable.** An example: The background-image property isn't inherited. If you choose a background graphic for fave, this property isn't passed down to child elements. To find out whether a property is inheritable, you'll need to look up the property in the CSS property index (which is currently located at *www.w3.org/TR/REC-CSS2/propidx.html)*.

By defining basic styles for your document's root element, you are in effect establishing default styles for your entire document—but only for those styles that are inheritable.

Grouping Selectors

To cut down on the amount of typing when creating a style sheet, remember that you can group elements in two ways. You can name more than one element when you write a rule (the rule applies to all the elements), and you can include more than one declaration in a rule.

Here's an illustration of grouping three selectors, which all share the specified style:

```
author, title, date { font-size: 10pt;
                      font-weight: bold;
                     }
```

You've already seen examples of grouped declarations. When you write them, be sure to separate each declaration with a semicolon, as in the following:

```
paragraph {     color: silver;
                font-family: Arial;
                font-size: 14pt;
          }
```

Using Advanced Selectors

You've already seen plenty of examples of *type selectors*, which match any element that has the selector's name. CSS enables you to write many other types of selectors. Here are the types of selectors you can use. Table 16.2 presents these selectors in action with their syntaxes.

- **Universal selector.** Matches any element.
- **Descendent selector.** Matches a specified element one or more levels beneath a specified parent element.
- **Child selector.** Matches a specified element one level beneath a specified parent element.
- **Adjacent sibling selector.** Matches a specified element that exists at the same level as a specified sibling element.
- **Attribute selector.** Matches a specified element that has the specified attribute set to a certain value.
- **Pseudo-elements.** Matches a specified element's first line or first letter.
- **Pseudo-class.** Matches elements containing an unvisited link, a visited link, an active link, or an element on which the user has positioned the mouse pointer.

Table 16.2 Examples of Advanced CSS Selectors

Example	Description
*	Matches any element (universal selector) `* {font-size: 12pt}`
cat	Matches any <cat> element (type selector) `cat {top-margin: 0.5in}`
cat mouse	Matches any <mouse> element that is a descendent of a <cat> element (descendent selector) `cat mouse {color: red}`
cat>kitten	Matches any <kitten> element that is a child of a <cat> element (child selector) `cat > kitten {color: white}`
cat.first-line	Matches the element's first line (pseudo-element selector) `cat.first-line {margin-left: -0.5in}`
cat.first-letter	Matches the first letter of any <cat> element (pseudo-element selector) `cat.first-letter {font-size: 18pt}`
cat + dog	Matches any <dog> element that is immediately preceded by a <cat> element (adjacency selector) `cat + dog {font-weight: bold}`
cat[name="Skip"]	Matches any <cat> element that has the name attribute set to "Skip" (attribute selector) `cat[name="Skip"] {color: silver}`
cat#skip	Matches any <cat> element that has an ID attribute set to "Skip" (id selector) `cat#skip {font-family: Arial}`

xref:link	Matches an <xref> element containing a hyperlink that has not yet been visited (pseudo-class selector) `xref:link {color: blue}`
xref:visited	Matches an <xref> element containing a hyperlink that has been visited (pseudo-class selector) `xref:visited {color: purple}`
xref:active	Matches an <xref> element when it is activated by the user (for example, by clicking it) (pseudo-class selector) `xref:active {color: red}`
title:hover	Matches a <title> element when the user has positioned the mouse over it (pseudo-class selector) `title:hover {color: red}`
textbox:focus	Matches a <textbox> element when the user has selected it (pseudo-class selector) `textbox:focus {color: yellow}`

Defining Block and Inline Elements

When you write rules for your XML elements, remind yourself that you're not working with HTML and that you need to decide whether your elements will be block elements or inline elements. For any element with content that shows up on the screen, you need to supply one of the following properties:

- **display: block.** If you assign this declaration to an element, the browser creates a *containing block* for the element. If the declaration is assigned to a text element, each element's content forms a separate paragraph. Every block has margins, borders, padding, and many other properties that you can control.

- **display: inline.** If you assign this declaration to an element, the browser does not create a containing block. For text elements, this means that inserting the element doesn't cause a paragraph break. Instead, it generates an *inline block*, the dimensions of which are determined by the dimensions of the containing block as well as by the content's intrinsic properties (such as a font's line height or the dimensions of a graphic).

From Here

In this chapter, you learned the fundamentals of CSS, including CSS syntax, CSS selectors, and the important distinction between block and inline elements. In the next chapter, you'll examine the CSS properties that you'll find most useful for inline and block element formatting.

17

Assigning CSS Styles to XML Elements

In the previous chapter, you learned that you must use the display property to define XML elements as inline or block elements. Once you've done this, you can write rules that assign presentation styles to these elements. In this chapter, you look at the most commonly used CSS properties for inline and block element styles.

This chapter (and those to follow) aren't intended to provide an exhaustive treatment of CSS Level 2; that would require a separate book! What you'll find here is coverage of the properties you're likely to find most useful for displaying your XML data.

Defining Root Element Styles

To choose an overall color scheme for your XML document, you can add a background color or image to the root element, just as you'd assign a color or image to the BODY element in an HTML document. In an XML document, the root element is the container for all other elements.

Background Options

You can choose from the following:

- **Background color.** Background colors can do wonderful things for your document, as long as you give some thought to how they will look with the other colors you've used. You will need to devote some thought to default text colors so that everything works harmoniously.
- **Background image.** Background images add depth and beauty to your document, but they can make your document difficult to read. If you're planning to use a background image, make sure it is something that won't interfere with your text's legibility. And again, you will need to think about text color so that the overall color scheme works harmoniously.

Browsers don't display background images and background colors at the same time. You can define both for a given document, but the background image takes precedence. In case the browser cannot load the background image for some reason, it displays the background color. If you use a background image, you should also define a background color, just in case the graphic isn't available for one reason or another.

Adding a Background Color

To add a background color to your document, use the CSS background-color property to define the root element. (You can actually use this property for any element, not just the root element.)

PROPERTY	background-color
PURPOSE	Specifies the background color of an element
INHERITED	Yes
VALUES	Color code or mnemonic
DEFAULT	Defined by browser

Here is how to add a background color to your document. In this example, <fave> is the XML document's root element:

```
fave        {  display: block;
               background-color: black;
            }
```

Note that you must define <fave> as a block element. If you don't, CSS won't establish a containing block for it, and your color choice won't show up.

Adding a Background Image

Adding a background image to your document is just as easy as adding a background color, but there are many more options. Here's the background-image property definition.

PROPERTY	background-image
PURPOSE	Inserts a graphic in an element's background
INHERITED	Yes

VALUES	url
DEFAULT	Defined by browser

To specify the URL, you type url, and then enclose the absolute or relative URL within parentheses, as in the example that follows. The syntax is a bit weird, so take special note of this example (which uses a relative URL):

```
sailing {display: block;
         background-image: url(sailboat.jpg)
        }
```

Using Fonts

From a presentation standpoint, one of the Web's major shortcomings is the lack of a smoothly functioning mechanism to support authors' font choices. With HTML, you could assign a fixed font name to a given element, but you couldn't be certain whether the font you chose was actually present and installed on the user's system. CSS Level 1 started to improve the situation by introducing font name matching, providing a mechanism by which browsers can use similar fonts if the exact match isn't available. The Level 2 specification introduces a mechanism by which browsers can download a font from the Internet, if necessary.

Generic Fonts

When you specify a generic font name (see Table 17.1), the browser looks for an installed font that has the font's characteristics. For example, suppose you format an element with the sans-serif generic font. If somebody is browsing your page using a Mac, she will see Helvetica. If, instead, she's using Windows 95, she will see Arial.

Table 17.1 Generic Font Names

Name	Looks like
cursive	Script
fantasy	Comic
monospace	Courier
sans-serif	Helvetica or Arial
serif	Times Roman

The only downside here is that you can't get too specific about which font you would like the browser to use, and that takes a lot of the fun and artistry out of designing your document using fonts. Still, this is a lot better than the default font situation, in which browsers display documents using the same, old, boring default fonts.

The "Take Your Pick" Route

There is another way to solve the font problem: Give the browser a list of font options so that it can check to see whether any of them are installed on the user's system. You can use the font-family property to do this. Here's the font-family property definition:

PROPERTY	font-family
PURPOSE	Defines font typeface and alternates (in order of preference)
INHERITED	Yes
VALUES	Font names or font family names, in a comma-separated list (in order of preference). Font family names: serif, sans-serif, cursive, fantasy, monospace
DEFAULT	Determined by browser

See the following example of the font-family property applied to a root element style definition. This defines a family of related system fonts (fonts installed on the user's system), any one of which can be used for the base font of the document (the font that is supposed to be used unless there is some specific instruction to the contrary):

```
fave  {  display: block;
         font-family: Helvetica, Arial,
         "Avant Garde", sans-serif
         }
```

In this property definition, you see a list of fonts (four of them), separated by commas. It tells the browser to look for the Helvetica font. If that's not found, the browser looks for the Arial font. If Arial is not found, the browser looks for Avant Garde. Only if the last font isn't found does the browser fall back on the default font.

Note that "Avant Garde" is surrounded by quotation marks; this is necessary for font names of two words or more. Also, notice that the last font in the list is the generic sans-serif, as a fallback in case none of the others are present.

Choosing a Font Size

You add font size specifications with the font size property. Here's the property definition:

PROPERTY	font-size
PURPOSE	Defines font size
INHERITED	Yes
VALUES	Absolute sizes (xx-small, x-small, small, medium, large, x-large, or xx-large), relative sizes (larger or smaller), font size measurement (in pts, in., cm, px, or em), or percentage in relation to parent element
DEFAULT	Medium

Downloading Fonts with CSS Level 2

The just-released Cascading Style Sheets Level 2 specification provides much better support for fonts; it supplies a method to support font downloading in case the font you've chosen isn't present on the user's system.

The key lies in the CSS Level 2 property called @font-face. (The @ sign tells the browser it's supposed to import some data.) Here's the @font-face definition:

PROPERTY	@font-face
PURPOSE	Indicates name and location of a downloadable font
INHERITED	No
VALUES	Includes a font-family descriptor and the url of the downloadable file, as shown in the example below
DEFAULT	Determined by browser

Here's an example that illustrates how to use @font-face in your style sheet. Note that @font-face is a command, and it comes before the rules that make use of the font:

```
@font-face {
    font-family: Shakespeare;
    src: url(www.historic-fonts.org/fonts/
    shakespeare)
    }

stage-direction { display: block;
                  font-family: Shakespeare;
                }
```

Character Styles for Inline or Block Elements

A number of CSS properties are used to define character styles, including emphases. You can use these to define inline or block elements. For example, you could create an element called <italics>, and write a rule that defines it as an inline element:

```
italics   {     display: inline;
                font-style: italic;
          }
```

You could also assign an italic style to a block element, such as the following:

```
heading-2 {     display: block;
                font-style: italic;
          }
```

Using Small Caps

The font-variant property enables you to choose small caps.

PROPERTY	font-variant
PURPOSE	Enables font variations such as small caps
INHERITED	Yes
VALUES	Normal or small-caps
DEFAULT	Normal

See the following example that shows how to specify small caps for an XML heading element:

```
heading-2 {  display: block;
             font-variant: small-caps;
          }
```

Determining Weight (Boldness)

With the font-weight property, you can specify the boldness of a font with precision.

Here's the property definition:

PROPERTY	font-weight
PURPOSE	Determines weight (boldness) of font
INHERITED	Yes
VALUES	Normal or bold. You can also specify a numerical weight ranging from 100 (light) to 900 (dark), or relative weights (bolder or lighter).
DEFAULT	normal

The following shows how to specify bold for an element called "emphatic":

```
emphatic  { display: inline;
            font-weight: bold;
          }
```

Adding Space between Letters

To create special effects, you can add extra spacing between letters.

PROPERTY	letter-spacing
PURPOSE	Adds to the default spacing between characters
INHERITED	Yes
VALUES	Specify a length
DEFAULT	normal

Here's a heading element that adds space between characters:

```
heading-2 {  display: block;
             font-variant: small-caps;
             letter-spacing: 1pt;
          }
```

Adding Text Decorations

With the text-decoration property, you can specify a number of special emphasis formats, including line-through (strikeover), line-over, and blinking text.

Please use blinking text sparingly! Many Web users find blinking text to be annoying, distracting, and hard to read.

PROPERTY	text-decoration
PURPOSE	Adds decorations (such as strike-through) to text
INHERITED	Yes
VALUES	none, underline, overline, line-through, or blink
DEFAULT	none

The following illustrates a text paragraph element formatted with a first-line indent:

```
body-text {  display: block;
             text-align: justify;
          }
```

Getting Control of Block Element Layout

The following sections introduce the most useful properties for controlling the appearance of any block element in your XML document.

Text Alignment

To align text (left, center, right, or justified), use the text-align attribute. Here's the property definition:

PROPERTY	text-align
PURPOSE	Controls horizontal alignment of text

INHERITED	Yes
VALUES	Left, center, right, or justify
DEFAULT	Left

Here's an example of text alignment added to a heading element's style:

```
heading-2 {  display: block;
             font-variant: small-caps;
             text-align: center;
          }
```

Text Foreground Color

To color all the characters within an element, define the element using the color property. The property definition follows:

PROPERTY	color
PURPOSE	Specifies the foreground color of an element
INHERITED	Yes
VALUES	Color code or mnemonic
DEFAULT	Defined by browser

The following illustrates the use of this property in the heading element example:

```
heading-2 {  display: block;
             font-variant: small-caps;
             text-align: center;
             color: red;
          }
```

Text Indentation (First Line)

Document designers sometimes like to indent the first line of each paragraph of text. With CSS, you can do this, too. You use the text-indent property.

Here is the property definition:

PROPERTY	text-indent
PURPOSE	Indents the first line of text
INHERITED	Yes
VALUES	Any valid length or a percentage of the element's width
DEFAULT	0

The following illustrates the use of this property to control first-line indentation in a text paragraph:

```
body-text {  display: block;
             text-align: justify;
             first-line: 0.5in;
          }
```

Line Spacing

To control line spacing, use the line-height property, defined as follows:

PROPERTY	line-height
PURPOSE	Specifies the height (the distance between the baselines) of each line of text in an element
INHERITED	No
VALUES	Specify a number to multiply with the current font height, a length, or a percentage of the current font size, or auto (same as font size)
DEFAULT	Auto

The following illustrates the use of this property to add double spacing in a text paragraph:

```
body-text {  display: block;
             text-align: justify;
             line-height: 2;
             first-line: 0.5in;
          }
```

Understanding the Box Formatting Model

As you've already learned, block elements create a *containing block* when you place them in your document. In this section, you learn about the containing block's properties.

Properties of the Containing Block

The CSS Level 1 style sheet specification envisions a box formatting model, in which each element resides in a rectangular box. A box can fit within a box, like Chinese boxes.

In Figure 17.1, you see how the various boxes fit together, using three separately defined properties:

- **Margins.** Transparent space indented from the document window.
- **Borders.** Rules in a variety of styles.
- **Padding.** Space that is placed between the borders and the object.

Table 17.2 introduces some useful terminology for talking about the box formatting model.

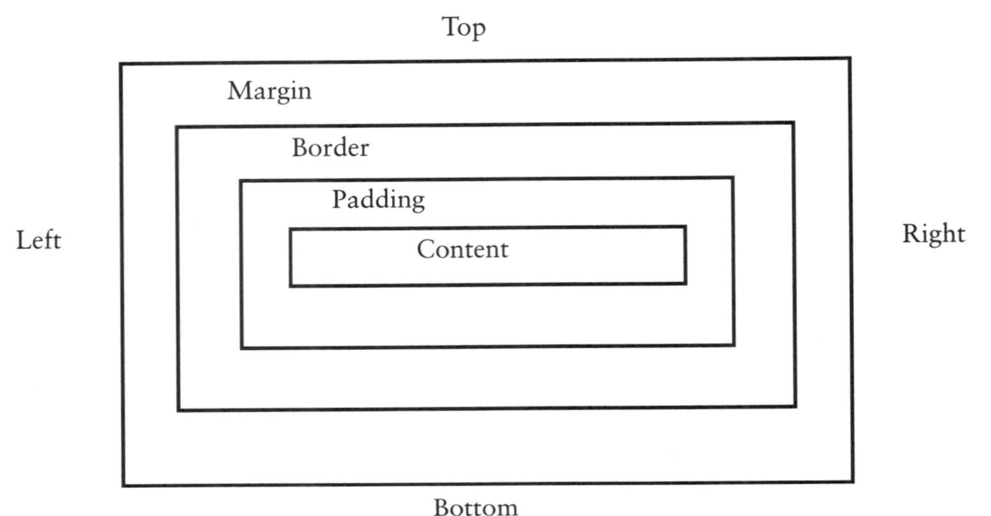

Figure 17.1 The CSS box formatting model.

Table 17.2 Useful Terms for Box Formatting

Term	Definition
left outer edge	The left edge of the box, taking into account the margin, border, and padding.
left inner edge	The left edge of the enclosed content.
right outer edge	The right edge of the box, taking into account the margin, border, and padding.
right inner edge	The right edge of the enclosed content.
top	Top of the box, including the margin, border, and padding.
bottom	Bottom of the box, including the margin, border, and padding.
width	Width of the enclosed content. If you box a

	replaceable element (such as an image), the default width is the width of the replaced element. (If you specify a different width, the browser resizes the element.) If you box a block-line element, the default value of the width is "auto," which means that the browser calculates the element's width so that the seven horizontal elements (left and right margin, border, and padding, plus the content itself) equal the width of the parent element.
height	Height of the enclosed content. If you box a replaceable element (such as an image), the height is the height of the replaced element. (If you specify a different height, the browser resizes the element.) If you box a block element, the default height is calculated by the current line height settings (which depend on the font size you choose).

CSS Box Formatting Model: Rules

You can independently place rules on any side of the element: top, right, bottom, and left. In addition, you can also independently adjust the size and color of each border.

To create borders, you can define the border properties independently using separate properties for the top, right, bottom, and left sides. These properties include color and width. You can also define border styles (including dotted and dashed lines).

The easiest way to define borders, though, is to use the border shorthand property, which enables you to specify all the borders at once. You can also use the shorthand property to determine which borders are added, either all four or any combination of individual borders. Begin by examining the properties for individual borders; you will learn how to use the border shorthand property at the end of this section.

Border Colors

To define the color of borders around an element, you can use the following properties: border-top-color, border-right-color, border-bottom-color, and border-left-color. The following property definition sums up all four of these:

PROPERTY	border-top-color, border-right-color, border-bottom-color, and border-left-color
PURPOSE	Specifies one of the four border colors individually
INHERITED	Yes
VALUES	Specify a color code or mnemonic
DEFAULT	Value of the color property for the current element

Instead of defining all these border color properties independently, you will find it convenient to use the border-color shorthand property, defined as follows:

PROPERTY	border-color
PURPOSE	Provides a shorthand means of specifying color settings for all borders
INHERITED	Yes
VALUES	Specify colors for the top, right, bottom, and left borders, in that order. If you specify only one value, it applies to all four sides. If you specify two values, you define the top and bottom. If you specify three values, you define the top, bottom, and sides (left and right), respectively.
DEFAULT	Not defined

The following example shows how borders can be placed around all four sides of a block element:

```
review    {  display: block;
             border: thin blue solid;
          }
```

In the border-color style, as in other shorthand border styles, you can specify from one to four borders, but you will need to learn how. Table 17.3 sums up the technique used to specify borders, depending on the number of values you type. For example, if you type "border-color: navy white," you've typed two values.

Table 17.3 Specifying Borders in Border Shorthand Styles

Specified nos.	Border location
one	The value applies to all four sides.
two	The first value defines the top, while the second value defines the bottom.
three	The first value defines the top, while the second value defines the left and right. The third value defines the bottom.
four	The values apply to the top, right, bottom, and left, respectively.

Border Widths

Just as you can define colors for the four borders independently, so too can you define widths. As with colors, there are separate properties for the width of all four borders, and there is a shorthand border-width property. Let's look at the separate properties first. Here's the element definition for border-top-width, border-right-width, border-bottom-width, and border-left-width.

PROPERTY	border-top-width, border-right-width, border-bottom-width, and border-left-width
PURPOSE	Specifies the width of a specific border
INHERITED	Yes
VALUES	Specify thin, medium, or thick; or type a length
DEFAULT	0

Here's the property definition for the border-width style, which gives you a shorthand way of defining border widths for all four sides:

PROPERTY	border-width
PURPOSE	Provides a shorthand means of specifying width settings for all borders
INHERITED	Yes
VALUES	Specify lengths for the top, right, bottom, and left borders, in that order. If you specify only one value, it applies to all four sides. If you specify two values, you define the top and bottom. If you specify three values, you define the top, bottom, and sides (left and right), respectively.
DEFAULT	Not defined

Border Styles

In addition to border colors and widths, you can also choose border styles (dotted, dashed, solid, double, groove, ridge, inset, outset). Not all of these styles are supported, even by ostensibly CSS-capable browsers, so use styles other than solid with caution.

As with colors and widths, there are separate styles for the individual borders and a shorthand property that enables you to define them all. Here is the property definition for the border-style-top, border-style-right, border-style-bottom, and border-style-right properties:

PROPERTY	border-style-top, border-style-right, border-style-bottom, and border-style-right
PURPOSE	Specifies the color of the box's bottom border
INHERITED	Yes
VALUES	none, dotted, dashed, solid, double, groove, ridge, inset, outset
DEFAULT	Value of the color property for the current element

Here's the property definition for the border-style shorthand property:

PROPERTY	border-style
PURPOSE	Provides a shorthand means of specifying color settings for all borders
INHERITED	Yes
VALUES	Specify styles for the top, right, bottom, and left borders, in that order. If you specify only one value, it applies to all four sides. You can choose from none, dotted, dashed, solid, double, groove, ridge, inset, outset.
DEFAULT	Not defined

Summing It All Up: The Border Shorthand Property

Do you have to write a zillion style specifications to add borders to your elements? Nope. You can use the border shorthand property. Here is the definition:

PROPERTY	border
PURPOSE	Provides a shorthand means of specifying all types of properties for all borders
INHERITED	Yes
VALUES	Specify any value used in the border color, border style, or border width properties
DEFAULT	0

CSS Box Properties: Padding

Padding is inserted between the element and the borders. As with margins and borders, you can add padding all around or to each of the sides independently. You can specify the size of the padding.

Defining Padding for Individual Padding Zones

The following properties add padding zones individually to the top, right, bottom, or left sides of an element. The padding appears between the element and the border.

PROPERTY	padding-top, padding-right, padding-bottom, and padding-left
PURPOSE	Provides a means of specifying settings for individual padding zones
INHERITED	Yes
VALUES	Specify a length or percentage of the enclosing element
DEFAULT	Not defined

Using the Padding Shorthand Property

Here is a shorthand property that enables you to define all padding zones at once:

PROPERTY	padding
PURPOSE	Provides a shorthand means of specifying settings for all padding zones
INHERITED	Yes
VALUES	Specify lengths for the top, right, bottom, and left padding zones, in that order. If you specify only one value, it applies to all four sides. If you specify two values, you have defined the top and bottom. If you specify three values, you define the top, bottom, and sides (left and right), respectively.
DEFAULT	Not defined

CSS Box Properties: Margins

To create margins, you use the CSS margin properties. In CSS, the term *margin* doesn't refer to the whitespace found around the edges of a page in a printed medium, but rather the whitespace around a block element. The term *indent* might be more appropriate, although you can use negative measurements to "outdent" margins too.

As with borders, you can define margins independently by using the individual properties (here, margin-left, margin-right, margin-bottom, and margin-top), or you can use the shorthand property (margin) to define them all at once.

You'll find the shorthand property much easier to use than the individual margin properties; it enables you to set all the margins at once.

Defining Margins Individually

Here are the properties you can use to define margins individually.

PROPERTY	margin-left, margin-right, margin-bottom, and margin-top
PURPOSE	Specifies the width of the box's bottom margin
INHERITED	Yes
VALUES	Specify a length or a percentage of the containing block
DEFAULT	0

Using the Margin Shorthand Property

You can define all four margins at once with the margin shorthand property. Like other shorthand properties that you'll learn in this chapter, it's vastly preferable to typing out separate definitions of the left, right, bottom, and top margins. Here is the definition for the margin shorthand property:

PROPERTY	margin
PURPOSE	Provides a shorthand means of specifying settings for all margins
INHERITED	Yes
VALUES	Specify lengths for the top, right, bottom, and left borders, in that order. If you specify only one value, it applies to all four sides. If you specify two values, you define the top and bottom. If you specify three values, you define the top, bottom, and sides (left and right), respectively.
DEFAULT	Not defined

CSS Box Properties: Controlling Element Size

By default, the boxed element's width and height are set to auto, which means the following:

- **Width.** The browser sizes the element's height based on the size of the original replaceable element or the line height of text.
- **Height.** The browser sizes the element's width based on the size of the original replaceable element. For text blocks, the auto setting sizes the width dynamically based on the available space after margins, borders, and padding are taken into account.

You can override these settings by using the width or height properties or both.

Using the Height Property

Here's the definition for the height property:

PROPERTY	height
PURPOSE	Specifies the height of an element
INHERITED	No
VALUES	Specify a length or a percentage of the containing block, or auto
DEFAULT	auto

Using the Width Property

Here is the definition for the width property:

PROPERTY	width
PURPOSE	Specifies the width of an element
INHERITED	No
VALUES	Specify a length or a percentage of the containing block, or auto
DEFAULT	auto

CSS Horizons

This chapter has explored the essentials of creating CSS style sheets for your XML documents, but there isn't room to mention many of CSS's more advanced features. These include:

- **Floating elements.** You can float any block element to the left or right of a containing block, so that text flows around it.
- **Absolute positioning.** You can fix an element's position anywhere within a containing block so that it

doesn't move, even if text or elements are inserted above it.

- **Three-dimensional positioning.** You can fix element positions so that they appear in overlapping layers; in this way, you can position text over a graphic image, for example.
- **Fixed positioning.** You can fix an element's position relative to the display window, providing XML authors with an answer to HTML's frames.
- **Automatic numbering of elements and list items.** For XML authors, this is an important substitute for HTML's automatic numbering capabilities, which don't exist in XML.
- **Pagination for printing.** You can insert page breaks and specify print margins.

From Here

In this chapter, you learned a great deal about how to control XML document presentation using CSS style sheets. You learned how to assign background colors and images to your XML document's root element. You learned how to use fonts and character emphases, and how to control basic block element formats such as text alignment and line spacing. You learned more about the CSS box formatting model, and explored the many properties for adding margin, borders, and padding to your block elements. In the next chapter, you examine the XSL proposal and learn what XSL can do that CSS can't.

18

Advanced Style Sheets with XSL

Although Cascading Style Sheets (CSS) will meet the needs of most readers of this book, there's a more advanced style sheet language in the works. It's called Extensible Style Language (XSL). Currently, XSL is in the hands of a W3C working group, but the language isn't past the proposal stage, and much is expected to change. Consequently, this chapter serves only to introduce XSL concepts and to illustrate some of the areas where it may prove useful.

What's Wrong with CSS?

The basic problem lies in the fact that CSS is a *declarative style sheet language*. A declarative language (of any type) can be used to declare what something is, but it can't really undertake any procedures (at least on its own) to *do* something to the declared data. As you learned in the previous chapter, CSS includes some rudimentary section numbering capabilities, but it lacks the *procedural* capacity to generate numbered pages for printed output. That's a very serious deficiency, and it's not easy to remedy, given the basic fact that CSS is a declarative rather than a procedural language.

What's So Great about XSL?

XSL is a *procedural* style language. This means that it doesn't merely declare which style goes with which element. (As you'll see, it can do this, and you can even incorporate CSS into XSL to pull this off.) Far more importantly, XSL can *process* an XML document and generate output on the fly. In XSL terminology, the result of an XSL operation is output called a *flow object*, which is in the form of a tree composed of formatting containers (blocks and subblocks). You'll learn more about this concept later in this chapter. For now, let's look at the significance of the fact that XSL processes XML data rather than merely assigning styles to elements.

One major gain lies in the area of printing, which CSS doesn't handle very well. XSL output could take the form of a file written in a printer-savvy language such as PostScript or RTF—or, for ease of display on the Web, HTML. Unlike CSS, which tells the browser how to display an XML document, XSL takes the data in this document, processes it, and generates completely new output. And just what it generates is up to the XSL application's designers.

The fact that XSL is a procedural language enables users to do other things that aren't possible with CSS, such as rearranging and sorting content for output purposes.

In general, XSL will appeal to those who view XML data as a resource for applications, rather than something to be viewed directly by means of a visual browser. XSL is a perfect ancillary to applications that take XML data and perform processing operations on it; XSL fits in as an ideal way to add good-looking presentation styles to the final displayed output (which may contain only a small subset of the data actually stored in the XML document).

Who's Working on XSL?

XSL is being shaped by a working group chartered by the World Wide Web Consortium (W3C). This activity got going after three companies (Microsoft, Inso, and ArborText) submitted a very well-thought-out proposal, which will very likely form much of the basis of the final W3C Recommendation. For the latest information, check out the Consortium's web site (*www.w3.org*).

XSL and DSSSL

One way to look at XSL is to view it as a simplified version of the Document Style Semantics and Specification Language (DSSSL), the SGML-associated style programming language introduced in Chapter 2. That's not quite accurate, though, since XSL draws a lot from CSS. What's more, XSL draws on the familiar XML syntax rather than requiring you to learn something entirely new (as DSSSL does).

Essentials of XSL

Without going into the details of XSL, here's an overview of how the language works. Essentially, you write *construction rules*, which specify how to locate elements in the source document and transform them into objects for the flow object tree (the generated output). You can add styles to the rule that specify how the output is supposed to look.

Construction Rules

A construction rule consists of two parts: a matching pattern and a result. The simplest matching pattern names an element:

```
<element>
    <target-element type = "novel">
</element>
```

This pattern selects all the <novel> elements in the document.

As for actions, you need to specify what type of flow object you're going to create. (Recall that XML provides no means to distinguish between block and inline elements, so you have to do this for each element you want to display.) Examples of flow objects are block elements such as paragraphs, tables, and lists, as well as inline elements (called *sequences*).

When you write the construction rule, you can specify styles as well as the flow object type, as in the following example:

```
<paragraph       font-size="12pt"
                 line-spacing="24pt">
    <children/>
</paragraph>
```

This part of the construction rule creates a paragraph flow object, with the specified formats. The <children/> element specifies that all the element's children inherit these styles.

Looking at a Complete Rule

Here's the complete construction rule for the <novel> element:

```
<rule>
    <target-element type = "novel">
    <paragraph  font-size="12pt"
      line-spacing="24pt">
      <children/>
    </paragraph>
</rule>
```

This rule takes each <novel> element and produces a flow object tree consisting of a series of paragraphs in which each <novel> element is formatted as a paragraph (12 pt. type and double line spacing).

Transforming the Output

Since XSL is generating output on the fly, there's no reason why you can't generate output in some other markup language, if you like. Here's the same rule written so that the element's children are formatted as <H2> elements in HTML:

```
<rule>
    <target-element type = "novel">
    <H2><children/></H2>
</rule>
```

XSL Horizons

This brief introduction is intended only to illustrate the essentials of how XSL works. As you might imagine, the language has many more options and possibilities, including the following:

- **Pattern matching.** As with CSS selectors, you can write much more sophisticated matching patterns than the simple ones illustrated here. For example, you can write matching patterns that retrieve only those elements in which a certain attribute value has been specified.
- **Filtering.** You can write construction rules that sort the output—for example, by alphabetizing items in a list.
- **Repetition.** You can specify that a given element's content appears more than once—for example, a header at the top of every printed page.
- **Numbering.** You'll be able to specify automatic numbering in the output, but the current proposal doesn't handle this yet.
- **CSS support.** You can write *style rules* that enable you to assign the same, named style to more than one element.
- **Macros.** You can write a series of commands that specify how a flow object is to be put together.

- **Scripts.** XSL fully supports ECMAScript, the standardized version of JavaScript.

As this section suggests, XSL could grow into a very useful tool—especially if the promised support from printed output materializes. That's one area that CSS doesn't handle well, and isn't likely to, considering that it's a declarative language. For now, XSL is mainly used to transform XML data into HTML output for publication to the Web.

---

*For the latest news concerning XSL, check the World Wide Web Consortium's home page (*www.w3.org*).*

From Here

With this chapter, you've come to the conclusion of Part Five. In Part Six, you look at some of the vocabularies that have been developed with XML.

Part Six

Exploring XML Vocabularies

19

Channel Definition Format (CDF)

If you're wondering about whether XML can really work on the Web, rest assured. It already does. In version 4.0 of Microsoft Internet Explorer, Microsoft Corporation implemented an XML vocabulary called the Channel Definition Format (CDF), created an XML-based vocabulary for CDF, and developed an XML processor to read CDF information and pass it on to Internet Explorer. Tens of thousands of Web sites are using CDF to enable users to subscribe to these sites and receive regular notifications of site updates.

CDF is worth exploring for at least three very good reasons. First, it's an excellent illustration of how one of XML's design goals can be implemented—namely, by supporting a range of applications. CDF information doesn't appear on-screen. Instead, the XML processor passes the information to special code within Internet Explorer, which displays a wizard that helps the user choose subscription options. Second, it's useful. Although CDF is currently supported only by Internet Explorer, it's still a great way to enable this browser's users to keep in touch with your site. And third, CDF illustrates the analytical process one must go through to create a new vocabulary. As you'll see, the CDF design takes into account the elements needed to specify update intervals and subscription options — and what's more, how to miminize adverse effects on the Internet should a site prove so popular that many thousands of people subscribe.

Introducing CDF

How would you like your Web page to be positioned on the Windows desktops of hundreds or even thousands of visitors, so that changes to your Web page are automatically downloaded and displayed for them to see? That's what you can do with push publishing. In contrast to pull publishing, where people have to find your page and go to it deliberately, push publishing brings your page to users' desktops. Once they've subscribed, they don't need to do anything to see site updates. It's all automatic. What's more, changes are downloaded in the background, and in their entirety, so users can browse your page while they're offline, if they wish.

How CDF Channels Work

Microsoft's Channel Definition Format (CDF) requires users to create a separate file (with the CDF extension) that's written using the special CDF elements. Created with XML (and defined by a DTD), CDF is easy to learn. Anyone who knows HTML can quickly create a CDF file that enables users to subscribe to a Web site.

When visitors access a page with CDF capabilities, they can click a link that enables them to initiate and configure the subscription. After clicking the link, they see the dialog box shown in Figure 19.1. They can choose from the following options:

- **Adding the page to the channel lists, without subscribing.** The channel lists appear in the Channel Explorer (a special window that appears when users click the Channels button on the standard toolbar), the Channels folder within the Favorites menu, and the Channel Guide, a window that appears on the desktop when the Active Desktop is enabled.

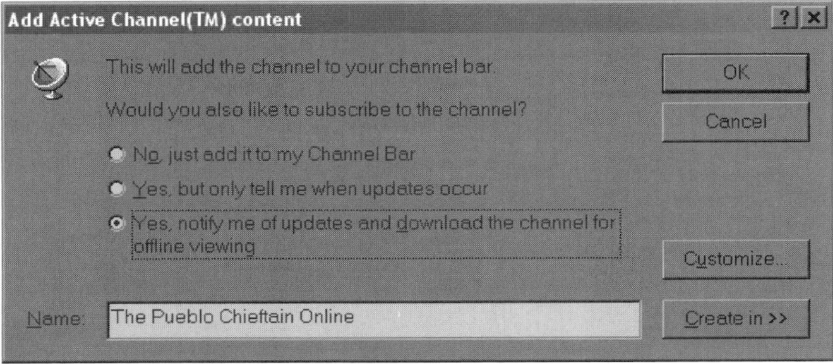

Figure 19.1 Initiating the subscription.

- **Subscribing with notification of updates.** Users see a flag next to the page's title, but Internet Explorer doesn't automatically download the page. If users choose this option, they can also choose to receive notifications via e-mail. (This doesn't require any effort on the user's part; the mail originates from within Internet Explorer once it detects that your site has changed.)
- **Subscribing with notification of updates and automatic downloading of new content.** As in the previous option, they can, if they wish, receive notifications via e-mail. Users can choose to download only the page to which they subscribed (the default option) or all the content specified by the channel. By default, the downloads take place at the publisher's recommended schedule, or the user can choose other downloading times (daily, weekly, or monthly). Users can also determine how much to download; for example, they can choose to download all the pages linked to the subscribed page up to a link depth they specify. This feature is especially attractive to Web users who would like to download extensive amounts of content at night when they're not using their computers, and then view the content offline during the day.

After users subscribe, they'll see the page in the Channel Explorer, as well as the other channel lists. Clicking the page brings it up very quickly if the user chooses to download the content.

In addition to inserting content within the various channel lists, you can also direct content to windows on the user's desktop and to the user's screen saver.

Randomizing Accesses

What happens if thousands of users subscribe to your page? With other subscription schemes that assign a fixed update time, the updating activity could overwhelm your server. That's why CDF incorporates a novel scheme to randomize updating (within given schedule parameters that you specify).

Creating a CDF Channel

To transform an existing Web page into a channel to which MSIE version 4 users can subscribe, you need to create a logo, an icon, and a CDF file, and upload all of these to your server. In addition, you need to add a link to the page you want to "push." In this section, you'll do this the easy way, without worrying about the many available options. As you'll see, it's really easy to do this – try it!

Creating the Logo

So that your page will display properly within Internet Explorer's various channel-related lists and dialog boxes, you need to create two graphics. The first, sized 80 by 32 pixels, is your channel's logo. This doesn't have to be elaborate, but it does have to be exactly 80 x 32. You can create this graphic using a graphics program such as Paint Shop Pro.

Creating the Icon

Next, you need to create an icon that's exactly 16 by 16 pixels. This isn't a lot of space, so don't try to cram in too much detail.

Creating the XML Channel File

The last file you need is the channel definition file, which is written in XML. You can easily modify the following file to create your subscription. Edit and save the file, naming it channel.cdf. (You can use any filename you want besides "channel," but you must use the cdf extension.)

```
<?XML VERSION="1.0" ENCODING="UTF-8"?>
<CHANNEL HREF="URL of your page">
<TITLE>Your Title Here</TITLE>
<ABSTRACT>Your Abstract Here</ABSTRACT>
<LOGO HREF="URL of your 16 x 16 icon"
STYLE="icon"/>
<LOGO HREF="URL of your 80 x 32 logo"
STYLE="image"/>
</CHANNEL>
```

Looks like HTML, doesn't it? Here's how to modify the above code, line by line:

- ` On line 1, just copy the example exactly (<?XML VERSION="1.0" ENCODING="UTF-8"?>). This tells the browser that the file to follow conforms to XML version 1.0.
- On line 2, modify the CHANNEL element to contain the URL of the Web page you're offering for subscription.
- In the TITLE element (line 3), type a brief title. There's room for about 40 characters in MSIE's channel bars, so don't exceed this amount.
- In the ABSTRACT element (line 4), type a description of your site – what it's about, what it has to offer, why people should subscribe. You can type two or three sentences here. It will show up in an extended tool tip box.

- On line 5, type the URL of your icon.
- On line 6, type the URL of your logo.
- Don't forget the CHANNEL element's end tag.

That's all there is to it!

Carefully check your work to make sure you've typed everything correctly. In particular, note the peculiar XML syntax for close tags: />. Don't forget the slash!

Adding a Link

To enable users to subscribe to your site, just create an ordinary hyperlink (using the A element) on the page you want to push. Link to the CDF file you created. Be sure to tell users that the link works only if they're accessing the page with Microsoft Internet Explorer version 4.

Uploading the Channel Information

To test your CDF file, you must upload the following to your server:

- Icon
- Logo
- CDF file
- New version of page with hyperlink to the CDF file

You must upload all of these in order to test your work, unless you're running a Web server on your computer. CDF requires a Web server.

Testing the Channel

After you've uploaded the CDF file, use MSIE version 4 to access your page and click the link you inserted. You should see a dialog box that enables you to specify subscription preferences. (If you don't, there's an error in the file. Carefully check your typing, upload the corrected file, and try again.)

Specifying the Schedule with CDF

The easy-to-use CDF file just introduced doesn't specify a schedule. This means that your page won't get updated unless the user deliberately updates the content. That's not likely to happen very often. To specify an update frequency, use the SCHEDULE element.

Introducing the SCHEDULE Element

This element is designed to avoid a potentially huge problem. If you could specify an absolute update time, what would happen if your page became popular and thousands of browsers tried to update at the same time? Your server would go down. So the SCHEDULE element specifies a time frame within which updates can occur; a single update will occur within this period. You can also specify an earliest time within the time frame, as well as a latest time, to gain some control over the update timing; nevertheless, the browser is free to choose a random update time within these constraints.

The SCHEDULE element must appear directly beneath the first CHANNEL element, as shown here:

```
<?XML VERSION="1.0" ENCODING="UTF-8"?>
<CHANNEL HREF="URL of your page">
```

```
        <TITLE>Your Title Here</TITLE>
        <ABSTRACT>Your Abstract Here</ABSTRACT>
        <LOGO HREF="URL of your 16 x 16 icon"
        STYLE="icon" />
        <LOGO HREF="URL of your 80 x 32 logo"
        STYLE="image" />
        <SCHEDULE>
        <INTERVALTIME day = "1">
        </SCHEDULE>
</CHANNEL>
```

Specifying the Time Interval

To define the time interval, you use the intervaltime attribute. Valid values are day, hour, and min (minute). If you set the interval time to day = "7," you're telling the browser to update the page once per week. If you set the interval time to day = "1," you're telling the browser to update the page once per day.

You can also define hourly schedules. If you set the interval time to hour = "6," you're telling the browser to update the page four times per day. Beginning at midnight, there are four periods within which updates will occur: midnight to 6 am, 6 am to 12 noon, 12 noon to 6 pm, and 6 pm to midnight.

Minute schedules work the same way: They establish the number of minutes during which an update occurs once. If you specify a time interval of min = "90," one update will occur within each 90-minute period.

If you specify an earliest time or latest time, you can control the earliest time and the latest time within which an update will occur during the interval. You can do this with the EARLIESTTIME and LATESTTIME elements, which are nested within the SCHEDULE element. For example, suppose you've created a 24-hour interval. If you specify an earliest time of hour = "2" and a latest time of hour = "6," you've told the browser to update the page only between 2 am and 6 am each day. (This isn't a very good idea, though, because most people don't leave their computers running all night.) If you leave out the EARLIESTTIME and LATESTTIME elements, the browser chooses a time at random within the interval you've specified.

Specifying the Beginning and Ending Dates

Optionally, you can specify the beginning and ending dates for the subscription. You do this by using the startdate and enddate attributes of the SCHEDULE element, and specifying a date using the following syntax:

```
YYYY-MM-DD (example:  1998-02-20)
```

Sample Schedules

The first sample schedule establishes a daily interval, with an update occurring sometime between 9 am and 6 pm. The updates run from January 1, 1998, to December 31, 1998, with no further updates after that time.

```
<Schedule StartDate="1998.01.01 End-
Date="1998.12.31">
    <IntervalTime DAY="1" />
    <EarliestTime HOUR="9" />
    <LatestTime HOUR="18" />
</Schedule>
```

Here's a weekly schedule. There's no beginning or end date, which means that the schedule begins when the user subscribes and doesn't end at any particular time. There's no earliest or latest time specified, which means that the update takes place at a random time during the week.

```
<Schedule>
    <IntervalTime DAY="7" />
</Schedule>
```

From Here

In this next chapter, you'll look at another XML vocabulary, the Synchronized Multimedia Integration Language (SMIL), which could bring to the Internet a new, nonproprietary markup language for multimedia authoring.

20

Synchronized Multimedia Integration Language (SMIL)

Pronounced "smile," the Synchronized Multimedia Integration Language (SMIL) is an XML-based language for writing TV-like multimedia presentations on the World Wide Web. In contrast to currently available Web tools, there's no easy way (short of extensive programming) to implement timed or synchronized multimedia presentations, such as showing an image for 20 seconds while an audio track plays. Currently, SMIL is a Proposed Recommendation of the World Wide Web Consortium (W3C)—the particulars may change when the final recommendation is issued—but the language is stable enough to discuss it here. The W3C's SMIL working group includes key industry players such as AT&T/Bell Labs, Microsoft Corporation, Netscape Communications, Philips, RealNetworks, and Sun Microsystems.

Like CDF, SMIL is written with the realities of Web publishing in mind. It's simple—there are only six elements to learn—and it's amazingly flexible. Recognizing that Web bandwidth is often severely limited, SMIL enables authors to create multiple presentation choices for differing bandwidths. In addition, SMIL recognizes the diversity of multimedia object types on the Web; it can work with audio, MIDI, video, text, images, and graphics; and it's extensible by design, so that new multimedia types can be handled without having to reinvent the language from scratch. And despite its simplicity, SMIL's underlying design embodies an extremely clever mathematical concept that gives SMIL enormous flexibility. (Here's another reason to think about leaving vocabulary creation to the experts—here, people who have a great deal of experience trying to deliver multimedia via the Web, and the mathematical background to build incredible flexibility into a very simple DTD.)

This chapter discusses the most recent version of SMIL, which has not yet been finalized by the World Web Consortium (W3C). Some of the elements and attributes discussed in this chapter may change when the Consortium publishes the final version.

This chapter introduces SMIL and shows how easy it is to incorporate SMIL markup for synchronized multimedia presentations. As you'll see, anyone who knows HTML can learn SMIL in short order. (Here, I'm assuming you've learned at least a bit of HTML, so I won't go into concepts such as relative and absolute URLs.) And the results are cool. Imagine a page in which an image appears; a few seconds later, some text appears beside it, and a sound starts playing. The presentation could go on for hours, if you wish, with text, images, sounds, videos, and animations popping up and doing their thing, all under your direction. And all without programming!

Start with a SMILe

Creating a SMIL file is easy—just as easy as creating an HTML file. You can use any word processing or text editor program that can save output as plain (ASCII) text. SMIL files should contain nothing but SMIL markup, and you should save them using the standard SMIL extension, *.smi.

Anyone who knows HTML can create a SMIL file in short order. However, there are some important differences between SMIL and HTML. Keep the following in mind when you're creating SMIL documents:

- **All elements must be in lowercase letters.** You may be used to typing HTML element names (such as <BLOCKQUOTE>) in upper case so that you can distinguish the element name from surrounding text. Don't do this with SMIL!
- **All attribute values must be surrounded with quotation marks.** HTML is lax in this regard, but SMIL isn't.
- **All markup must conform to XML syntax rules.** This includes using XML's distinctive tag-ending characters (/>).

How SMIL Documents Are Organized

Every SMIL document begins and ends with SMIL tags, as follows:

```
<smil>
</smil>
```

Within the <smil> element, you can place a head and body (just as in HTML):

```
<smil>
          <head>
          </head>
          <body>
          </body>
</smil>
```

Within the head, you can place the following information:

- A title, much like the title of an HTML document.
- A META element, giving the document's author, title, and copyright information (again, much like the corresponding HTML element).

The <head> element is optional. However, if you use the <head> element, you must also use the <body> element.

Go to the <head> of the Class

What's in the <head> element? As just noted, you can insert a title (using the <title> element) and a <meta> element. Both are optional.

Using the <title> Element

If you insert a <title> element, your SMIL document's title will be displayed on the browser's title bar. This element is just like the corresponding HTML element of the same name. Here's how to insert a title:

```
<smil>
          <head>
             <title>Here's my presentation's
title</title>
          </head>
          <body>
          </body>
</smil>
```

Using the <meta> Element

The <meta> element enables you to provide information about your presentation. Again, this element works in much the same way the corresponding HTML element does—with the HTML element's corresponding limitations. The lack of a standardized language for describing a document's contents severely limits the usefulness of the <meta> element. Still, you can use it to describe the document's title and subject in a way that might increase its discoverability by certain search engines (the ones that examine <meta> elements for titles and subject keywords).

Here's an example <meta> element, which works just like the corresponding HTML tag:

```
<head>
          <meta name = "author" content=
"Jane Smith" />
          <meta name = "keywords" content =
"Rappahannock River" />
```

```
            <meta name = "title" content =
    "Rappahannock River Vistas" />
    </head>
```

Remember, to conform to XML syntax, your SMIL tags must close with the nonambiguous />, and every value must be enclosed in quotation marks.

You can use as many <meta> elements as you wish. For example, you may wish to rate your page with one of the PICs rating services, such as the Recreational Software Advisory Council (RSAC), located at *www.rsac.org*. At this site, you can register your SMIL document by filling out a questionnaire; the result is a <meta> element that you can paste in your SMIL document. Be sure to edit the HTML code so that it's XML-compliant. (See the note above.)

Additional Elements in the <head>

Besides the <meta> element, you can use *either* of the following elements in the <head>:

- **<layout>.** This element determines how the elements in the document's body appear within the displayed page. If you don't use this element, the application determines the layout.
- **<switch>.** This element enables SMIL authors to create alternative presentations with varying media types, ranging from most to least desirable. This is a great option if you want to develop a Web presentation for use under varying bandwidth conditions.

If you don't include either of these elements, the SMIL application uses the defaults. For now, let's go on with the rest of the SMIL document's structure; later sections return to the <layout> and <switch> elements.

Building a <body>

Like an HTML document, a SMIL presentation packs the visible (or audible) material into the <body> element. Just as the BODY element in HTML implicitly defines the sequence of elements that follow, so too does SMIL's <body> element implicitly define a <seq> element, in which the child elements occur in a timed sequence. Within the <body>, you can include explicit <seq> elements, as well as <par> elements (which play two or more media sources simultaneously). You'll learn how to start using these two elements in this section, but let's first take a look at ways to include media objects.

Types of Media Objects

SMIL distinguishes between two types of media objects:

- **Media objects with intrinsic duration,** such as a sound that plays for one minute. These are called *continuous media.*
- **Media objects without intrinsic duration,** such as graphic images or text. These are called *discrete media.*

To insert media objects into your SMIL document, you use the following elements:

- **<animation>.** An animation, such as an animated GIF or a ShockWave animation.
- **<audio>.** A sound file.
- **<img>.** A graphic image.

- **<video>.** A movie or video clip.
- **<text>.** Ordinary text.
- **<textstream>.** Streaming text, such as a stock ticker.
- **<ref>.** Any other media object that doesn't fall into the above categories.

Specifying Media Sources

To specify the source of a media object, you use the src attribute, just as you would with HTML's IMG tag. As with HTML, you should also specify alternate text (using the alt attribute) for the benefit of people browsing with media options unavailable. If you specify a title for the object, the browser may display this (for example, in a yellow tool tip box). Here is an example of a specified media source location:

```
<audio src= "sound.wav" alt = "drums" title
= "Drum roll"/>
```

Note that this example uses a relative URL, which refers to a sound file stored in the same location as the referring document. SMIL uses the same URL standard that HTML does, so you can refer to relative URLs as in the above example, or specify an exact location by spelling out the location with a full URL.

Playing Media Objects in Sequence with <seq>

The <seq> element enables you to define the sequence in which media objects play. Here's an example that plays three sounds in a sequence:

```
<seq>
          <audio "sound1.wav"/>
          <audio "sound2.wav"/>
```

```
        <audio "sound3.wav"/>
</seq>
```

Playing Media Objects in Parallel with <par>

The <par> element enables you to play two or more media objects simultaneously (in parallel). Obviously, this wouldn't be a very good idea if you're playing sound clips, but it's great for displaying audio and video simultaneously, as in the following example:

```
<par>
        <audio src = "sound1.wav"/>
        <video src = "movie1.mov"/>
</par>
```

Controlling Timing

Synchronization isn't possible unless you've a way of controlling timing. With SMIL, you can specify timing in a number of ways, which are illustrated in this section.

Using SMIL Clock Values

SMIL enables you to specify full clock values (hours, minutes, and seconds), partial clock values (minutes and seconds), or timecount values (a specified number of hours, minutes, or seconds). Here's how to express these clock values:

- **Full clock value:** 02:30:03 (2 hours, 30 minutes, and 3 seconds)
- **Partial clock value:** 30:03 (30 minutes and 3 seconds)
- **Timecount value:** 3s (3 seconds)

For timecount values, you may use the following abbreviations:

- **h** for hours
- **m** for minutes
- s for seconds
- **ms** for milliseconds

If you don't specify an abbreviation for a timecount value, the application defaults to seconds.

Specifying a Delay

If you specify a delay, the media object starts playing later than it would without the delay specification. In a <seq> element, inserting a delay results in an inactive period between the playing of the sequence media objects. In a <par> element, adding a delay to one of the objects causes the object to start playing later than the other ones.

To add a delay, you use the begin attribute with any of the media object elements described above. For example, the following specifies a delay of 5 seconds before the second sound starts playing:

```
<seq>
         <sound src = "sound1.wav"/>
         <sound src = "sound2.wav" begin =
"5s"/>
</seq>
```

In a <par> element, all the elements start displaying immediately, by default. However, you can use the begin attribute to control timing, if you wish. In the following example, the graphic starts displaying 30 seconds after the sound starts playing:

```
<par>
          <img src = "picture1.png" begin =
"30s" />
          <sound src = "sound1.wav"/>
</par>
```

Specifying Clip Begin and End Times

Within a continuous media object such as a video clip or sound, you can specify clip beginning and ending times. This differs from a delay; the clip beginning time specifies how far into the clip's time frame the object starts playing. In other words, the object starts playing right away, but it "fast forwards" to the point you specify. Suppose, for example, you want to skip the first 10 seconds of a sound. You could specify this as follows:

```
<src = "sound1.wav" clip-begin = "10s" />
```

In this example, the sound starts playing 10 seconds into the recording.

You can also specify an end time, if you wish to stop playing the object before it reaches its conclusion. You do this with the clip-end attribute, as follows:

```
<src = "sound1.wav" clip-end = "65s" />
```

In this example, the sound plays until it reaches the 65-second mark.

You can combine the clip-begin and clip-end attributes, as in the following:

```
<src = "sound1.wav" clip-begin = "10s" clip-
end = "65s"/>
```

Here, the sound starts playing 10 seconds into the recording, and stops 65 seconds into the recording. You don't hear the recording's first 10 seconds; you only hear the next 55 seconds of the recording.

Timing Discrete Objects

SMIL enables you to time discrete media objects, such as text or images. By default, any discrete object you insert is timed according to its position in a <seq> element—and bear in mind that the whole <body> constitutes an implied <seq> element. In the following example, the graphic image will appear after the first sound:

```
<seq>
          <sound src = "sound1.wav"/>
          <img src = "graphic1.png"/>
</seq>
```

In the next example, the graphic image and the sound begin displaying at the same time:

```
<par>
          <sound src = "sound1.wav"/>
          <img src = "graphic1.png"/>
</par>
```

You can add timings to discrete objects by using the dur (duration) attribute. In this attribute, you can use a clock value or "indefinite." The following example starts displaying the image when the sound stops playing, and displays it for 10 seconds:

```
<seq>
          <sound src = "sound1.wav"/>
```

```
            <img src = "graphic1.png" dur =
"10s"/>
</seq>
```

Nesting <seq> and <par> Elements

You can create a virtually infinite variety of effects by nesting <seq> and <par> elements.

In the following example, Sound 1 starts playing. When it finishes, Sound 2 and Video 1 begin playing. When they are both finished, Sound 3 plays.

```
<seq>
          <sound src = "sound1.wav"/>
              <par>
                  <sound src =
"sound2.wav"/>
                  <video src =
"video1.mpg"/>
        </par>
          <sound src = "sound3.wav" />
</seq>
```

In the following example, Sound 1, Video 1, and Video 3 all start playing at the same time. When Video 1 finishes, Video 2 starts:

```
<par>
          <sound src = "sound1.wav"/>
              <seq>
                  <sound src =
"video1.mpg"/>
                  <sound src =
"video2.mpg"/>
        </seq>
```

```
            <sound src = "video3.wav" />
</par>
```

Making Objects Repeat

If you'd like a continuous media object (such as a sound) to repeat or even loop indefinitely, you can do so by using the repeat attribute. You can use repeat with <seq> or <par>. If you specify an integer as the repeat attribute's value, the objects within the element repeat the number of times you specify. If you specify "indefinite," the objects repeat until the user exits the window.

Here's an example of a sound that plays three times:

```
<seq repeat = "3">
         <sound src = "welcome.au"/>
</seq>
```

Controlling Layout

Whenever you use the <par> element, you can have more than one media object going at a time. If you wish, you can specify how you want these elements laid out. To do so, you use the <layout> element, which you insert in the <head>. The <layout> element enables you to define display regions, which you name by means of the <region> element.

In the following example, two display regions are defined using a simple coordinate system, in which the region begins at the top left corner. The offset measurements (in pixels) specify the region's beginning point using the top and left attributes. If you wish to control the region's height and width, you can do so by using the width and height attributes.

In the following example, two regions are defined. The first is displayed 10 pixels from the top of the window and 10 pixels from the left. The region's height is fixed at 240 pixels. The second is displayed 300 pixels from the top of the window (thus allowing room for the first region) and is also indented 10 pixels from the left.

```
<head>
          <layout>
               <region id= "region1" top =
"10" left = "10" height =
        "240" />
               <region id = "region2" top =
"300" left = "10" />
          </layout>
```

To add media objects to regions, you use the region attribute of the media object element, as in the following example:

```
<video src = "video1.mov" region =
"region1"/>
```

Creating Alternative Presentations

If you would like to make sure that your presentation looks and sounds good on systems of varying quality, you can use the <switch> element. Basically, <switch> works by means of test conditions, including the following:

- **system-bitrate.** This is the number of bits per second that the system can handle. You specify the bitrate using an integer (whole number). For example, you may specify one presentation for users whose system bitrate is 20,000 (an appropriate figure for users of 28.8 Kbps modems) and a second version for systems with a bitrate of 40,000 (appropriate for 56 Kbps modems).

- **system-screen-size.** You specify this using the familiar "width x height" measurement, in pixels. For example, system-screen-size = "1280 x 768" specifies a screen size of 1280 pixels across and 768 pixels down. You can use this test to create alternative presentations for people using smaller screen resolutions.

Here's an example of a <switch> element that's used to create alternative versions of a presentation for fast and slow modems:

```
<switch>
          <par system-bitrate = "40000"/>
              <seq>
                  <sound src =
"sound1.mp3"/>
                  <sound src =
"sound2.mp3"/>
              </seq>
          </par>
          <par system-bitrate = "20000"/>
              <seq>
                  <sound src = "sound1.au"/>
                  <sound src = "sound2.au"/>
              </seq>
          </par>
          <par>
</switch>
```

Adding Hyperlinks

Ready for the icing on the cake? Up until now, I've been describing SMIL as if it were a static presentation language, designed for creating canned sequences. But it's much more than this.

From the beginning, the SMIL team envisioned SMIL as means for creating *interactive* presentations. You add interactivity by means of hyperlinks, which work very much the same way they do in HTML documents—but with one very important exception. In HTML, when you click on a hyperlink, you go off to a different page. With SMIL, you have a very appealing option: If you prefer, you can incorporate the linked material within the current page, so that it replaces content that would otherwise run. Alternatively, you can pause the ongoing presentation while the user explores the linked material.

Using the SHOW Attribute

To create a hyperlink in a SMIL document, you use the <a> element, which looks and works much like its HTML counterpart. Here's an example:

```
<a href = "presentation-2.smi" show =
"replace">
<video src = "video1.mpg"/>
</a>
```

In the above example, if the user clicks the link, the SMIL player goes to presentation-2.smi and plays that file's contents *instead* of playing video1.mpg. After presentation-2.smi is finished, the current presentation resumes.

The SHOW attribute takes the "replace" value by default. If you omit the SHOW attribute, the linked presentation replaces the <a> element's content.

If you would like to start the linked presentation in a new window, you can use the SHOW element's "new" value instead. This value tells the SMIL player to display the linked presentation in a new window, and leaves the current presentation running. Because this could be confusing (particularly if both presentations have sound), you may wish to use the "pause" value instead; show = "pause" displays the linked presentation in a new window, but pauses the original presentation until the user reactivates its window.

Because no SMIL players have been implemented (at this writing), it's unclear just how users will tell that a link exists. SMIL enables you to embed a link in a complete media object, such as a graphic—and in this respect, it's very much like using HTML's A tag to embed a link in an image, as in the following example: <A href="help.html"><IMG src = "help.gif" > </A>. In order to inform users that the image contains a link, most HTML browsers surround linked images with an ugly blue border. You can suppress this and add a note explaining that the image contains a link. It's up to the SMIL player vendors to decide how to handle this. If SMIL players don't provide distinctive borders for objects containing links, you'll need to include a text object that explains what happens when you click on the object containing the link.

Linking to Targets

In HTML, you can link to targets (named locations in the destination document). For example, if you link to resume.html#experience, the browser jumps to the target named "experience" and displays this at the top of the new page. SMIL also enables you to use targets, but they're much more logically implemented. Instead of jumping to named text anchors (as in HTML), you jump to media objects with assigned IDs. Here's an example:

```
<a href = "presentation-2.smi#video2">
<video src = "video1.mpg"/>
</a>
```

In this example, the link goes to the file named presentation-2.smi and locates the media object with the ID "video2." It starts playing the linked presentation from that point on.

You can assign an ID by using the ID attribute in any media object element, as in the following example:

```
<video src = "video2.mpg" id = "video2"/>
```

Embedding Multiple Links in Objects

In HTML, you can create *imagemaps*, in which portions of a graphic image are linked to other documents. If you click on one of the defined regions, you activate the hyperlink. SMIL's <anchor> element enables you to do much the same, except that you can use this capability with any media object (including videos and animations).

To embed two or more links within a media object, you use the <anchor> element and define coordinates using the coords attribute.

Note the following:

- To define the coordinates, assume that the object's upper left corner lies at left = 0, top = 0.
- You specify the clickable region by listing the region's four corners in the following order: left, top, right, bottom.

- For horizontal measurements, you measure from the left; for vertical measurements, you measure from the top. You can do so in pixels or percentages.

Here are a couple of examples:

- **coords = "0,0,200,200."** This region starts at the object's top left corner, and extends 200 pixels right and 200 pixels down.
- **coords = "200,200,350,400."** This region starts 200 pixels from the left and 200 pixels from the top of the object. The region ends 350 pixels from the left edge and 400 pixels from the top edge.
- **coords = "0,0,50%,50%."** This region starts at the object's top left corner, and ends halfway to the object's right edge and halfway to the object's bottom edge.

Here's how to use the <anchor> element to embed a couple of links in a video:

```
<video src = "video3.mpg">
          <anchor href = "about.html" coords
= "0,0,50%,100%"/>
          <anchor href = "help.html" coords =
"50%,0%, 100%, 100%/>
</video>
```

This divides the video into two equally sized rectangular panels: one on the left and one on the right.

SMIL Horizons

This chapter presents enough of the SMIL standard to get you started in synchronized multimedia production—and most SMIL authors will use little more than what's covered here. Still, there's more to SMIL, and some of it will prove of very great interest indeed to anyone doing professional multimedia production.

Here's an example of SMIL's riches for professional multimedia production. All the media objects can use the clip-begin attribute, as explained earlier, to specify a beginning point other than the object's normal beginning. In addition to the clock timings I discussed, you can also specify specific video frames; for example, you could start a video at precisely the frame you want. You can specify frames for the clip-end attribute, too. This feature will probably prove more interesting to professional rather than amateur multimedia producers, since it requires that you understand a lot of esoteric things about frame rates and the standards used to specify them.

From Here

In the next chapter, you'll find brief descriptions of some additional XML vocabularies that are now under development.

21

More XML Vocabularies

You've just looked at a couple of XML vocabularies in detail. What else is going on in the XML world?

This chapter introduces a number of proposed XML vocabularies in a variety of subject areas, encompassing interests such as genealogy, astronomy, and Internet commerce. The intent here isn't to be comprehensive—there are dozens, if not hundreds, of XML projects underway even at this early stage in the game. What's presented here are brief introductions to some early XML ventures that, taken together, illustrate the wide range of XML development now underway. Some of these efforts stem from huge, well-funded corporate research departments, others from loosely knit consortia of companies and researchers, and still others from the efforts of individuals. They illustrate how Internet-based knowledge communities are learning how to use XML to mark up their documents and make information more easily accessible on the Web.

Astronomical Markup Language (AML)

Astronomers have accumulated a wealth of information concerning the heavens, but there's a problem: Much of this information is currently stored in proprietary databases that are not easily accessed. Worse, the information is made available in a variety of publication media and formats. Some of it is stored in preprints or published articles, more is to be found in tabular form, and still more in a host of incompatible database formats.

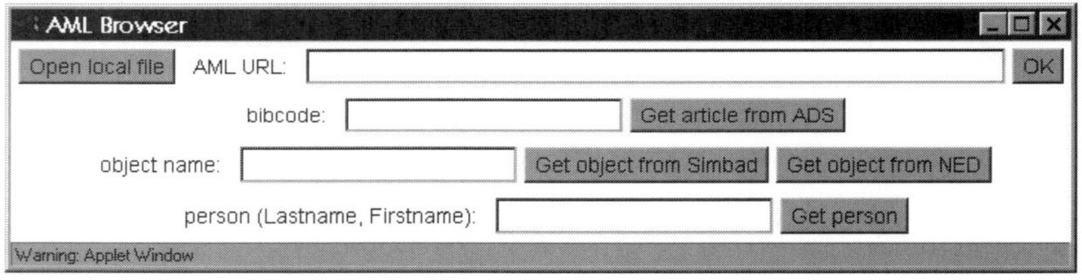

Figure 21.1 The AML Browser enables searches for astronomical data.

The Astronomical Markup Language (AML), a project led by Damien Guillaume of the University of Ulster, will help resolve these problems by creating a common metadata format for all types of astronomical information. (Metadata means—literally—data about data.) By

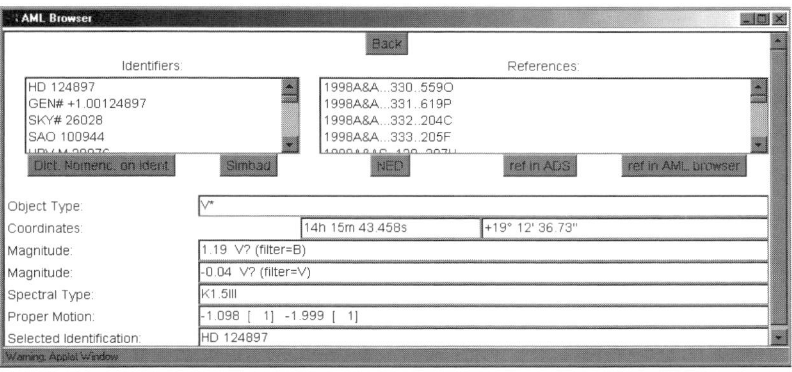

Figure 21.2 Retrieved data for Arcturus (AML Browser).

creating a format for marking up astronomical data with metadata, AML will enable astronomers to search a variety of sources for information about specific astronomical objects, bibliographic items, and even people in the astronomy business. An AML-enabled search tool could give astronomers access to all of this information with the same, easy-to-use interface.

AML is supported by a comprehensive DTD (located at *www.infm.ulst.ac.uk/~damien/these/AML.dtd*) that defines the markup needed for all the various forms in which astronomical data is stored, including databases, tables, and articles. A glance at the DTD shows why subject-related expertise is so important when it comes to crafting a new XML vocabulary; most of the DTD's tags won't mean much to nonastronomers, but they're grist for the mill for anyone trained in the profession of astronomy.

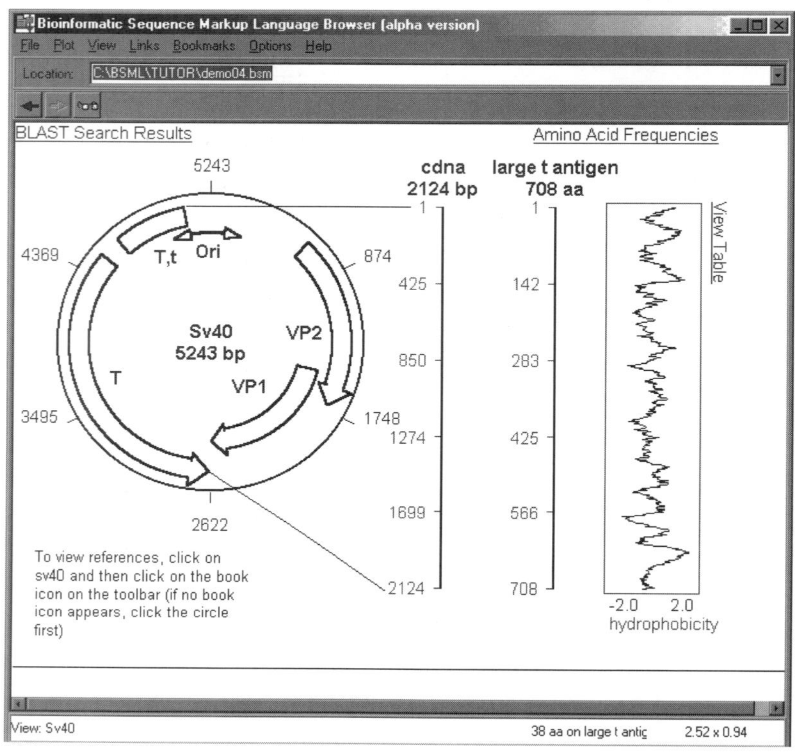

Figure 21.3 Bioinformatic Sequence Markup Language browser.

In concert with the Java-based AML Browser, AML shows the potential of XML to enable searches for astronomical information. The browser enables users to search for astronomical objects, bibliographic items, or astronomers. Figure 21.2 shows the results of a Web search for astronomical data concerning the star Arcturus.

Bioinformatic Sequence Markup Language (BSML)

Currently one of the hottest areas in biomedical research involves mapping DNA, RNA, and protein sequences; this is an essential step toward understanding the genetic basis of disease processes. Computers play a key role here by enabling the graphic display of genetic information. At the same time, they frustrate researchers by imposing proprietary data and file formats that discourage cross-platform sharing of genetic information (and discourage the widespread publication and retrieval of such information on the Internet). To solve this problem, TopoGEN, a Columbus, Ohio-based biotechnology company, is developing the Bioinformatic Sequence Markup Language (BSML), a public domain protocol for displaying genetic information graphically in a cross-platform environment. Once BSML is finalized and comes into general use, genetic sequencing information will become widely available on the Internet.

Like the Astronomical Markup Language (AML), BSML lends itself to a customized browser that's specifically designed to take advantage of BSML's discipline-specific graphics possibilities. (See Figure 21.3.) TopoGEN has already developed a BSML-enabled browser, shown in Figure 21.3, that integrates HTML capabilities; with this tool, a researcher can access a wealth of genetic information on the Internet and display the results graphically.

What about data that's already been encoded in proprietary databases? BSML's toolkit includes a number of Java applets that automatically translate data retrieved from databases into BSML. This is an important component of a strategy to ease the transition to nonproprietary markup.

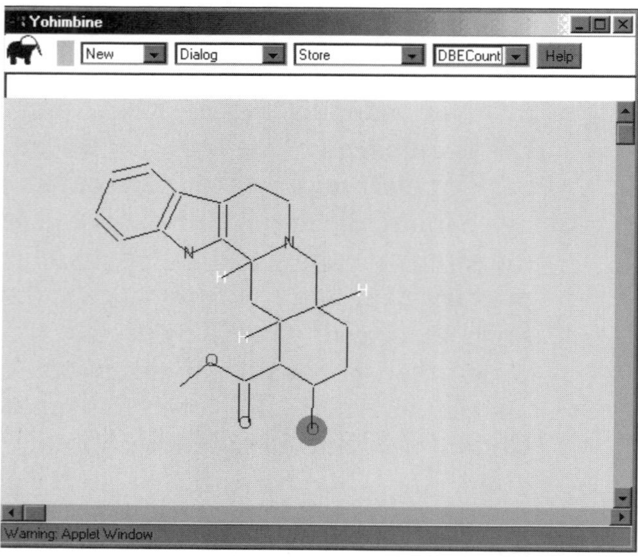

Figure 21.4 Chemical Markup Language (CML) document.

Chemical Markup Language (CML)

One of the earliest XML vocabularies to be developed is the Chemical Markup Language (CML), a project spearheaded by Peter Murray-Rust. The argument for CML closely resembles the one made for BSML: Chemical information is currently housed in a dizzying variety of incompatible proprietary database formats, discouraging the exchange of information among researchers. CML enables chemists to encode virtually any kind of chemistry-related information so that it becomes available over the Internet. Currently under development are a variety of

Java-based tools, including Jumbo, the first XML browser. (See Figure 21.4.) Jumbo enables chemists to browse structured chemical documents; the program displays browsable graphics of chemical data.

GedML

If you're a genealogy buff, you've probably heard of the GEDCOM standard; it's a well-known method of encoding genealogical information for computer representation and processing. Created by the Family History Department of the Church of Jesus Christ of Latter-day Saints (known as the LDS Church), GEDCOM stands for Genealogical Data Communication. But GEDCOM has the same set of problems that afflict other proprietary standards: It doesn't provide any means for making data available on the Web, discourages data exchange with users of programs that employ varying data formats, and—worst of all for a family-tracking standard—it doesn't handle foreign language characters very well. That's what led Michael Kay to develop GedML, a genealogical markup language supported by an XML DTD. GedML provides a good example of how individuals can create workable XML DTDs and, in so doing, address a genuine need in their communities.

Information and Content Exchange (ICE)

Suppose you've created a Web site, and you're offering some information that's of genuine value to the people who access your site. You've discovered another Web site that offers additional information of interest to your customers, and you've linked to it. But you'd like to do more. You'd like to work out a business agreement with this second site so that you could mutually benefit by promoting each other. But how?

Currently, there's no way to set up site-to-site cooperative ventures without a lot of expensive, time-consuming programming and customization. That's going to change when the Information and Content Exchange (ICE) standard sees the light of day, according to its proponents. These include most of the Web publishing industry's heavyweights (including Vignette Corporation, Firefly Network, Microsoft, and Yahoo). Using ICE, business partners will be able to specify just which information they're willing to share with other online providers and under what conditions. In addition, ICE provides the tracking and monitoring capabilities needed to transform content licensing into a going enterprise. What's more, ICE will enable all of this without compromising security and without requiring businesses to acquire intimate knowledge of their partners' Web publishing system.

What's likely to come out of the ICE proposal? According to the ICE consortium, you'll see a number of unprecedented sites on the Web, including Web superstores in which the various "shelves" are automatically stocked and updated by suppliers.

Mathematical Markup Language (MathML)

Web browsers currently do not support math expressions well, but that's about to change. Recently approved as a World Wide Web Consortium (W3C) Recommendation, the Mathematical Markup Language (MathML) should provide the markup tools needed to make math available on the World Wide Web.

Unlike most of the vocabularies discussed in this chapter, MathML isn't intended to be hand-coded. Authoring and displaying are both handled by MathML-enabled programs. The major browser publishers have already announced that they will build MathML support into their products, so it shouldn't be necessary to use special viewing software. For now, though, MathML authors need to include a Java applet with their pages so that the

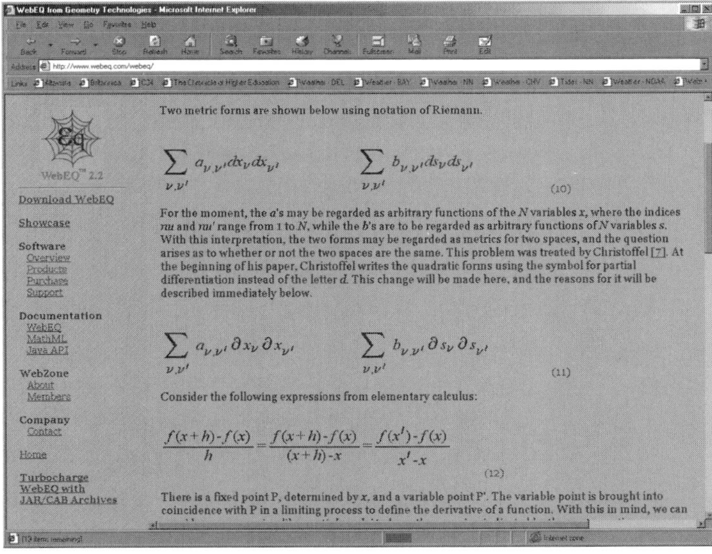

Figure 21.5 MathML enables rich mathematical markup on the Web.

MathML equations appear within the Web browser's display. (See Figure 21.5.)

WebEQ (*www.webeq.com*) exemplifies the new generation of MathML-savvy authoring tools now becoming available. The program enables authors to use easy, visual techniques to create equations within HTML documents; all the MathML coding is done automatically.

Precision Graphics Markup Language (PGML)

You've probably looked at a lot of graphics on the Web. What you may not realize is that all of the ones you've seen are bit-mapped graphics, unless you've equipped your browser with some kind of special plug-in software. Bit-mapped graphics are made up of thousands of tiny dots, and they're good for some purposes. However, they have one serious drawback: they can't be enlarged. If you blow up a bit-mapped graphic, it looks terrible—you can see the dots. For some time, the World Wide Web Consortium (W3C) has been looking for a vector graphics standard for the Web. In vector graphics, images are made up of individual objects, each of which is mathematically represented. You can size and scale a vector graphic to your heart's content, and it won't lose its quality. Even better, vector graphics often take up less disk space than bit-mapped graphics, and this means they'll download faster.

The Web needs a vector graphics standard, and it's under development, thanks to a consortium headed by Adobe and including IBM, Netscape, and Sun. This consortium has proposed the Precision Graphics Markup Language (PGML), which will use the same imaging model as the popular PostScript page description language that powers high-end printers. While we're on the subject of printers, it's worth mentioning that PGML is also designed to enable high-quality printing of Web documents, which isn't possible now.

Like the Mathematical Markup Language (MATHML), PGML isn't designed to be coded or read by humans; it's too complex. When and if it's implemented, PGML will be enabled by graphics programs and processed by PGML-savvy browsers. Currently, PGML isn't official; the Adobe-led consortium has submitted PGML to the W3C as a proposed standard, but the standardization process is (at this writing) in the initial stages.

Resource Description Framework (RDF)

One of the Web's most serious shortcomings is the lack of a universally accepted means of expressing *metadata*, or information about the type of information a Web page contains. For example, suppose you're looking for a page about spices in Indian cuisine. You'll retrieve more than 750,000 pages, most of which aren't at all relevant to your search question—most are ads for Indian restaurants promising "savory spices." At the root of the problem is the lack of a metadata system that would enable you to exclude restaurants' ad pages in favor of the cooking tips you're looking for.

There's no shortage of proposals for metadata systems, but none has gained widespread acceptance. With the advent of the Resource Description Framework (RDF), a collaborative project spearheaded by the World Wide Web Consortium (W3C), a metadata framework may finally become available. Perhaps it would be more accurate to say "frameworks," because RDF is a complex framework for *creating* metadata frameworks and making them available in computer-readable form.

Why not just create a simple, universally applicable metadata set? Impossible, say RDF's proponents; the job of creating metadata vocabularies is best left to members of the communities that will create and share their knowledge on the Internet. What RDF does is to enable these communities to create and declare such vocabularies using a common underlying structure. Using RDF, members of a community can define an unambiguous resource description vocabulary and encode their documents with this vocabulary. The vocabulary is written in XML by means of a DTD that defines strict rules for expressing metadata logically. Because the vocabulary is expressed in RDF, which is computer-readable, an XML-savvy browser can "learn" the semantics of the vocabulary by consulting its DTD, and perform smart searches on the described data.

Among the many metadata vocabularies that are finding expression in RDF are the following:

- **Platform for Internet Content Selection (PICS).** The PICS standard supplies a means for rating Web sites according to a variety of content-rating schemes, including some designed to protect children from sites containing adult content.
- **The Dublin Core.** This is a simple set of metadata categories that any Web author can use to identify a document's content, including Title, Subject, Description, Source, and Publisher.
- **Linux Metadata.** This is a proposed vocabulary for expressing information about Linux software so that it's more easily retrieved on the Web.

Ontology Markup Language (OML)

The Web's packed with information, but very little of it can be read and understood by machines. It's expressed only in human-readable text. But wouldn't it be cool to turn the entire Internet into some sort of artificial brain, one that could respond to questions, such as "How many different species of frogs exist in tropical Costa Rica?" If OML bears fruit, you might be able to ask such questions—and what's more, get an answer.

Short for Ontology Markup Language, OML provides a way to mark up information about *ontologies*. In artificial intelligence (AI), an ontology is a formal description of the relationships among facts and claims in a specialized field of knowledge. Suppose we're talking about mutual funds. You could write a Web page about a mutual fund that says something like the following:

```
The Humbug Fund specializes in the techno-
logy sector. As with any sector fund, the
usual risks are multiplied by reliance on a
single sector--in this case, one that's
especially volatile (subject to rapid price
fluctuation). The Humbug Fund isn't for the
faint of heart, but the rewards can be
great: Over the past five years, the fund
has averaged a 35.2% gain.
```

The above paragraph contains a number of *claims* about the world, all of which are subject to formal representation. For example, it's claimed that the Humbug Fund is a sector fund—and implicitly, that sector funds are one type of mutual fund, distinguished from others by unusually high risk. But the Humbug Fund has also been a solid performer, racking up good gains over the past five years.

With OML, you could annotate your page so that, in addition to the human-readable text about the Humbug Fund, you also make *machine-readable* claims available, of the following sort:

```
Humbug Fund is a mutual fund.
Humbug Fund is a sector fund.
A sector fund is a kind of mutual fund.
A sector fund invests in one industry sec-
tor.
A sector fund is more volatile than nonsec-
tor funds.
A volatile fund has rapid price fluctua-
tions.
The Humbug Fund rose 35.2% annually over the
past five years.
A gain of 35.2% over the past five years is
excellent performance.
```

So how do you do the annotation? As with many XML vocabularies, this isn't something you'd want to do by hand, unless you spend your spare time playing around with metaphysics and symbolic logic. For most knowledge areas, you'll make use of existing ontological frameworks, so that you don't have to figure out just how to express the core relationships and identities. And what's more, you'll use a Java application to add the OML code to your page. Once you've chosen the ontology you want to use (such as "mutual funds"), you'll see drop-down boxes that enable you to make the claims you want to make. The Java application generates the code automatically and pastes it into your document.

Sound futuristic? Well, it is. OML is in its infancy. But there's already a demonstration version of a very similar Java application, called the Knowledge Annotator. This program doesn't annotate in OML (yet); it was designed to annotate Web sites using a predecessor of OML called SHOE (short for Simple HTML Ontology Extensions). SHOE is SGML-compliant; OML will make SHOE conformant to XML.

What can you do with SHOE? It's a big job to write an ontology; you'll be better off making use of a pre-existing one (several have been written already). One such vocabulary, created for demonstration purposes, defines all the various entities and relationships found in computer science departments, such as "graduate students" and "not having tenure."

Once an ontology has been created, the next job arrives: adding SHOE-compliant code to your HTML pages. With hand coding, this would be a huge job. Here's where software can step in to simplify an application tremendously. In Figure 21.6, you see Knowledge Annotator, a Java applet that enables anyone to code a page with SHOE annotations using a predefined ontology. Here, you see the code describing a series of claims made about an artificial intelligence publication.

If you'd like to know more about SHOE, visit the SHOE Home Page at *http://www.cs.umd.edu/projects/plus/SHOE/index.html*.

Outbreak Markup Language (OML)

When there's an outbreak of communicable or food-borne diseases, it's essential that the word gets out as fast as possible. Currently, information about such outbreaks gets around in a variety of formal and informal ways. If the person reporting the outbreak follows a standard format to get the information out, it's more likely that this

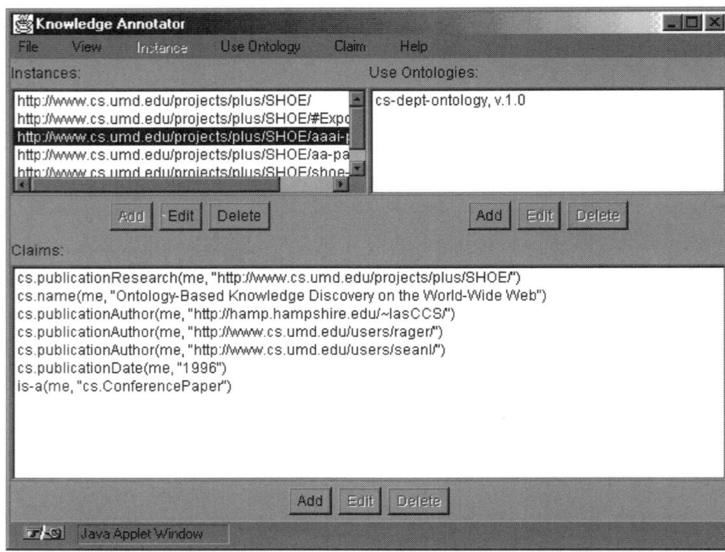

Figure 21.6 Encoding a page's claims in machine-readable form (SHOE)

information will prove useful. That's the purpose of the Outbreak Markup Language (OML), a project coordinated by David Orenstein, publisher of *Outbreak*, an online information service specializing in emerging diseases (*www.outbreak.org*). Still under development, OML is a simple, easy-to-use markup langauge that's defined with XML.

In contrast to many of the XML vocabularies, OML is designed to be very easy to understand and use; no special software is needed to create an OML document. A complete OML document contains some or all of the following information:

- Name of disease/disease agent/health event

- Date and source of report
- Date of first case/occurrence of event
- Location
- Number of cases and number of deaths
- Country of origin
- Product recall
- Whether this notice is an update
- Complete narrative description
- Confidence (whether information is believed to be reliable)

OML documents can be as simple as the following:

```
<outbreak>
          <who>
            <who-location-common-name>
              Kinshasha, Zaire
            </who-location-common-name>
          </who>
          <what>
            <what-common-name>
              Ebola
            </what-common-name>
          </what>
          <where>
            <where-common-name>
              Kikwit, Zaire
            </where-common-name>
          </where>
          <when>
            <when-report-made>
              19950518
            </when-report-made>
          </when>
          <description>
            Cases of Ebola are appearing at
the hospital in Kikwit....
```

```
            </description>
    </outbreak>
```

With so many XML vocabularies appearing that require powerful, Java-capable computers and special software, it's refreshing to see an effort to develop a simple vocabulary such as OML. Why is it made so simple? Realism. Health officials in many countries don't have the computer resources necessary to run complex applications and Java. With OML, anyone who has access to ASCII-based e-mail can generate and send an OML document.

Signed Document Markup Language (SDML)

Computers are great, but they have a number of drawbacks: It's a hassle to print envelopes, and it's impossible—at least currently—to sign an electronic document in a way that would stand scrutiny in a court of law. New printers will surely solve the envelope problem, and SDML (short for Signed Document Markup Language) may provide support for digitally authenticated signatures. With SDML in place, you'll be able to write checks and sign contracts on the Internet.

Developed by the Financial Services Technology Consortium (FSTC), a consortium of banks, financial services providers, national laboratories, research universities, and government agencies, SDML enables the complex sorts of signatures business requires, such as co-signing, endorsing, and witnessing. Integrated with cryptographic tools such as digital certificates and encryption, SDML documents can be verifiably traced to their origin and proven to have survived Internet transfer without alteration.

They also have the feature of nonrepudiability, which means that a third party who receives a signed document can prove that the signer really did sign the document, even if the signer later wishes to claim that no signature was made.

Currently, SDML is under development; initial work focused on creating an SGML DTD for SDML, but future development work will use XML.

XML/EDI

Businesses have been exchanging data electronically for more than a decade, thanks to Electronic Data Interchange (EDI), an international standard for exchanging a huge variety of business information (including air freight invoices, student transcripts, return merchandise authorizations, product service notifications, and dozens more). But EDI has never been a picnic to implement. In order to exchange data using EDI, two businesses had to agree to link up via a secure private network, and they then had to agree to use the same proprietary application in order to exchange data. EDI defines the format for the various business documents it supports, but the task of specifying the encoding for electronic interchange was left to proprietary vendors.

Can EDI work on the Internet? The first prerequisite is security, and that's on the way; for example, recently introduced protocols enable businesses to implement *virtual private networks* (VPNs) on the Internet, and they're highly secure. The second prerequisite is an open, non-proprietary means of encoding EDI data. That's the job of XML/EDI, a project spearheaded by the XML/EDI group, a consortium of individuals from dozens of companies interested in fostering electronic commerce. Current projects include creating XML DTDs for specific EDI document types, such as book order forms, and developing Java applications that will support the use of EDI on the Internet.

From Here

With this chapter, you come to the end of this book. What's next in your exploration of XML? Although it's too early to say just how browser publishers intend to support XML in their products, it's clear that XML, CSS, XSL, and the Document Object Model (DOM) are going to revolutionize the way information is presented and processed on the Web. Microsoft's implementation of DOM in preview releases of the firm's Internet Explorer 5.0 browser suggest that the browser's XML processor will make XML data directly and easily available to scripts for further processing. CSS adds yet another dimension of potential interactivity, because CSS Level 2 enables Web authors to display or hide styles based on user input. Web pages of the future will combine HTML, XML, CSS, and DOM. Together, these technologies will transform Web publishing into a platform for inexpensive, ubiquitous application development.

Index

D

F

N

O

P

Q

R

S